IT'S WHAT'S INSIDE THE LINES THAT COUNTS

★ ★ ★ ★ ★ ★ ★ ★ ★ ★ ★ ★ ★ ★ ★ ★ ★ ★

Baseball Stars of the 1970s and 1980s Talk About the Game They Loved

The Baseball Oral History Project
Volume 3

FAY VINCENT

Simon & Schuster

New York   London   Toronto   Sydney

Simon & Schuster
1230 Avenue of the Americas
New York, NY 10020

First Simon & Schuster hardcover edition March 2010

SIMON & SCHUSTER and colophon are registered
trademarks of Simon & Schuster, Inc.

For information about special discounts for bulk purchases,
please contact Simon & Schuster Special Sales at
1-866-506-1949 or business@simonandschuster.com.

The Simon & Schuster Speakers Bureau can bring authors
to your live event. For more information or to book an
event contact the Simon & Schuster Speakers Bureau at
1-866-248-3049 or visit our website at www.simonspeakers.com.

Designed by ISPN Publishing

Manufactured in the United States of America

10 9 8 7 6 5 4 3 2 1

Library of Congress Cataloging-in-Publication Data

Vincent, Fay.
   It's what's inside the lines that counts : baseball stars of the
1970s and 1980s talk about the game they loved / Fay Vincent.
—1st Simon & Schuster hardcover ed.
   p.   cm.
   1. Baseball players—United States—Interviews.   2. Baseball—
United States—History—20th century.   I. Title.
   GV865.A1V57   2010
   796.357092'2—dc22   2009053014

ISBN 978-1-4391-5921-7
ISBN 978-1-4391-6331-3 (ebook)

To Elden Auker, whose encouragement was vital

CONTENTS

INTRODUCTION

Some ten years ago, a friend gave me a set of tapes of interviews Larry Ritter had done as the basis for his captivating book *The Glory of Their Times*, and I was enthralled to listen to old-time ballplayers talk about their days in baseball in the early part of the twentieth century. This book, the third in a series, is a direct product of that chance encounter with the superb work that Ritter had done.

My decision to try to emulate Ritter led to some forty-five interviews of ballplayers and to the deposit at the Hall of Fame in Cooperstown of the videotapes of those interviews, with the hope that over time fans of our wonderful game would be able to see these fine players tell their stories. By preserving these tapes we preserve the essence of what makes baseball unique.

At the outset of this Oral History Project, my friend and mentor Herbert Allen encouraged me and helped me to finance the effort with a generous grant. The Hall of Fame receives the author's share of the proceeds from this book, and has graciously begun to find ways to make the tapes available to fans and students of baseball. In doing the interviews, I have been assisted by good friends Claire Smith, Murray Chass, eminent baseball writers; my good friend Walter O'Hara; Dick Crago, the longtime announcer at Dodgertown in Florida; and Jon Pessah. My editor at Simon & Schuster, Bob Bender, and I edited transcripts of the videotapes to create this manuscript. We tried to faithfully record the comments of the interviewees, correcting minor grammatical mistakes and occasional errors caused by the inevitable lapses of memory after several decades. Thanks also to Jim Gates, Bill Francis, Gabe Schechter, Freddy Berowski, and Tim Wiles at the Hall of Fame for their help with the introductions to the ballplayers and to Pat Kelly at the Hall of Fame for the photographs. And, once again, I acknowledge the enormous contribution of my colleague George Cooney, whose production crews have ensured that our videotapes are highly professional. My thanks to them and to all the others who have worked with us to make this such a rewarding undertaking.

My dear friend Bart Giamatti claimed baseball was essentially oral history and he loved to hear and retell baseball stories. This book is replete with good stories and I hope it captures some baseball moments that would otherwise have been lost. These superb players talk of magical games, relate memorable experiences, and explain what it means to be a professional. I very much hope you find it both interesting and instructive.

WILLIE MCCOVEY

Topping out at six feet four inches tall, Willie McCovey earned the nickname "Stretch" as he embarked upon a dominating major league career, mostly playing first base for the San Francisco Giants. As a sign of things to come, McCovey went 4-4 in his July 1959 big league debut against Hall of Fame pitcher Robin Roberts. He would complete the season with a .354 batting average and National League Rookie of the Year honors.

Teaming up with fellow slugger Willie Mays, McCovey would pursue a career in which his power hitting was also matched with excellent defense and sound baseball judgment. As noted by his manager Clyde King, "I'd hate to think where we'd have been without McCovey. He played when he was hurt and came through when he was hurt." He also said, "In my opinion, Willie is the best-fielding first baseman in the National League. In fact, he's the best I've ever seen on thrown balls. Stretch saved our infielders a great many errors this season."

As to McCovey's baseball acumen, King remarked, "He's the kind of guy who is good for an organization because he has such a good baseball mind. His judgment is very sound. He knows how to evaluate opposing players."

With respect to his opponents, McCovey was an intimidating figure at the plate. "I'm not afraid of any pitcher," he said. "I've been pitched almost every way, and I've hit every kind of pitch. There wasn't much else to do in Mobile." This thought was echoed by manager Sparky Anderson, who stated, "Here's a guy who is the most feared in baseball. If you pitched to him instead of around him, he'd hit eighty home runs." And, according to Walter Alston, "McCovey didn't hit any cheap ones. When he belts a home run, he does it with such authority it seems like an act of God."

As a dead-pull, line-drive-type hitter, he often faced defensive shifts by opposing teams. McCovey was not flustered by this tactic, noting, "Those shifts don't really worry me a lot. Sometimes they're successful. Other times they hurt a team's defense. Of course, the shifts don't mean anything at all if I can hit the ball over the top of them. Sometimes [I] hit through it, sometimes opposite, and sometimes bunted."

Willie McCovey retired from major league ball after twenty-two seasons. His career numbers place him in a special pantheon of talent: 521 home runs, 1,555 RBIs, 1,229 runs, and 2,211 hits. Along with his Rookie of the Year Award, he also won the National League Most Valuable Player honors in 1969, was a six-time All-Star selection, and captured three National League home run crowns.

In 1986, McCovey received baseball's highest honor when he was elected to the National Baseball Hall of Fame. His reputation as a quiet, unassuming ballplayer remained intact as he said, "And now I have become a player on the most distinguished team of all. It's a new family in a way, a family of men whose accomplishments in baseball and in life set them apart from all others; and I'm truly honored and blessed with this ultimate adoption, if you will, by the game that I played so hard and loved so deeply."

Of all the great guys that came out of Mobile, I'm the only one really that came out of Mobile proper. Hank Aaron is from Mobile, Billy Williams, and we can go on and on. But most of those guys were born outside of Mobile proper. I was really born right in Mobile.

Willie McCovey

We were eight boys, two girls. I was number seven of the ten. And for some reason, I was the only athlete. I don't know why. A couple of my brothers thought they could box, but they couldn't. So it didn't take them long to realize that they couldn't make a living boxing.

We were playing baseball off the streets of Mobile, I can remember that, right in front of my house, and the paper boys were coming around with the Extras. Extra, Extra, read all about it, the death of President Roosevelt. I remember that, for some reason, very vaguely, you know? I was born in 1938 and I don't remember a whole lot about 1945 other than that, to be honest with you. But I do remember that.

We didn't have any ballparks to play in. Most of the open fields weren't open to us. Although a little later, for whatever reason, we became pretty friendly with the white kids and the sports guys of Mobile, and we started playing games against them. And I think we were the only southern team that was able to do that.

The white kids came out with uniforms, they had this full equipment. They had nice-looking cheerleaders cheering them on. And we came out in dungarees and some Levi's and things like that and homemade gloves, just a couple pieces of leather sewed together.

I was my own coach. So I just went by things that I read or whatever. You know, I listened to the radio because there was no TV then. The games were on radio. They were re-created, although at the time we didn't know that. I tell you, they sounded live, like it was happening just then. Once a week, the Giants, the Dodgers. Mobile was a Dodger farm team at the time, the Mobile Bears. So naturally, we followed the Dodgers closer. And then Jackie Robinson breaking the color line with the Dodgers made the Dodgers even more of a favorite down in Mobile. But they had a Double-A team, Southern Association. So we could go follow that whole game and watch the Mobile Bears play. The guys that played for the Bears, we saw them work their way up to Brooklyn to play with the Dodgers.

My very first idol, I think, was Whitey Lockman because he was with the Giants. And I liked the Giants for whatever reason, I guess because of Whitey, although the Dodgers were my favorite because of Jackie. I don't know why I liked Whitey Lockman, and of course, I got to meet Whitey because we became teammates with the Giants later on. He coached me at first base.

Billy Williams and I knew each other. We played against each other down there. Billy was from a little town called Whistler. And of course, Aaron lived out that way, too. And our league at the end of the year would meet Billy's league, so, you know, we almost always played against each other in the playoff game, a championship game or whatever you want to call it at the end of the year.

Henry Aaron was a little older. Yeah, we all idolized Henry because by the time we were on our way, Henry had already signed up to play in the Negro Leagues. So, we followed him and his exploits with the Negro Leagues before the Braves signed him.

I wanted to play in the Negro Leagues. I thought that was the only place we'd get to play, really, until Jackie broke the color line. So, for me, at the time, that was our major leagues.

Satchel Paige is from Mobile. Satchel used to come down during the winter and we would all gather around the little oak tree. We had a little oak tree where all the guys kind of hung out. And Satchel used to come down to the oak tree and would tell us stories about what went on the last year in the league, tell us stories about Josh Gibson and Cool Papa Bell. And we'd sit there half a day listening to Satchel.

God, he told us a lot of stories, a lot of it I have forgotten. He would tell us about how good Josh Gibson was. He was, I guess, the Babe Ruth of the Negro Leagues. He could really hit. They were unbeatable then when he and Josh were on the same team. But he would tell us stories about Cool Papa, who was probably the fastest human being alive at the time. One of those stories that used to go around about Cool Papa was he was so fast that he could turn the light switch off and be in the bed before the lights went out. That's how fast he was. But Satchel told us, well, he'd run his way over from first base and steal second and third on me. And Satchel said, I looked over at him one day after he had done that and said, now, let me see you beat my fastball across home plate. Well, he had a million of them. I've forgotten most of them.

It was either get into sports and play sports or get in trouble. And unfortunately, most of the guys down that way got in trouble. They went the other way. But fortunately, I hung out with the guys who liked sports. We played all sports. But baseball was the one we thought would allow us a better career, mostly because of the Negro Leagues. And then after Jackie signed, we figured, hey, there's a chance to go into the major leagues now.

At that time, we figured, you could have a longer career playing baseball. So that's why most of the good athletes signed to play baseball at that time.

The Giants had a scout named Alex Pompez. And all scouts have what they called bird dogs, who are not scouts per se, but they knew scouts in the different organizations. So they looked out for good players in that neighborhood where they grew up. And this guy Jesse Thomas was the head of the playground where we used to go and play. And whenever there was a player that Jesse Thomas thought had some ability or some future or whatever, he would call Alex Pompez and let him know. That's how I got invited to the Giants minor league training camp.

I was in Los Angeles at the time. I left Mobile just to spend some time with my brother, who was living in Los Angeles. And after I got

Alex Pompez

to L.A., I decided I wanted to stay. My brother said, well, you got to get a job. So I went to the employment office and started to register for a job.

This was '55. And my mother called me. This was in January or February in '55. My mother called me and said, Jesse Thomas wants you to come home. He wants to send you down to the Giants training camp. I thought she was kidding at first. But I knew my mother wouldn't kid me. So I went back home to Mobile and there was a bus ticket waiting for me to go to Melbourne, Florida.

That's where all the Giants farm teams trained. And like a week or so before their farm teams would report, they would invite a bunch of guys like me, who were unsigned, that were sent down by bird dogs to try out. They chose up sides and we played against each other. And of course, in that camp were myself, Orlando Cepeda, Felipe Alou, and Jose Pagan. Yeah, all those guys were taken there. That's the best one they ever had. So we all got signed that spring. And then after we were signed, they would assign us to different farm teams.

I signed for $75 a month. And little did I know that, behind my back, my mother called and negotiated $500 for herself. She turned out to be a good agent. I didn't know it.

I signed with Sandersville, Georgia, with the Georgia State League. That's the Deep South. And even though I grew up in the segregated South, I had never heard some of the things I was called in that league, so I still got some of the stuff that Jackie had to go through. It was still prevalent at that time, you know?

The other African-American guy on the team was born and raised in New York, and he couldn't take it. He quit, he went home. So that left me the only one.

I got death threats and things. Back home we were able to mingle with the white kids in Mobile and, you know, I never got anything like that.

The person I liked the most—and she didn't realize how much trouble she was getting me in—was our manager's wife. She was like

Miss America, she was gorgeous. Pete Parlick played second base and managed, so he was a player-manager. I used to walk home from the ballpark. And naturally, I lived in a different neighborhood than the white guys did.

Pete's wife would always come around and pick me up and drive me home. And, you know, me driving home at midnight with her, she didn't realize that's a no-no. But she didn't care. I got a lot of threats from that.

After Georgia, I went to Danville, Virginia, in the Carolina League. It was the only team in Virginia with the league, everybody else was in Carolina. So a lot of the same stuff but not quite as much as the Georgia State League. After that, I went to Dallas in the Texas League.

In my first year in the Georgia State League, I led the league in home runs and RBIs, so I figured then there was some promise. And the next league was Class C, after the Class D where I broke in. But I was good enough to skip Class C and go to Class B, which was the Carolina League. I had another good year in that league. I played with a guy by the name of Leon Wagner, Daddy Wags, who was like a great home run hitter in that league. He hit over 60 home runs in that league. I think he hit 66. And, I mean, just throughout the league. And I hit right in front of him in the lineup. I didn't realize how much respect I had against other pitchers until that year when they would walk me to pitch to him. He was having that incredible year, but they would still rather pitch to him than me. So that's when I started gaining the respect at the plate.

One thing is I didn't fraternize. That's the one thing. There were a lot of guys who did. So the guys didn't get to know me very well, so I kind of evoked that presence to the pitchers. And, you know, I just turned into a good hitter. I could think at the plate. I didn't give in to pitches. I didn't swing at a lot of bad balls and things like that. So all that added up, I guess.

We were embarrassed to strike out during my era. For some reason, that's no big deal now. I guess the guys figured that out now, so it's nothing for them to strike out 150, 200 times.

Unfortunately, I got hurt that year, so I didn't really play a full year at Dallas. I sprained my ankle and tore up my knee. It was just bad. First time I started having problems with injuries is in Fort Worth, Texas, when Dallas was playing Fort Worth. And that's when I first started sampling the Dodgers-Giants rivalry. That's where it started, in the Texas League. At Fort Worth with the Dodger farm team. Dallas was the Giants farm team. So, we didn't like each other.

That's when I met guys like Tommy Davis, and we became lifelong friends. We always had this rivalry going, who was gonna have the best year, and that carried on through when I got to the major leagues.

We were in the Pacific Coast League together. The Giants called me up in July, and of course, everybody knows I went 4-4 against Robin Roberts. And I got back in the clubhouse, and the first telegram they handed to me was from Tommy, congratulating me. He said, I'm taking over Dallas here now that you're gone.

Dallas was a good town. I like Dallas a lot. But I spent a lot of time in the training rooms, unfortunately. And the real time I got back to play, I had a pretty good year, enough to be moved up the next year. So, that's when you know you've done well, if you don't have to go back to that same league again the next year.

When I had to have knee surgery, they sent me to New York. And when I was released from the hospital, they wanted me to stick around in New York so they could check it.

That's when the scout introduces me to Willie. And he told Willie that, well, I had to stick around about a week. Willie said, oh, he can stay with me. So, I stayed in Mays's house for a week, and talk about a thrill. So he takes me around Harlem. He and Junior Gilliam of the Dodgers were really good friends. They played a lot of pool. So I used to tag along with them all over Harlem, into pool halls and whatever, you know, sitting around, and both of them were good.

* * *

Giants had about thirteen or fourteen farm teams at that time, from Class D right up to Triple-A.

And every one of those leagues, they had about three farm teams in each one of those leagues, you know, in various places. So naturally, there was a first baseman on every one of those teams that was competing for that one job in the major leagues. I'm playing first base on the Double-A team, the Dallas team, and a guy came up to me and started talking to me about playing first base and about gripping the bat. That guy was Bill White.

And he was giving me advice. And I said, boy, it's the guy that one day I'm probably gonna be fighting for this first-base job, and he's down here giving me advice. And that's when I decided, you know,

Willie Mays

that's the way I want to be. I want to be able to help guys. That's when I knew the Giants organization was more of a family, too, because that's when I realized how much guys in the organization were trying to help each other. They were the type of guys who weren't jealous of anybody because they were playing the same position.

In 1959 I was having such a good year in Triple-A. I was hitting over .370 when they called me up, leading the league in everything, everything possible. Yeah. In a way, I wanted to keep that year going because I would have liked to have seen how good a year I could have really had if I had stayed there. But my, we're going to the big leagues, you know, that was it. So, they called me up. And that year I was having in Triple-A just continued when I got up here, you know, going 4-4, and just continued throughout the year.

And then, I'm Rookie of the Year up here. So, it's one of those crazy years, you know?

The weather wasn't a big problem that first year in San Francisco. It wasn't until we moved to Candlestick in 1960 that the weather became a factor.

There was an interesting story about the invisible triple that I hit, as they called it. I hit a ball into the outfield. We played the Dodgers at night. It was just a routine fly ball to center field. And Duke Snider never did see it, because of the fog. I kept running. I got to third base and they called a delay in the game. I didn't remember how long a delay we had, maybe around twenty-five minutes.

I bunted a triple one night. Mays was on first and I bunted, and there was nobody there, so Mays goes from first base on the ball, but when he kept running, I kept running. So I ended up on third base and Willie scored.

Willie was always the center of attention. Everybody gathered around Willie because he had that infectious laugh. You knew he was around because he had that laugh. Everybody gathered around Willie asking questions. And he was a giver. Yeah. He gave guys the shirt off his back, you know, even visiting players.

There might have been a guy that might be a little better hitter or there might have been a guy had a little more power or whatever, but when you put everything together, he was it, the greatest player I ever saw. And he didn't really have to work hard at it. That was what's so scary. I was wondering, if this guy worked hard totally, how good would he be? Because all he did in the off-season, like I said, we'd go to the pool hall and play pool, lie around the bedroom and watch TV. And then the first day of spring training, he was playing like it was midseason.

While we were all huffing and puffing trying to get in shape, he was already ready for Opening Day, you know. He was just amazing.

Orlando Cepeda and I signed the same time. We were together in that tryout camp. And Cepeda actually was signed as a third baseman. They sent him off to Kokomo to play, which wasn't even a Giants farm team, but they just kind of traded him off, so I don't know. It was almost like they weren't expecting him to move up very far in the organization, so they sent him off to Kokomo. And he had a great year, because Cepeda can hit. I mean, he can hit, yeah. And I guess it was during that time he was transferred to first base, I guess, and started playing first base.

Felipe Alou and I used to ride to the ballpark together. We even bought a car together, you know? Because that winter, I played baseball in his hometown in the Dominican Republic. And since I couldn't speak Spanish, he moved away from his family to move in with me down there so I'd be comfortable, because I was ready to go home since I couldn't understand Spanish. So he said, oh, no, I'll move in with you.

He and I bought a car together. And he got called up to the Giants before me. And I sold the car and sent him his share. He likes to tell that story because he didn't think he'd ever get back, you know, he'd never get any money from that sale, but I sent him his share of the car.

When I got called up, they moved Cepeda to third base that day, since he had played some third base. So that first day he played third

Orlando Cepeda

base and I played first. And he didn't play it very well, so he decided to try left field.

He probably could have been a better left fielder, but he didn't really want to play out there. So when Alvin Dark took over the team, Alvin came to me and said, I'd like for you to try playing left field. Are you open to it? We would have a much better team. So I said, yeah, I'll gladly play left field. So he handed me a left-handed glove and I went out there and played, and to my surprise, I liked it out there, yeah. I tell people, how can you not like playing beside Willie Mays? But I ended up liking it. And I thought that's the way it was gonna be because we had a good team with me in left field and Cepeda playing first base.

We knew it was history when we had the three Alou brothers in

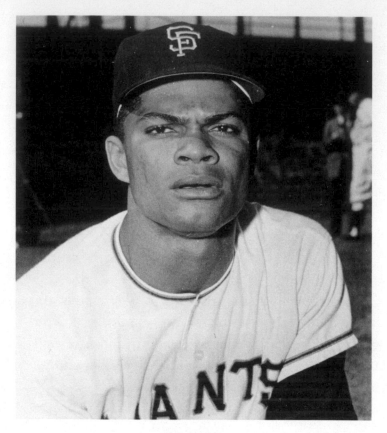

Felipe Alou

the outfield. But we knew all of them were good. And we were just looking forward to the day when they would be out there. We thought it would be history in the making. So it finally happened. And then that day that all three of them started, I hit three home runs in the game.

They were all different. Matty was a little guy whom they couldn't outrun, and so was Felipe. In spring training, we would play intersquad games. And Felipe'd hit a ball to shortstop, and we had trouble throwing him out at first base. He was so fast, you know. That's when I woke my eyes up to how fast this guy was, and Matty was the type of guy who, you know, was kind of a slap hitter, and bunted a lot to get on. Jesus was just kind of an average player. He didn't have the tools those other two had, but he was good enough to be a major leaguer. But Felipe was head and shoulders the best of the three.

Juan Marichal was a great pitcher. And I put emphasis on pitcher. Guys who are mostly throwers know they can throw in the high nineties so they just want to blow it by everybody. But at that age, Juan was a pitcher. He could still change speeds on the ball, change his delivery and throw all those curveballs when most pitchers would be throwing a fastball. And he just knew how to pitch. And everybody wondered how he got that much knowledge at that age to know that much about pitching. You don't usually learn that until you're almost at the end of your career, really. He knew it then and that's what everybody noticed about him right away, I guess. So he was just such a great pitcher.

Oh, he was right at the top. Yeah. Unfortunately, though, he never won a Cy Young, you know. For some reason, I don't want to say why, but for some reason he was always overlooked. And then he was right there every year. And one of those other guys always got one or two votes more than him for whatever reason.

He was such a good guy, such an easygoing guy. I mean, if you didn't like Marichal, you couldn't like anybody.

Nineteen sixty-two, World Series, Giants against the Yankees, Game Seven, two outs, bottom of the ninth, Ralph Terry on the mound, Matty Alou on third, Willie Mays on second. I go to bat. First base is open. So the first thing on my mind was, oh, shoot, I'm not gonna get to hit, because I'm thinking they were gonna put me on. Of course, Cepeda is over there, who's a good hitter. But since Terry is a right-hander and I'm a left-handed hitter it made sense to put me on. Plus, I had hit Terry really well during that Series. I hit a home run off him in the second game of the Series. I tripled off him in that particular game and then scored. So, naturally, you'd figure he's not gonna pitch to me.

And their manager, Ralph Houk, he goes out to the mound to talk to him. And that's what I was figuring that he went out to talk to him about. But Ralph says just pitch to McCovey, which he did. Everybody knows what happened. Well, the first ball I hit, I pulled it foul. Everybody was saying it would have been a home run but it wouldn't have been, it wasn't hit that far. I hit it pretty far down the right-field line but it was a foul. And that's when I realized they were gonna pitch to me. So it was either the next pitch or the next pitch after that, that I hit the line drive. Although he will tell you differently, Bobby Richardson was almost playing me out of position because everybody played me to foul. They even had exaggerated shifts on me. I couldn't believe some of the shifts they were pulling on me. He was playing close to the second-base bag. No second baseman ever played me there. And that's exactly where I hit the ball. And he was standing right there.

It happened so fast. I think I took one step, and that was it. It was over. I was depressed, naturally, because I felt I had let everybody down, especially myself, because I wanted to be the man to win the Series. I always liked being up in situations like that.

I remember the *Peanuts* cartoon that came after that. I got to meet and know Charlie Schulz, the creator of *Peanuts*, really well. He and I played golf a lot together. And I guess the first one was, well, they had the box of Charlie Brown sitting down. And then in the last box, he said, why couldn't McCovey hit the ball two feet higher, or something like that?

In 1963 we had the three-way platoon. Harvey Kuenn came over from Cleveland in 1960. He played for Detroit, and then he was with Cleveland when we traded for him. When Cepeda didn't play, I played first base. When Harvey didn't play, I played left field. So I was kind of the swing man that year.

That year I led the league in home runs with 44. Even made the All-Star team for the first time. Hank Aaron and I tied for the home run lead, and we both hit 44. We both wore 44, and we're both from Mobile.

* * *

One of the biggest thrills of my career was that I hit cleanup in the 1969 All-Star game in Washington. I was the MVP at the All-Star game that year, I hit two home runs. I remember hitting one off Blue Moon Odom, and one off Denny McLain. So when I look back to all those guys in the lineup—Aaron and Mays and [Ernie] Banks—and the MVP at the All-Star game, you know, it doesn't get much better than that. In most of the All-Star games that I played in, I usually hit fourth and Mays would lead off. Hank Aaron would hit third, and I'd hit fourth.

Nobody played right field like Clemente. Nobody. He would come into a visiting ballpark and he could play that right-field fence as though he played there all year, better than the player that played it.

My first year in the majors the Pirates came to town. The bottom of the eighth inning, Harvey Haddix was pitching, good left-handed pitcher. Then Willie came up to me and said, if you're patient now— Willie was on first base—he said, if you're patient, give him a few pitches. Willie would steal second base. And if you get a hit, you can be a hero. So I did. I took a pitch. The second pitch, I took it. Willie stole second. The next pitch, I hit to right field, and Willie scores. But Clemente plays it off the wall, and I made the turn at first base. He already had the ball behind me. Threw me out on the turn.

Everybody has a pitcher that gives a little more trouble than other guys. And I had my trouble with Bobby Veale, who pitched for the Pirates, a big, tall left-hander. I had one good year off of him that I can remember, maybe one good month, I should say, not a whole year. Boy, I was happy with that month. All the good pitchers are going to give you problems at one time or another, naturally, but he might have been the most consistent one.

Sandy Koufax threw hard; he developed pinpoint control. So he wasn't the type of guy who like was going to trick you at the plate. It was, here it comes, and let me see you hit it. And most of the time you didn't. He was the greatest. I mean, when we would play, we'd always go on the road together, the Dodgers and the Giants, and they would either follow us to a town or we would follow them to a town. So we could always look back at the scoreboard at the Dodgers, see what they were doing. And if we saw a bunch of zeroes on the scoreboard, we knew who was pitching for the Dodgers.

I hit Don Drysdale probably better than I hit anybody, so I didn't have any problems with Drysdale. Bob Gibson came across as being pretty mean. He was gonna let you know who was in control out there. If you stood too close to the plate, he was gonna back you up a little bit. He was gonna get you off the plate. He was never gonna fraternize with you. So you never knew what he was thinking out

Bob Gibson

there. And you better not show him up. Even when you got a home run or something off him, you better just run around the bases as though you've been there before, not put on all these antics like these guys do today. I didn't get really what you'd call really knocked down like a lot of guys do. But Drysdale would knock Willie down a lot. I was the one that hit him well and he didn't knock me down at all, never did.

Nineteen sixty-nine was my MVP year, 45 home runs, led the league; 126 RBIs, led the league; batted .320, fifth in the league, pretty close to a triple crown. But it was 1968 when a lot of people thought I should have won. That was Gibson's fantastic year, and they gave him both awards, Cy Young and MVP. Hitters didn't think pitchers deserve that MVP award. They have their own award, the Cy Young. And that's the only time I've seen Mays speak out publicly that he thought I should have won that year. I led the league in both home runs and RBIs in that year, too. And the only guy that had a higher batting average, I think, was Pete Rose, because, you know, that was the so-called year of the pitcher.

I was just kind of in the zone that year, and it's just hard to explain, it's just like, you just know nobody can get you out. I've heard people trying to tell stories like that, the ball looked like a basketball or something. It never looked that big to me but I just felt like I was gonna get a hit all the time. I just felt this guy can't get me out, you know? And it's just a good feeling to have that feeling.

I was playing on a two-year contract and I was rewarded by Horace Stoneham by his tearing up that contract and giving me more money the next year, which he didn't have to do. It was kind of unheard of in that time to sign even a two-year contract, which I had done. You're always taking a chance when you sign up for a long-term contract. It just so happened I had a better year in the middle of that contract. And I didn't go back and ask for that, he just volunteered it to me. He said, I'm gonna tear up that contract and give you more money because you deserve it.

I don't remember what my salary was. Maybe $45,000, $50,000, that was big money then. If you made $100,000, that was the ultimate. I made more my last couple of years than I made in my peak years. But it just seems to work out that way.

Gaylord Perry was a real Giant, although he bounced around to a lot of teams, as you know, but he signed as a Giant. Great pitching prospect, one of the better pitchers during his early years here. We all hated to see him go. He was quite a guy, you know? He had a place down in Portola Valley, down in the peninsula there, a little old-fashioned wood-sided big spread down there. And on his big spread, he was constantly working on the yard, because he had quite a few acres. So, Gaylord would come up with an idea that he would invite

Gaylord Perry

the players to come down to his place, but he said, dress casual. And when they got there, he'd put them all to work. He was smart.

But I tell you, boy, he was a great teammate. He was one of those type of pitchers when you threw at one of his batters, he was gonna get you. He protected his hitters. And the funny story, we had a rule on our team when Alvin Dark was here, that if one of the pitchers on another team threw at one of our best hitters, you didn't throw at their best hitter like most teams did. You got the pitcher. That was the rule we had. And I got beaned once, although the pitcher wasn't really trying to do that, I know that.

We played the Cleveland Indians in an exhibition game. And the pitcher that was up to hit the next time, in one of those situations, was Gaylord's brother Jim Perry, and Gaylord knocked him down. So, when you hear those stories about him knocking his mother down, Gaylord was that type of guy. He really protected you.

The umpires would come out there, almost undress him, try to find Vaseline or whatever they thought he was using, and the very next pitch after they got going, undressing him and toweling him a little down, the next pitch would be the best one he threw all game. He was amazing.

Then in 1973 I was traded. Willie had gotten traded to the Mets. Stoneham was gone. The Giants had changed ownership and Bob Lurie had taken over the team. I was placed under the 10-5 rule at the time, so I had to okay the trade. It wasn't like I woke up one day and listened to the radio and found out I was traded somewhere. This was something that Horace Stoneham and I had talked about. He was losing a lot of money, so he was getting rid of all his high-priced players and he wanted to make sure they were happy, so he would ask us, me and Mays, where we wanted to go.

And we talked about some of the ballparks that I could hit, where I had good years, and some of those teams where I didn't want to go to. Because he thought that, with that short right-field wall in Detroit, he thought, God, I'd hit 50, 60, 70 home runs a year. But I wanted to stay in the National League and I wanted to stay in California, so that's why San Diego was the perfect fit. Buzzie Bavasi, who was with the Padres, we all three were on the phone. And I let them know then that this is where I wanted to end my career. So, they all agreed that we could make that happen. But they thought if I came down I could save the franchise.

That last year with the Padres, I didn't sign that year. You could play out your option if you wanted to, and then you were free to go to anywhere you wanted. So, I didn't sign that year. I was playing out my option that last year. So I got traded from the Padres to the A's. But since I wasn't signed, I wasn't gonna even report to the A's. And Chub Feeney talked me into reporting because Chub used to be my general manager, Horace Stoneham's son-in-law.

So, he said, you'll tarnish your reputation by not reporting because you'll get a lot of bad publicity if you don't report. He said, you have too good an image to do that. So I said, well, I'm not gonna sign with them, but I'll go and finish out the season, which had only like about three weeks or so left. So I figured, I can put up with Finley [owner of the A's] for that little time. So I did report, but that team was really in disarray, everybody on that team at the time, and they really had a chance to win it that year. But everybody just couldn't wait till the season was over, so they could get out of there.

So, I was glad when the season was over. So, I could go back to spring training that next year with the Giants, which I'd already arranged to do. But I talked to Bob Lurie and, of course, he honored the gentleman's agreement that I had with Horace and brought me back to spring training with no guarantees that I was gonna make the team. But I made the Comeback Player of the Year that year.

I pride myself as being the only Giants Hall of Famer that actually retired as a Giant. Everybody else retired with other teams.

Early in that 1978 season I hit my 500th home run. It took forever for me to do that because we had a lot of reporters who followed me from the year before waiting for me to hit it. And I just got tired with all those reporters following me around, asking me, when are you gonna do it? When are you gonna do it? So when I did it, it was more of a relief than anything. That was in Atlanta against the Braves—Jamie Easterly, the little left-hander. We had a lot of young players on the team that year, Jack Clark and a bunch of guys, and then they were all, they were happy, it seemed like they were happier that I did it than I was.

I didn't know what the Hall of Fame was, to be honest, when I was at Mobile. I just wanted to play. I would have played for nothing, to be honest with you. I just wanted to play that bad.

The players now are a lot bigger, stronger, faster, a lot of them are more athletic, but I think the guys in my era knew how to play the game more than the guys of today. Otherwise, they had more baseball instincts, you know, knew the fundamentals of the game. Guys nowadays, they make unbelievable dives and catches and things that, I mean, I'm impressed with some of the catches and things I see nowadays. But I just don't think they know all the fundamentals of baseball. A lot of them learn that at the major league level rather than learning it in the minor leagues.

It seems like most of the big league teams now are spending their money in the Dominican Republic rather than over here to give the black players a place to play. I hear they finally started looking in that direction now, I don't know. But I know they spent a lot of money in the Dominican Republic to build facilities down there. And as you know, many of the players on the clubs now are coming out of the Dominican Republic.

It was an honor for someone to ask you for an autograph, and we didn't mind signing autographs. But with autographs so valuable now and people selling your autograph, that's why I think most guys are skeptical about signing autographs nowadays. The adults, they put these kids up to come and ask you for an autograph. And they give them a couple of bucks. Then the next day, you see your autograph on eBay, where they've sold it. And everybody puts the guys down now because they won't sign autographs, but that's one of the reasons.

It was an honor when the Giants named part of the ballpark after me, McCovey Cove. And that only really came about when they decided to do the statue of Mays and named the street out there Willie Mays Parkway, or whatever they call it. There was a writer for the *San Jose Mercury* who thought I meant more than Mays, and who asked why haven't they done at least something for me.

So, it was really that writer who got together with Peter Magowan, with Larry Baer, actually, and discussed what they were gonna do. Well, they said, there is this statue already planned for him. And this writer said, you know, if McCovey had played here, if he hit 100 home runs, he would have hit that body of water back there. So, Pete said, why don't you call that McCovey Cove? And then Barry Bonds made it famous because he hit a lot of home runs in there. But I don't think they were looking at that when they decided to name it McCovey Cove. They were just thinking of what I might have done had I played here.

I just hope I left a legacy that lets people know how much I love the game. And I really mean what I said, that I would have played it for nothing, but I thought you can't make a living playing it for nothing. But I would have, I wanted to play that badly. I loved being a Giant. I mean, I grew up as a Dodger fan because of Jackie Robinson. But there is nothing like the Giant family. From Horace Stoneham to Peter Magowan, and now, a new guy coming in, I think he's gonna be just as good as everybody else. That's kind of the legacy I'd like, to be remembered as just a really nice guy.

JUAN MARICHAL

When high-kicking pitcher Juan Marichal arrived in the major leagues, he seemed destined for greatness. On July 19, 1960, the twenty-two-year-old righty, who was in Class D ball just two years earlier, made his big league debut by tossing a one-hitter—only the third player to pitch a one-hit game in his major league debut—and striking out twelve batters, as the San Francisco Giants defeated the Philadelphia Phillies, 2–0. He not only retired the first nineteen batters but had a no-hitter going with two outs in the eighth inning.

After the game, Marichal was asked if he was worried about winning. Teammate Orlando Cepeda, translating for the Spanish-speaking rookie, just smiled, not even asking Marichal for the answer to that question. "Juan said he expected to win," Cepeda said. "He always expects to win."

Win he did, finishing with six 20-victory seasons and a 243–142 record over sixteen years. Along the way he had a no-hitter against Houston in 1963, was named to ten All-Star teams, tossed 52 shutouts, and completed 244 starts. The ultimate honor came with his induction into the National Baseball Hall of Fame in 1983.

"The symbol of his artistry . . . was the windup, with the high, graceful kick that left the San Francisco Giants hurler poised precariously on one leg like a bronzed Nureyev before he swept smoothly forward and pro-pelled the baseball toward the plate," was how sportswriter Ron Bellamy described Marichal in 1973.

Marichal, who began playing baseball on the dusty sandlots of the Dominican Republic, mesmerized hitters with his changeups, off-speed curves, sliders, and his famous kick-to-the-sky delivery.

While most pitchers are lucky to have two effective pitches—curveball and fastball—Marichal had eighteen, maybe twenty, according to fellow Hall of Famer Cepeda. "He throws a fastball from here [gesturing over-hand], here [gesturing sidearm], here [underhand]. He throws the curve-ball from here [overhand], here [sidearm], and here [underhand]," Cepeda said. "He has eight different speeds on his fastball. He can throw his curve so it will take a week. He can throw a screwball so it will do a tango if he wants."

Longtime opponent Hank Aaron once explained, "He can throw all day within a two-inch space, in, out, up, or down. I've never seen anyone as good as that."

Hoping to capture Marichal's signature pitching motion, columnist Jim Murray, who was honored with the 1987 J. G. Taylor Spink Award for excellence in baseball writing, wrote in 1968: "Every hitter in the league can tell you what size shoe he wears, what color it is, what the label is and how many spikes it has on it. The first thing Juan Marichal does on the mound is put his foot up in the batter's eyes. He kicks his leg so high in the air some batters can't recognize him when he has both feet on the ground."

Marichal, nicknamed the "Dominican Dandy," understood pressure when at age seventeen he was ordered to pitch for his country's air force team. The squad soon found itself in jail for ten days after losing a double-header, Marichal dropping one of the games 1–0. Perhaps it was ex-periences like that that helped Marichal become one of the greatest pitchers of his era.

Juan Marichal

I started playing baseball when I was seven years old and playing with the kids. I loved the game and right from the beginning I wanted to be a baseball player. My older brother, Gonzalo, he used to help me with balls and bats. When we started, we used to make our own ball and bat. We used to climb a tree and cut a branch, let it dry, and make a bat.

Baseball in that town, Manzanillo, was played on a small golf course, with the people from the Grenada Company—that was the name of the company; it was owned by American people.

They used to play golf there, and we used to go and find golf balls. So we used that golf ball, enlarged it with stockings and thread, and we kept rolling it there. It would get bigger and then when we got it to the size of a baseball, we took it to a shoemaker for a cover if we had a peso or two to pay him to put the cover on; otherwise, we put a nylon on it. We called it a *gangora*. And we'd tie them up real tight, and that's how we played. That's how we played in those days.

I remember leaving my house for school, and if I found somebody playing baseball on my way to school, I never got to school because I stopped and played baseball with those kids. When my teacher told my mother, ah, she was—well, I shouldn't say mad but she was—she didn't like what I did and I did that so many times. And she used to ask me, what are you going to do when you grow up? And I said, I'm going to be a baseball player. But I didn't know about Major League Baseball. I didn't know that you can make money playing baseball.

I just wanted to be a baseball player because in my country there was a team, the national team, that played all over the world representing the Dominican Republic and I—at that age, I wanted to be one of those players. And when I was nine years old my brother-in-law took me to see that team, and on that team was a guy named Bombo Ramos, a right-handed pitcher, that threw sidearm. He pitched the afternoon game and when I saw that man, I went back home and told my friends that I wanted to be a pitcher like Bombo Ramos. At that time I used to play shortstop because I wanted to play every day, you know, with the kids, and I loved to hit.

So after that day I went back home and started throwing the ball all over the place. Yes, I wanted to be a pitcher. So, in 1955, I played my first organized championship at age seventeen, or sixteen going on seventeen. So we won the whole thing. You know, over there you got different places that you had to play against, like, my team was on the west side of the island. We won the whole thing there, then we had to play the central part of the island. So we beat every team there, then we had to face the capital and south, east, and north. We won the whole thing. The following year, 1956, I played for a team, the city of Manzanillo, and that team was owned by the United Fruit Company, a big company that spent lots of years in my country.

They used to have a real good baseball team. They recruited a lot of kids from the country to play on their team and I was one of them. So the same thing happened. We won our zone, then we went to the central part, we beat everybody. Then we were playing in the capital. For the first time in my life I pitched in the capital, against the university named USA, Universidad Autónoma de Santo Domingo. So I faced that team, and I was lucky enough, I pitched a shutout against that team. Then we faced the south and we faced the east—and the east was a city that everybody knows, because it produces so many major league players today, San Pedro de Macorís. So we played San Pedro, and the last team we had to face was the Dominican air force.

They used to call it Aviación Militar Dominicana. They came to Manzanillo to play against my team. I played the first game in the morning and I beat them 2–1. The next day about eight o'clock in the morning somebody knocked on my door. I went out and opened the door, and there was a lieutenant, with the uniform and everything, with a telegram. I was—for a minute I was a little bit shaky, you know. I said, what did I do wrong, you know, to have this guy here looking for me? He handed me a telegram saying be at the Dominican air force immediately. Now I was shaking. I ran, took a bath, put my clothes on, and went home to see my mother.

I say my mother, and don't mention my father, because I never, never met my father. I was three years old when he passed away. So I never met him. So I went to my home. I showed the telegram to my mother. She didn't know what to do. She was upset about the whole thing. She claimed later that the reason she was acting that way was that she considered that I was a kid and did not belong in the air force. But I waited and I waited and I waited for her decision, and about four o'clock in the afternoon the same lieutenant came back with another telegram. When she saw the second telegram she said, son, you can't say no to those people. When she said those people she meant the big dictator of the Dominican Republic, Rafael Leonidas Trujillo Molina.

And his son was chief of the air force at the rank of general.

When she said you can't say no to those people, I think I was waiting for that answer. So right away, I packed a little bit of clothes and I took a bus to Santo Domingo. I got to the base, they welcomed me to the team, and I spent fourteen months in the air force. Now, we are talking about 1957. We had to do the same thing that we did when I was with Manzanillo. I considered the Dominican air force the best team in the country. In fourteen months I lost three games. Now we had to face Manzanillo, which had been my team a year before, in 1956. We got there; we lost a doubleheader. I pitched one of those games and I lost—we lost both games on Sunday. When we came back to the base the general, Ramfis Trujillo, formed a commission to investigate why we had lost two games.

In the meantime they put everybody in jail: manager, players, and coaches. They were in Manzanillo investigating. I don't know what they found out, but we spent ten days in jail until they came back.

During that time I played for the air force there were about three or four scouts. I remember one from the Yankees, I remember one from the Dodgers, I remember one from the Pirates, and a man who wasn't a scout, who was what they call a bird dog. He used to work for Alex Pompez, the Giants scout then in the United States and the Dominican Republic. So, this man's name was Horacio Martinez, he used to be a shortstop and then he played in the Negro Leagues, a good shortstop, couldn't hit, but they say that he was the best glove ever. So he talked to my brother. Everywhere I went, I pitched good most of the time.

He told my brother that he was interested in signing me. So my brother told him, well, I don't think he's ready but I can make an agreement with you that when he's ready you would be the one signing. So I was in the country playing all over the place, and one day he told my brother or my brother told him that I was ready, so the Giants sent him to see me at the base and they wanted to sign me and my brother said, what type of money is he going to get? Well, we can offer him $500. I was so happy, not because of the $500 but because I was going to be a professional baseball player, something that I dreamed of since I was seven years old.

I wanted to be a baseball player. So Horacio Martinez and the president of the Escogido Baseball Club came to the base, they got me out, and that day, September 16, 1957, I signed my contract, my first contract to become a professional baseball player. There was a team for the United States, Las Estrellas de Willie Mays, and they promised me on the signing that they were going to take me to see that team at Santo Domingo.

So I went to see Las Estrellas de Willie Mays on the same day that I signed my contract and I saw Willie Mays for the first time step up to home plate. He faced a left-handed pitcher and I think that the pitcher wanted to throw the ball before he was ready, so he called time, he dug a little bit in the dirt, and the next pitch was over the left-field fence. I can never forget that, that night. That was beautiful. The following year, 1958, they send me to Sanford, Florida, where the Giants have the minor league camp. They used to have major league camp in Phoenix, Arizona, and minor league camp in Sanford, Florida. For the first time I left my country, with a group of players—Manny Mota, Danny Rivas, Fred Velazquez. We belonged to the same team in Santo Domingo, to the Escogido Baseball Club.

We got to Sanford and I was shocked. I can tell you that I was shocked when I saw that the Latin and the Negro couldn't be together with the white players, because we never saw that in my country. But it didn't bother me, because I wanted to concentrate on being a baseball player. I got to a Class C team, and I don't think the manager liked me too much, because he had more experienced baseball players. They moved me from Class C to Class D. I don't know if you remember this man, Buddy Kerr, used to play shortstop way back for the New York Giants. He was my manager, and what that man did for us was unbelievable, he was like a father to us.

We broke camp in Sanford and we had to ride in a Greyhound bus all the way to Michigan City, Indiana, and they have places where you stop to refuel and places where you can eat. But, in those places we couldn't go through the front door. So this man Buddy Kerr always all the time was with us when we had to go through the back door or through the kitchen, and I really, really, really have some respect for that man. I love him. He passed away some time ago, but let me tell you I never met such a wonderful person as Buddy Kerr. In Michigan City, we couldn't stay in the hotel with the white players. So they had to rent rooms for us to stay with black families. One of the things that really got me was the cold weather.

In early March you can see the trees, like, no leaves, you know, and I thought, oh, my God, how can that happen to those beautiful trees? I didn't know at that time that the seasons change from winter to spring to summer, and that later on those trees were going to get leaves, they were going to get green, and it really, it really surprised me. In the Dominican, the trees never lose their leaves because we don't have any winter, we don't have spring—maybe a little bit, but not winter, it's summer most of the time. So we were there, we had three or four Latinos on the team, and one of them was a Cuban guy from Key West, and he was our interpreter because we could hardly say, "Give me a glass of water," in English.

When we were on the field and the manager wanted me to do something he always was there with the manager to be sure that I understood what the manager was telling me. At that time there was no pitch count, no limit. So, at the beginning I won 21 games in the regular season and 2 in the playoffs. Altogether I went 23–8 with a 1.87 ERA. I pitched 245 innings and I struck out 246, my first year at Class D. When the season was over I went back home. Some announcer in the Dominican called me Juan Veintitrés—I don't know if you remember Pope John XXIII—because of the 23 games that I won. I had a pretty good year in the Dominican playing for Escogido. We became a champion in that year. We won the Winter League championship.

The following year, 1959, I was assigned to Class A, Springfield, Massachusetts. We got to Springfield, the season started, I was pitching pretty good and at that time I pitched exactly like Bombo Ramos, nothing but sidearm. So, right before the season was over my manager, Andy Gilbert, came up to me one day and said, why do you throw like that? You know, the question really surprised me because this guy had seen me for two years already and he never asked me that question. I didn't want to go through the story about Bombo Ramos, so I told him, well, that's how I learned, and then he said, You never have any arm problems?

When he asked me that I said to myself, well, I'd better tell this guy the whole story. So I said, listen, when I was a little kid I went to see this guy named Bombo Ramos in my country and after I saw him I wanted to become a pitcher like him. So I started throwing like him. So he said, do you want to learn how to throw overhand? I said to him, what would be the benefit if I learn? He said, well you would be a much, much better pitcher against left-handed hitters. So when I heard that, I right away said yes, I want to learn. So he took me to the bullpen, with two baseballs and a catcher. I started to throw overhand but it seemed to me it was impossible to do it without kicking my leg, and that was the day that I started to kick my leg so high. I felt like I was throwing a little bit hard with good control, and I fell in love with the style.

And I end up winning 20 games in Class A and I lost 10, I think. When the season was over, they assigned me to Tacoma, Washington. But before I got to Tacoma, they invited me to Phoenix with the big club, with no contract, just invited to spring training. I was so happy when I got to Phoenix and saw all those guys, all major leaguers, and all that, and the manager was Alvin Dark. He told me you're going to pitch batting practice, so almost every day, I was pitching batting practice. In those days they didn't have that protection, the screen in front of you, so that you can throw from the mound with the screen and to protect you. One day, a week later, they told me, "You're not going to pitch today, so you can take a day off."

I went to the outfield and shagged balls, and all of a sudden the pitching coach came up, Larry Jansen, and said, Juan, Alvin changed his mind, he wants you to pitch batting practice. At that time, from pitching batting practice every day I got a real, real, real bad rash from my supporter—you could see blood on both of my legs in there—so I hadn't put on a supporter or cup that day. I was afraid to tell him that I had to go to the clubhouse and put my supporter on, so I went to the mound to try to pitch batting practice, and I remember the first pitch I threw, the hitter hit a line drive and hit my right testicle. Let me tell you I said so many things—I said, how can this happen to me, how can you have such bad luck?

They sent me to the hospital in Phoenix for about five days. Then they decided to send me to Sanford, Florida. The only thing that I was doing every day was putting a bag of ice in there because it got swollen and I could hardly move. I never forgot that trip from Phoenix to Sanford. I didn't know one word of English, so I was afraid I'd get lost in the airplane. But luckily enough I got there, I got to Miami. From Miami it was a bus ride to Sanford. I got there, and I spent the whole spring training seeing a doctor every day. Couldn't throw, couldn't practice, couldn't do anything, but they kept me in there on the Triple-A roster.

When we broke camp, we went to Tacoma, Washington. That was the first year that the Giants Triple-A team was in Tacoma. Before it was in Phoenix, where McCovey, Orlando Cepeda, Felipe Alou, Andre Rodgers, and Willie Kirkland, all those guys came from there. But now they had moved the franchise to Tacoma. When we got there it was raining every day. We had to wait like eight days before we played the first game. People used to say that the president of that team was very tight with money. If you asked him for a raise, you never got it. So I was there and I was pitching pretty good, I got 11 wins, and I told people that the reason the Giants called me up was that I had asked Tacoma's president for a raise.

I was pitching in Sacramento in 1960, two days before they were going to play the Triple-A All-Star game. They told me every member of that team was going to get a beautiful watch, and I was happy because I was picked to be the starting pitcher in that game. So I was pitching against the Sacramento Bees—I beat them 2–1—and about twelve o'clock, maybe eleven-thirty at night in the clubhouse, I was taking a shower, happy because we won, this and that. The trainer came up to me and said, Juan, the Giants just called you up. Now I was happy because I was going to San Francisco, but I was sad because I wasn't going to get my watch.

But let me tell you, the next day, the same trainer drove me in a bus to San Francisco. When we got to Candlestick Park I walked through that door and Orlando and Felipe Alou were there. They seemed happy and proud to have another Latin on the team, so they grabbed me and introduced me to every player in the clubhouse, and I'll never forget when I shook Willie Mays's hand. I said, oh, my God, now I know why he is so great. So good a hitter, so good a player, and when I went in and shook Willie McCovey's hand and saw his body I couldn't believe it. I felt like I was in heaven, you know, and I started thinking about when I was seven years old and I used to argue with my mother: She wanted me to go to school and I say, no, I'm going to be a baseball player.

She said, when you grow up and you get married and create a family, how are you going to support your family? I said, don't worry, Mama, you're going to be so proud when you hear my name on the radio. That was the only thing I said to her because I could not talk about money because I didn't know about that.

I was happy when I got there. At that time the manager was Tom Sheehan, because they just had released Bill Rigney. He told me, he said, listen, you're going to throw batting practice to keep in shape. But you're going to watch every team that comes by. You watch them and you're going to pitch on July 19. I got there July 10, so that kept me nine days just throwing batting practice and watching all the teams. So, that day came and I remember going to the mound in the bullpen to warm up. I felt great, I felt good, and when they were announcing the lineup and they came up to my name, I felt something that I never, never felt before, some chill in my body, and I said to myself, I hope this will go away because there is no way I can pitch with this kind of feeling. So, now they played the national anthem. I walked from the bullpen to the mound with the batboy at my side and when I got to the mound, I gave him my jacket and the towel.

I started throwing to the plate, you know, the seven pitches you are allowed, and I got that feeling, I felt the same way, and when I saw the leadoff man and the umpire called, "Play ball," the whole thing went away, and thank God that feeling went away, because there was no way I could have thrown a ball feeling that way. I got lucky, I pitched a one-hitter, and that one hit was by Clay Dalrymple, the Philadelphia Phillies' catcher, in the eighth inning. I didn't mind that he broke up my no-hitter, I was so happy that I won the game and pitched nine innings. So that's how my professional baseball career at the major league level started, with a one-hitter against the Phillies.

I always told my mother, you got to come and see me pitch in the major leagues. She said, I'm sorry, son, I don't fly in those planes—she used to say, those *"aparato"* (apparatus). I could never convince her to come to San Francisco, but she used to come to see me in the Winter League in the Dominican Republic.

Today I tell every youngster that wants to be a baseball player that you can do both. You can go to school and you can play ball. I never finished school, though. It was baseball, baseball day and night, and I dedicated myself to my profession. I think that when you want to be somebody, you have to try hard. You have to work hard, and the more time you put into something that you want and you like, the quicker you can be better. I didn't want to be just a baseball player. When I heard the names Sandy Koufax, Bob Gibson, Warren Spahn, all those big names, I wanted to be the same level as those guys, and to do that you have to work hard. You have to be dedicated to your profession. I never was a person that loved to go to a disco.

I think that I did well enough to win at least one Cy Young Award. Up until 1967, there was only one for both leagues. I remember when Dean Chance won it in '64. I remember when Mike McCormick won it in '67. At the All-Star break in 1967, I had a record of 14–4, and running in Shea Stadium I pulled a hamstring and after that I couldn't pitch, so they sent me to a doctor in Los Angeles. He said, well, if you don't want to lose him stop using him. That year I could have won another 20 games, but if you put that year with '68—I only won 14 in '67 and 26 in '68—combined that is 40 games. So that year broke my streak of over five straight years with 20 or more wins. Some of those 20-win years I didn't get one vote for the Cy Young Award. So I have to say there was something wrong with the system.

I faced a lot of good hitters. The guys you didn't want to see come to home plate were Roberto Clemente, Pete Rose, Billy Williams, Willie Stargell, Tony Davis—I don't know if you remember Tony Davis before he broke his ankle. Man, he was awesome, what a hitter.

I'm very happy that Andy Gilbert taught me how to throw overhand because by learning that, I was able to throw a slider. The only way you could throw sliders was overhand. I learned my overhand curve. I learned the pitch that I think kept me sixteen years at the major league level, the screwball.

When Ruben Gomez, a Puerto Rican pitcher, was with the Giants, I used to read a lot about Ruben Gomez's screwball. So, after I learned how to throw overhand, one day I went to Andy, I said, Andy, how do you throw a screwball? He said, Juan, I don't know. Don't ask me because I don't know. He said, but you throw a fastball this way, you throw a slider that way, you throw a curve that way, I think the screwball is backward. You have to turn your arm this way. He moved his arm and showed me what he thought was the way to throw it.

So, after that day, every time I was on the field and I was able to play catch with somebody, the only thing that I used to do was that. And two years later, I had one of the best screwballs in the major leagues. And that pitch was the one that kept me in the major leagues for sixteen years. I remember facing the Dodgers and Philadelphia, I used to face—one time I faced nine left-handed batters when I pitched against the Dodgers . . . and eight when I pitched against Philadelphia. And the only reason I could survive was the screwball.

The screwball is like a left-hander's curve to left-handed hitters. When you throw a screwball, the ball rotates from left to right. And it seemed to be a fastball but then, at the last minute, the ball started rotating away from the left-handed hitter. So it was very effective against left-hand hitters because they can't hit the ball with too much power unless they know how to go to the opposite field. But, when you have to change your swing, once you've identified the pitch as being not a fastball, but a screwball, sometimes it's too late to change and go to the opposite field.

Using the screwball, I think, can damage your arm. At that time I remember seeing Carl Hubbell. He was one of the best screwball pitchers of his time, and his arm got so bad that he used to carry his hand in his pocket because his arm got like this [demonstrates with his elbow]. And they used to tell me, look at Carl Hubbell, your arm is going to be the same way. Both my arms stayed the same.

I used to turn my body and throw from that position. When you throw overhand and kick your leg, you have to push hard to bring that leg down quick enough to be ready to release the ball. If you're not powerful with your right leg, the left leg is going to be floating in the air and you won't have good mechanics to finish. And I think that really helped my career, my high leg kick.

I remember, in the 1962 World Series, pitching in New York, I struck out Mickey Mantle twice and the next day there was a picture of him at home plate breaking his bat. And somebody asked him, you know, what was wrong with Juan Marichal? And I remember exactly what he said. He said, well, the thing about that guy is that he kicks his leg, then he looks like he's going to throw his glove in your face, and the last thing you see is the ball, and it's too late. You know, that made me feel great, when I heard that from Mickey Mantle, one of the best in baseball.

It made me feel good. I was proud of that game. The only thing was that I only went four innings because I hurt my index finger. Whitey Ford was pitching, I was trying to bunt the ball, the ball hit me, and I had to come out of the game. We ended up winning that game 7–3, but I was pitching the best game of my life that day. And I was winning 2–0 in the fourth inning. I didn't get credit for the win.

Something very funny happened in that 1962 World Series. We played the first two games in San Francisco. Then we moved back to New York and the Series was tied. When we got back to San Francisco, it's such bad weather we had a three-day rain delay. They used to send one team to work out in Modesto and the other team worked out in Stockton. And for us to play the last game, they brought into the field three helicopters to dry all the water out of the outfield grass.

And the infield, they raked the dirt. They raked it and put gasoline on it and burned it. And that's how we played the last game. Because there was so much water. As a matter of fact, that rainout helped the Yankees win, because there was a ball that Willie Mays hit to right field, and Roger Maris was playing right field, and Matty Alou couldn't score, because the ball stopped right where it hit the ground and stuck there. So Roger Maris grabbed the ball and threw to Bobby Richardson and kept Matty from scoring.

And everybody knows what happened next, that famous line drive that McCovey hit and the famous catch that Bobby Richardson made to end the Series and win that game, 1–0.

McCovey's line drive—you can't hit a ball harder than that. And when Bobby Richardson caught it, he went to the ground with both hands because the ball really hit his glove so hard and he was running to the left, so he went down and he came up—last out of the Series.

* * *

Every year, at that time, I used to go back home, and a lot of writers asked me what would be my goal, my next goal at the major league level, and the only thing I said to them was, be healthy, because I knew if I was healthy I would be able to pitch every four days. When I see writers in the playoffs and World Series talking about a pitcher that is going to come up with three days' rest, they'll blow that up so big, talking about a pitcher with three days' rest. I pitched all my life with three days' rest. Every four days, I was on the mound.

Today you got so many relievers. Yeah, you got the setup man, and then you have the closer. I think the managers are waiting to get that far with their starting pitching and to start making all those moves, you know, with that reliever, and the closer, and all that. I guess they think that they don't need a pitcher to go nine innings anymore.

I used to admire Clemente because of the way he played. He played to win. And every time he came to the plate, he wanted to get you. And you could see it. You could tell just by the way he walked to the plate. He used to hit a ground ball to the pitcher, to the mound. And if you didn't hurry up, he could beat you to first. He never gave up. And I think that's the way the game should be played.

I remember one time, there were like seven Latin guys on the Pirates, and we had Gil Garrido from Panama, Orlando Cepeda, myself, and Jose Cardenal. When we had a night game at eight o'clock, we used to go to the park at two o'clock in the afternoon and sit on the bench. The whole bunch talked baseball. And I remember, one day, they sat all together and talked about how this guy got me out, how I hit this guy. I sat outside the group, but I was listening. I heard Clemente say to Orlando and all, the pitch that gave me more problems was the fastball outside. And, you know, when I heard that, I said, my God, I was wrong. I thought he liked to hit that pitch to right field, but I was wrong, because the pitch that went to right field was the inside pitch. He was an inside-out hitter. And that was the

Roberto Clemente

ball he hit to right field like a bullet. So, I was pitching the next day, and I struck him out three times with a fastball. I threw like nothing but fastballs outside.

Hank Aaron—what a wrist. He would break the wrist and all of a sudden you'd see a ball leaving the park. And he wasn't the type of hitter who hit long balls. He used to hit it enough to go over the wall. He was a great hitter. And he never changed, whether the count was 1-2 or 2-0. He was the same type of hitter—tough, tough hitter.

I used to pitch him like, I would show him my fastball inside. And I was trying to get him out with the slider, outside corner. But you cannot pitch a good hitter just one way. You have to pitch him in and out, in and out, because if he knows you're going to pitch one way, he's going to get you. So, I used to throw him my whole variety of pitches, you know, slider, and even changeup. I used to get him out with the changeup.

Not too many people know Tony Gonzalez, who played for Philadelphia, but he was somebody that, no matter what I threw, he was able to put the bat on the ball. He sprayed the ball all over the field. I remember playing a game in Miami, what they're calling now the Legends Game. I was with one of the two Cuban teams, Marianao, and he was playing for Havana. I faced him, and I got him out. I told him, listen, it took me twenty-five years, but I did it. I really did it.

Gaylord Perry was a good buddy on the Giants, and I think the reason that he and I were doing so well was that we competed against each other. Our friendship was so great, so great, that we helped each other by doing that. I've got a lot of respect for Gaylord Perry.

We used to go to the infield every day, except the days we were pitching, to catch ground balls, and we'd bet a dollar. Every time you missed one was a dollar. And by the end of the season, we would end up maybe losing one or two dollars, no more than that. Sometimes we were even. And that's why we were in great shape to be able to pitch every four days, because of the conditioning.

You know, when Felipe got traded, after the '63 season, he got traded to Milwaukee for a pitcher named Bob Shaw. Bob Shaw used to throw a spitter; he'd keep a tablet underneath his tongue. When he came to the team, I remember we were in Pittsburgh, and he took Gaylord and me to the bullpen to teach us how to throw that pitch. So I went, and I don't know how many pitches I threw, but the next day, my elbow hurt for the first time in my life. And that was the only time I tried it in the bullpen. Never, never again. But Gaylord kept it up, and most of the time writers came out to me and said, is it true that Gaylord threw Vaseline and he threw this and threw that? And I said, no, he threw nothing like that. He was just good, that's why he got so many guys out. What happened, he wrote a book. In that book he admitted that he was throwing Vaseline, and I said to him one day, oh, my God, you made a liar out of me, because I always said you never threw that, and now you admit it. Gaylord is a great guy. Great guy.

Willie McCovey—a gentleman, a gentleman. He won so many games for me, with his bat, with his plays at first base. Great man. Good man. Willie Mays—my job was easy with a guy like him in center field, directing everybody, knowing how to play every hitter. When Gaylord and I were supposed to pitch, we would have a meeting to go over the opposing hitters, and most of the time it was only four guys: Mays, a catcher, Gaylord, and me. Four guys. And it was Willie who knew how to pitch to the guy, how he was going to play him, and if you made a mistake, if you didn't throw the pitch you were supposed to be throwing, Mays might charge a little bit to the left or to the right, so if you threw the wrong pitch, he'd let you know right away. Oh, yes. He let you know. He'd say, hey, what did we talk about in the meeting? You didn't do what I said. I guess, because of his experience, you know, his knowing baseball so well and being such a good hitter, he could anticipate the other guys. And that was good, when you could see what would happen next. That really helped you.

When somebody asks me about baseball players that I played with or I saw playing in my era, I always say that Willie Mays was number one in center field, and Roberto Clemente was number one in right field. And let me tell you, I don't care how much baseball you watch in your life, I don't think you're going to see two players like those two. And the way they played, the way they came out to the field to beat you. Clemente was that type of guy. He came out to beat you. And you had to try hard to get him. Willie Mays, same way, had so much talent. When you talk about five tools, those two guys had the five tools; complete ballplayers.

I saw so many good ballplayers. But for left fielder I have to say Barry Bonds, you know. With the bat he carried, I think everybody wanted to see him on the team.

The best catcher I saw was Johnny Bench. I hope that by saying this, I don't make my teammates that caught for me feel bad, but let me tell you, in those years that I won 25, 26 games, if I could've had a guy like Johnny Bench, I could have won over 30 games. That man was awesome. His arm, his glove, his bat, everything, everything. I pitched a few times with him behind home plate, in the All-Star game, and it was so easy for me. I was seeing like a wall behind home plate. I just threw the ball. And he was, like, doing nothing.

I used to throw five different pitches. And I used to work fast— maybe because of the wind and the dust in Candlestick Park. When I got to the mound I got my job done and went back to the bench right away, so I used to work fast for somebody who threw five pitches. And if you're waiting for the sign and the catcher puts up one and you want to throw number five, you have to wait until he gets to that number.

Another thing that I invented was running from the bench to the mound. People would say, why are you running? I would say, be- cause I want to get there before my players. That way, instead of seven pitches, I can throw ten, especially in bad weather, like in Candlestick. It's good to warm up well before you face the hitter.

My favorite parks to pitch in were Dodger Stadium and Shea. I used to love to pitch where the park was full of people. Loved that.

When you faced a pitcher like Sandy Koufax, the only thing that came up in your mind was, don't give up more than one run, because many times, he didn't give up more than one, or maybe none. So, when you go to the mound you're thinking about how good you have to do to beat that guy or you're going to end up sec- ond. When you face a guy like Sandy, man, he was awesome and beautiful to watch.

You know, I used to get outside the dugout, when he was pitch- ing, just to watch him. I enjoyed watching him. The command, you know. Johnny Roseboro behind the plate, good catcher. And, they used to combine perfectly, the command against the hitters and the pitch they were supposed to throw. Sandy only used to have two pitches, but the best two pitches you ever saw. Yeah. I mean, great, fastball that was, what do they call them, a rising fastball.

That pitch is hard to hit, because the ball rises. You know, when the ball comes straight, you can adjust. But when the ball rises, man, you see the ball coming and you're going to hit right here and the ball keeps going up, there's no way you can hit it, and same way with a curve, his breaking ball. It used to make a sound. If you're at home plate when the ball starts breaking, you can hear that thing breaking down.

I remember pitching against Sandy one day. I was hitting, and he threw me a curve. I started to swing about head high. And the ball started going down. I went down the same way and I broke the bat on home plate. True story.

Earlier in my career I faced Sandy three times, and one day, Alvin Dark said, I don't want to throw my best pitcher against their best. So, Sandy was number one for the Dodgers. Drysdale was number two. And he never, after those three games, he never put me against Sandy Koufax, never. So that's why I faced Koufax seven times and Drysdale twenty-nine times.

When Drysdale was on the mound, he meant business. He was a guy that didn't fool around. And if you hit a ball, you'd better start running right away. Don't stay there watching that ball leave the park, because the next pitch might go to your ear. Oh, yes. Those days, you know, he was able to throw it high, he was able to knock a guy down.

But Dark, he tried to stop that. In the National League the pitcher hit. So Dark came up with a rule, it's like, we're not going to get the best hitter from the other team, we're going to get the pitcher when he comes to the plate. And we stopped those beanballs because of that. They knew that if they got somebody from us, we were going to wait for the pitcher to come to the plate.

Bob Gibson was tough, tough. I always say that if Gibson in those days had to face his mother, he didn't care. He'd knock her down. Oh yeah, he was another one that, don't try to dig in, because you might have to hit out of that hole that you're making there. He didn't like hitters to come and dig. Well, baseball was different in those days. Today, I think a good pitcher is one that pitches in and out, and has good command of his pitches.

And he has to know the strike zone. Sometime you might hang it and somebody hits it. But, when you see a catcher put that mitt right there [outside], if you don't hit it, you might miss two inches this way [outside], and that's okay. Same way, if you want to pitch inside. If you miss, miss that way [inside]—but most of the catchers put a glove there, and the pitchers put it right over the plate.

And, those guys today, the hitters, they're too strong, that's why they hit so many home runs and have so many high averages, because their pitchers don't have enough command of their pitches.

Batters know what type of pitch I want to throw to get them out. But you have to outthink them. One day, you get them out with a fastball, and next time, they'll get something else.

Ferguson Jenkins was a competitor. And he wanted that ball. He was the type of guy that wanted to be there any day, any time, a real competitor. And, well, he's a Hall of Famer. And you see how many games he won, how many complete games. He was a great, great pitcher, and it was beautiful to watch him.

Warren Spahn, that old man. I used to love that guy. You know, we started a game in San Francisco and, zero, zero, zero, zero, all the way up to the ninth inning, zero, zero. The manager wanted to take me out. I begged him to let me stay in the game. I said to him, the weather is nice. You know, it's cool. I'm strong. I feel good. Let me stay a few more innings. So he did. He let me stay a few more innings. Now, the game is in the fourteenth inning. Now he really wants to take me out. So I come up to him and say, Mr. Dark, you see that man pitching over there? He said, yes, what about him? I said, that man is sixty-two years old. I'm only twenty-two. And nobody gonna take me out of here while that man stays on that mound.

Warren Spahn

That was a no-no. Alvin got so mad, but he let me stay. Now when I went out and pitched the fifteenth, I came up to the bench and I told him, that's it, I don't want to go any further. So he called the bullpen and told the bullpen coach to get the next guy ready, that I was coming out. That game was like, I go out to the mound. I got one, two, three, Warren Spahn goes out, one, two, three, and that was back and forth, back and forth, back and forth. So, in that fifteenth inning, I got the three men out. When I told Alvin that I wasn't gonna pitch anymore, he called the bullpen. But Warren Spahn went out and got the three men right away.

So when I saw those guys getting off the field, now we're supposed to take the field. I looked at my hat and my glove. I looked at the bullpen, now the relief pitcher started to come in. I grabbed my glove and my hat and I took off for the mound. For a minute, I thought it was gonna be two pitchers in there. So, lucky enough, I got the three men out. When my team was getting off the field, I waited for Willie Mays. You know, he came from center field, so I waited for him around first base, and I threw my arm over his shoulder and I told him, you know, I called everybody Chico. And I said, Chico, Alvin Dark is mad at me and I don't think I'm gonna be pitching any longer. So, he touched my back and said, don't worry. I'm gonna win this game for you. And he was the leadoff batter that inning. First pitch, boom, home run. Oh, my God. What a night, you know? I remember that ball leaving the park, you know?

And in 1999, when they played the All-Star game in Boston, they had this voting for the All-Century players. So they got me to tell my story about that game. So I told everybody, in the press conference. I didn't know that Warren told his manager the same thing, that he said that his manager wanted to take him out. And he said, oh, as long as that little kid is still pitching in there, nobody's gonna take me out of there.

Seventeen days before that, I had pitched a no-hitter against the Colt .45s. And what I remembered about that game, for the first seven innings, I had nothing on the ball. I was pitching with finesse, good control, but not good speed. And I was lucky enough to be pitching a no-hitter. And when I came off the bench in the eighth inning, for some reason, I looked at the scoreboard and I saw those zeroes. I don't know from where this fastball came. In the first seven innings, I struck out four batters. And in the last two innings, I strike out four. I ended up with eight strikeouts, but the fastball that I got in those last two innings was unbelievable. I don't know where that fastball came from because the first seven innings was, you know, pinpoint control, but that was it.

I remember pitching against the Red Machine. I told my pitching coach I was gonna pitch against the Red Machine. And I told Larry Jansen in the bullpen, he should come and watch this stuff.

How do you feel? He used to ask me, how do you feel? What do you do? And I said, Larry, I'm gonna pitch behind every hitter. And he placed his hand over his head and he said, oh, you're gonna get murdered. Don't do that. They'd kill you. I say, well, they might kill me if I throw the pitch that they might be waiting for. But I don't think they're gonna see that pitch.

So he said, please don't do that. I said, this is how I'm gonna pitch. I wasn't trying to throw the ball. I wasn't trying to be perfect. If I missed, okay, I missed. Nothing to it. I could see those guys waiting for that fastball. You can tell, the way they move and the way they squeeze the bat. And I ended up pitching a one-hitter.

Tommy Helms hit a ball, hit my foot, the ball rolled to third base. Jim Ray Hart picked it up, threw it to first, that was the only hit. I was behind in the count on purpose. But they never got that fastball. They might get a changeup, they might get a slider or a breaking ball, whatever. They never got the fastball that they were waiting for.

Jose Rijo was pitching for Cincinnati; he used to call me when he went to face any team. And I remember talking to him about the Mets hitters, and one of the guys was Darryl Strawberry. I said, don't pitch to him low. Don't pitch to him outside because he's going to get you. If you want, if you walk him with a ball inside, do that, but don't pitch to him. And let me tell you, I never saw a guy like Darryl Strawberry hit a ball low like he used to. Willie McCovey, same way.

Yogi Berra was a good high-ball hitter. And many times, I tried to get Joe Morgan inside and he kept hitting me. And after I retired, I used to come to the clubhouse when Joe went to the Giants. I saw Joe taking a shower and I said to myself, no wonder he hit me so well inside. His arms are so short. That's why he was so quick in hitting, because of the short arms. But most of the hitters, they can't hit the ball in there. They can't. So there's a spot where you have to try but you can't go one way. You have to be thinking about it when you come in, then you try to get them out.

When Orlando Cepeda got traded to St. Louis—Orlando and I,

we're brothers. We're good buddies. We got there, we went to St. Louis, and he invited me to his home for dinner. I was supposed to pitch that night. I went to the dinner, had a good time, good dinner, everything. When Orlando came to the plate, first pitch, he went down.

When I released the ball, I hollered, watch out. Oh, he never forgot that. He'd tell everybody.

What happened between Johnny Roseboro and me is a long story. And I hate to talk about that now because Johnny passed away.

It happened in a Friday-night game we played in San Francisco. Maury Wills went to the plate and he faked a bunt, and he went back with his bat and touched Tom Haller's, the catcher's, mitt. And

Johnny Roseboro

the umpire said it was interference by Haller, so he sent Maury Wills to first base.

Herman Franks got upset because of the call. So he told Matty Alou, when he came to bat, Matty, I want you to do the same thing that Maury did. And, you know, Matty was an expert with the bunt. So he went to the plate and did exactly what Maury did. And the bat touched Johnny's mitt, and Johnny got mad.

Gaylord and I, we were on the bench, standing there, just watching the strike zone. The park was packed. You couldn't hear anything. Johnny started hollering from the plate to the bench. We didn't know what he said. I started hollering to him. He didn't know what I said. And what I said was that that happened to Tom, and he didn't get mad. That's what I said to him. All of a sudden, when Orlando went to the plate and hit, he sent me a message through Orlando. When Matty went to replace him, another message with Matty. And there was a coach named Cookie Lavagetto that used to be with us. He sent me another message. All three messages were the same.

And he told them to tell me to shut my mouth if I didn't want to get one behind my ear. And you know, the next day, Saturday, we both came out from the tunnel in right field, and we sat in that dugout. And we, I forgot the whole thing. I forgot the whole thing. And we were talking to each other there. So, by the fifth inning, Herman told me, it's too windy, you're pitching tomorrow, so go home. So I left. And the next day, the game started, and that game was the last game I pitched against Sandy. The first hitter was Maury. Came to the plate, bunted, safe.

He stole second, stole third, fly ball to right field, he scored, one–nothing. When he came back to the plate the second time, I said to myself, if he bunts, he's gonna get hit because I'm gonna throw one inside. You know how they stop moving forward? So, oh, exactly the way I thought. He was bunting and I threw one inside. He had to go down on his back. Ron Fairly came up to the plate and I threw a pitch, almost a strike, and he went down, trying to tell everybody that I was knocking hitters down. They started hollering from the bench. I concentrated. I wanted to concentrate on my game. I didn't put too much attention to that.

When I came to bat, I said to myself, maybe they're going to throw one at me. But I knew that Sandy doesn't. I was 100 percent sure that he wasn't gonna do it. So I said to myself, take one pitch, and he threw straight pitch, a ball. Well, you can take one more, I thought. Second pitch was a strike, right in the middle of the plate. For some reason, I don't know why, I looked back and I saw Johnny. When the ball hit his glove, he dropped the ball and it rolled back. I just looked at that point, then I went back and looked at Sandy. And I stayed there with my bat on my shoulder. And Johnny shot that ball from behind that hit my ear.

I looked back and I said, what did you do that for? Let me tell you, he called my mother so many names that I couldn't take it. When he first said that, I said, what? And he said, you heard me, you so and so and so, and then he started charging. A lot of people said that I hit him in the head with a bat, sure. But with a swing that I didn't think could hurt anybody, because I just moved the bat forward trying to stop him from coming at me with all the gear and everything. Oh, my God, what a fight. That was ugly. And the next day after the game, the Dodgers went to New York and we went to Pittsburgh. And, you know, the press in New York, they talked about that incident and I was the bad guy, and I regret what I did. I always say so in public, you know?

The only incident that I ever had in baseball was that one. And I feel so bad because of what happened. But when they were leaving the hotel that Sunday to play us, they had a meeting on the bus and they talked to each other, saying, who do they want to get, and Johnny said, leave Juan for me. Leave Juan for me. So you know that that was well prepared. But five years after I got inducted to the Hall of Fame, I was sitting on a bench outside the hotel by myself, and Sandy came and he sat with me and he asked me, Juan, were you and Johnny friends?

I said, yes. We became friends. When I went to the Dodgers, he talked to the Dodger fans, and he told them to give me a warm welcome and forget what happened on that day. That was part of the game, this and that, and we became good friends. And after that, I invited him to my country to play in the Juan Marichal Golf Classic. He came and his wife, Barbara, and his daughter, and we're friends.

Sandy said, oh, my God, you don't know what a relief it is to hear you say that. I pretended that I didn't know what was going on.

I said, why? Why do you say that?

He said, well, you know what happened that day.

I said, yes, they told you to knock me down, and you said, no. I know that.

He said, how do you know?

Sandy Koufax

I said, because I know you.

And he said, yes, they told me to knock you down. And Johnny said, don't do it, let me do it. And that was the whole story. But by using the bat, I was the bad guy.

I was the first Dominican player to be elected to the Hall of Fame, the only one. That was one of the greatest days of my life. I never got so nervous on the field as I did on that stage in Cooperstown. I think that was something. And I feel so proud, not for Juan Marichal, for the whole Latin country, because I know what that meant to the Latin country and to my family and my country, my hometown. That was something that I will never, never, never forget, that day.

My mother knows that I have seen my dream come true, and my promise, because I promised her that when she heard my name on the radio, she was gonna be so proud and she was gonna tell her friends and other people. Most of the people in my hometown, they called me Manico. And I used to say to her, when you hear my name on the radio, you're going to say to them, that's Manico, that's my Manico, *Manico el mío*.

It was an aunt that gave me that nickname. Why? I don't know. But she's the one that gave me that nickname. And when I used to come and pitch in New York and I heard somebody from the stands say, Manico, I knew that was somebody from my hometown, and I turned back right away.

Two years ago, two or three, they erected a statue in San Francisco of myself. That Hall of Fame induction, and that day in San Francisco, with Mr. Peter Magowan and the board of the San Francisco Giants deciding and agreeing and voting in favor of putting a statue in front of the stadium, I think that was one of the greatest things that happened in my life. I love this game. I gave everything I could for that wonderful, wonderful sport, to play with dignity. And when somebody like Peter Magowan decides to do a statue of myself in the Pac Bell Park, I don't know how I could repay him for what he did for Juan Marichal and my family and my countrymen.

On that day, I had my whole family, I had the president of the Dominican Republic and the First Lady there, and about forty congressmen that came for that occasion. Those two occasions, I think I should put them together at the same level. They were the biggest days of my life.

DICK WILLIAMS

Regarded as one of the best managers at turning around a team's fortunes, Richard Hirschfeld "Dick" Williams spent thirty-four years in baseball as a player and manager. Williams began his managerial career in the Red Sox farm system in 1965 after a thirteen-year career as a utility player. He played with five teams but never really stuck in any one place. Of his time in Baltimore, Williams said, "The manager started me in this one game and I thought I was doing all right. But after seven innings I was taken out and replaced by some kid. . . . What was his name? . . . Roberts, Robbens, something like that? Oh yeah, now I remember. It was Brooks Robinson."

In 1967, after a brief stint as a minor league manager, Williams inherited a Boston Red Sox team that had finished next to last the previous season, and led them to an impossible dream—coming within one win of a World Series championship. "We didn't know how to study the game," explained Red Sox first baseman George Scott. "Dick showed us how to do it. He pressed the right buttons for everyone on that team."

After Williams led the Oakland Athletics to their second straight pennant and first of two consecutive World Series titles in 1972, eccentric A's owner Charlie Finley proclaimed, "Dick Williams is the best manager I've

ever had. I ought to know. I've fired enough of them." George Stein-
brenner thought the world of Dick Williams as well, trying unsuccessfully
to hire him twice—once after Williams had a falling out with Charlie Fin-
ley in 1973 and Finley wouldn't let him out of his contract, and once
again after the tragic death of Billy Martin in 1989, at which point Wil-
liams declared himself too old to manage again.

Dick Williams's cantankerous personality didn't sit well with every-
one, but as Williams explained, "I don't want to mellow. I'd rather be
known as a winner and a poor loser." But if accounts of his players are to
be believed, he did seem to mellow with age. In Williams's final season at
the helm in Seattle, outfielder Mike Kingery said, "He's been great to me
and other players. Very positive. When we do something well, he tells us.
And when we do something wrong, he encourages us."

In his twenty-one years of managing in the big leagues, Williams com-
piled a win-loss record of 1,571–1,451, captured four league pennants,
and won two World Series championships. After his retirement from the
game in 1988, it took twenty years for him to earn election to the National
Baseball Hall of Fame, an honor that fellow 2008 inductee Goose Gos-
sage felt was long overdue. "I was elated to see Dick got in, he deserved it.
He's one of the best managers of all time, in my opinion, and he's the best
manager I've ever played for. And that's taking in some great managers."

I was born in St. Louis, Missouri, in 1929 during the start of the
Depression. My dad, he was out of a regular job for a good five years.
My grandfather kept us going, kept the household together by own-
ing a grocery store. I went to school, elementary school, about three
blocks from Sportsman's Park in St. Louis, and they played day
games at that time. And we got out at three-fifteen, their ballgame
started at three, and I was a member, illegally, of the St. Louis Cardinals' and St. Louis Browns' Knothole Gang.

I used my brother's pass—he was three years older than me. You

Dick Williams

had to be ten. I'd head right on over there and get there in the bottom of the first or top of the second and did my homework when I got home. But I was a baseball fan ever since I can remember.

We sat down at the left-field line, the members of the Knothole Gang, and we were segregated also. On the left-field line, they kept the youngsters that were black separated from the whites. But whether we're black or white, we're all fans of Joe Medwick, he was a left fielder. And for the Browns, it was Chet Laabs, he was the left fielder. So they were the closest to us, so we rooted for them.

In high school, I was on a semipro club, played on Saturday and Sundays. It was sponsored at first by the St. Louis Cardinals, which I loved because I got to wear a Cardinal uniform. I even got number 7, which was Joe Medwick's number, so I was in hog heaven. And then the scout who furnished the uniforms for the Cardinals switched over with Branch Rickey to the Brooklyn Dodgers. So it became a Dodger-sponsored club.

And I was a Dodger from that point on. I graduated in 1947 and our commencement exercises were in the Rose Bowl, and that was on a Saturday night. I signed after commencement exercise on Saturday. I signed Sunday. My contract, they'd paid me for a full year and I played a half year. That was my bonus. I think it amounted to around $1,100. And then I went out making $120 a month. I was signed by a scout named Tom Downey. He signed Duke Snider and quite a few others. Monday I was on my way to Santa Barbara to play for the Dodgers Class C club. And from that point on, I was just eighteen. I was eighteen in May, and I joined them when school got out in the first part of June.

I went from Class C to Double-A in 1948. My first year in pro ball was the last half of '47. And I was having a good year. I went back to Santa Barbara and was doing well, and I went to Fort Worth. I joined that ball club as Double-A, ten days after Bobby Bragan got the manager's job there. He was a third-string catcher up at Brooklyn at that time. And it was an experience I'll never forget. Bobby took me under his wing, and it wasn't always good days. If you did something wrong, they'd let you know.

It was the Branch Rickey way, the way they wanted it played. And I went from C to Double-A to the major leagues from '47 to '51.

My first full year was 1948. In spring training, Vero Beach opened. It was an old navy, air force, or air corps barracks just outside Vero Beach. And Branch Rickey and Walter O'Malley, they leased or purchased land, I forget which, and they had five diamonds there. If you worked your way up—and this is before Holman Stadium was built—if you worked your way up to Diamond One or Two, they thought enough of you. At Diamond Five, where you had to battle the snakes on the way over to get to it, you might not be around too long. I was there two weeks before we ever played in a ballgame because they were drilling fundamentals into everybody. There were, at one time, I think they had twenty-nine farm clubs. They had three Triple-A clubs, two Double-A clubs, about five A clubs, the rest were all C and D. And there were, I don't know, about 720 players coming through there, counting free agents. So you had, there were twenty guys ready to take your job at any particular classification. And I was very fortunate.

It could take you seven years to reach the major leagues at that time with the options they would have. They kept you for four years and then they could option you out three years. As I said, in one year, I went from C to Double-A under Bragan, and I stayed there the last half of '48, all of '49, and all of '50. They didn't have to move me up. I went up to the major leagues under a Brooklyn contract from Double-A. Some fellows went up from Triple-A and a few went up from Class A. So it didn't make any difference where you played, according to Mr. Rickey.

I went back after having a real good year at Fort Worth in '49. I thought I was going to play at Hollywood, which was right near my hometown in Pasadena, California, but they didn't have to move me. They didn't have to worry about anybody drafting me, so I went back to Fort Worth. And I couldn't figure that out. So I asked for an audience with Mr. Rickey. And it was like an audience with the pope. And he said, son, you don't make your money in the minor leagues. You make it when you reach the major leagues. Later, I found out that under Mr. Rickey, you didn't make it in the major leagues, either. I mean, Jackie and Pee Wee were the two highest players, paid around $45,000 or $50,000 at that time.

Every minor league manager, plus all their scouts, all their executives, they were there in Vero Beach, and they made sure they taught you how to lead off a base, a one-way lead, a secondary lead. They taught you how to bunt, their way of bunting. Hitting the cutoff man, that was a must. If you didn't hit the cutoff man, it took the whole play out of kilter.

Just pounding fundamentals one after another, day in and day out for two weeks, how to hit the ball behind the runner. If there was a man on second, nobody out, your job, I don't care who you were, you had to hit the ball to make sure you at least advanced him to third. It was a game that was played like defense. You're gonna get runs but you better execute on defense to prevent them from having that fourth or fifth out in an inning. And this was Branch Rickey's style of baseball.

I worked it on a plus-and-minus basis as a manager. If I had a guy that advanced a runner, he got a plus in that event. If he failed to advance that runner with the man on second, nobody out, he got a minus. End of the week, I'd post the total pluses or minuses. I wouldn't say a thing. They knew what it was. And half the time, I had three or four or five prints ready. And when they ripped the first one down, I'd put it up again. But my coaches knew exactly the style I wanted done and it was successful with the Dodgers. The Yankees always beat us in the World Series, but it was successful in the National League.

June 1951, I reported to Brooklyn. I was there about two weeks working out, batting practice, extra batting practice, fielding practice, all that. When I pinch-hit for Gene Hermanski against Pittsburgh, in the ninth inning, we were getting beat 2–1. And on a 3-2 pitch by Bill Werle, left-hander, I hit about an eleven-hopper back to the mound. So that ended the game.

I was in the starting lineup for the second game, I was leading off and I went 4-5. I had a bunt base hit, I had two singles, and I hit a triple to right center. And we lost that game. Ralph Kiner was playing first, plus he hit a couple of home runs in both games, I think, and beat us one-handed. But I got off to a good start. Then it was probably another two weeks before I had a chance to pinch-hit or something like that. Jackie Robinson was like my big brother because we're both from Pasadena, California. I knew his brother Mack before I met Jack.

And playing in the minor leagues and living out in Southern California, they made *The Jackie Robinson Story*, I'm in that. I was the second baseman when Jackie hit a home run on his opening day against Jersey City. They shot that one day, and him rounding second. And the next day, they were shooting the pitcher throwing the ball for Jackie to hit. I'm the pitcher. So I was the pitcher—it was a low-budget film—I was the pitcher and the second baseman on the same play. But Jack treated me real well. I knew Duke Snider from being in Southern Cal. And I was a bench jockey.

I got the claim for fame being the next-best bench jockey to Leo Durocher and Eddie Stanky, and when I got up to pinch-hit or something, I got knocked right on my tail, but my first year was a thrill down to the end when Bobby Thomson hit the home run off [Ralph] Branca. That was my first year up.

At first, Jackie couldn't stay in the hotel with us in St. Louis. The next couple of years they allowed him to stay there. He and Don Newcombe and Campy [Roy Campanella] , they had to go to another hotel in the black neighborhood. It got better, but it still wasn't good. I mean, coming up, we used to barnstorm with the Braves coming north in spring training. And we'd keep our sleeping cars and we'd go to a hotel to dress. We'd change and leave our stuff there.

Jack couldn't do that. He had to change in the car. Campy did, Newcombe did. Junior Gilliam, when he joined us, Joe Black. It was still bad, especially in the South. But we'd play the exhibition games, they packed the place, and 90 percent of the people would be black. And, you know, in the outfield, we always had to cordon off the outfield to get more people in.

Jack was as good an athlete as you'd ever want to see. Willie Mays is the best ballplayer I ever watched. Jackie was twenty-eight when he got to the major leagues, Willie was twenty. If Jackie had had those eight years, I'd probably say Jackie was the best ballplayer I ever saw. He did everything you could have a player do.

My second year up against the St. Louis Cardinals in St. Louis, I went for a fly ball and separated my shoulder. And I couldn't throw a lick after that. I lasted thirteen years as a utility player. Paul Richards helped me there, when I was with Baltimore. I played six positions for him in a doubleheader. One day, he kept moving me around, percentagewise, so they wouldn't hit it there because I couldn't throw.

But I pinch-hit real well and lasted thirteen years. But I think my smarts, I knew what I wanted to do when I was still playing. And I was gonna stay in there playing as a utility player as long as I could before I went to managing. And then I had the opportunity from Dick O'Connell, Neil Mahoney, and Ed Kenney at Boston offering me that Triple-A job, which was unheard of at that time.

My first year in the major leagues as a manager, I'd managed two years for the Boston Red Sox at their Triple-A club in Toronto. We won the Governor's Cup both years. Half the players didn't care too much for me. The ones that I elevated to the major league club that I recommended, they knew my style of play and they let the other guys, before I even got there, know what to expect. But I was only two years removed from that major league ball club when I went to manage. I got a tremendous break. I finished my playing career in 1964, the last two years with the Red Sox, managed two years for their Triple-A club, which is unheard of.

I knew what type of club it was when I took over the Red Sox in 1967. We had one good player and two promising players that were surefire winners. That was Yaz [Carl Yastrzemski], and then we had Tony Conigliaro and Rico Petrocelli. I had a youngster who came up for me at Toronto, Joe Foy. He was a third baseman.

I had a first baseman who never even played Triple-A. He came up from Eddie Popowski at Double-A in Pittsfield, and that was George Scott. And I had another youngster that played centerfield in Reggie Smith. So I had a nucleus of a young ball club. And then I had Mike Andrews at second base. So I had a good young defensive infield. Yaz in left, Reggie in center, and Tony in right. Behind the plate, I had three different catchers. I had Mike Ryan, who was a great defensive catcher, probably the best one of all of them; Bob Tillman, who was my roommate my last year at Boston in '64; and then my other one was Russ Gibson.

And I started Gibson in the first game of the World Series in '67, later on coming in with Elston Howard, who would join us late in the year, and Elston really helped my pitching staff. He didn't hit much but knew everything about catching and did a tremendous job. So all the youngsters that came up that I had never run across, I figured in spring training, we're gonna do it the way I want it done. I have a one-year contract. If I'm going down, I'm going down my way, and it's been a successful two years at Triple-A. We took two days, a little more than two days to talk about all the offensive and defensive things that could happen in certain areas.

Half the club didn't know what the line was halfway down to first base, the double line. I put a set of rule books in each player's locker. Halfway through the year, I'd walk into the locker room and I'd see the rule book up there and put my hand on it. If there was dust on it, I knew they never picked it up. And usually, the fellow that made the most mistakes was the guy that didn't pay too much attention to me. And they found out it was successful, the way I wanted to operate it, and we had the talent to do it. And Yaz was having such a spectacular year. That first year, it was unbelievable.

Now I had inherited a pitcher I had never watched before in Jim Lonborg. Yaz was the MVP; Lonborg was the Cy Young winner; Dick O'Connell, the general manager, was the Executive of the Year; and I rode in on their coattails and I was Manager of the Year. This was all in my first year in the major leagues.

I was thirty-seven. I was the second-youngest manager in the majors, the youngest in the American League. But what a thrill. And we took the Cardinals to seven games in the World Series.

My very first Hall of Famer that I managed, and the last guy to win the Triple Crown, was Carl Yastrzemski. In 1967, he had a year that I've never watched a player have, whether he was playing for me or playing against me. He did everything when he had to do it. And he kept our club afloat. Plus we had Jim Lonborg, a Cy Young winner that year.

Yaz is the last Triple Crown winner. Frank Robinson won it the year before with Baltimore. But Yaz did everything for us. We got somebody on base, we knew Yaz was going to drive him in. And he prepared himself from day one that winter by work, having his own trainer up in the New England area, just outside of Boston. Yaz weighed only 175, 180 pounds at the most. But he went through some strenuous exercises, like they say Steve Carlton did.

His were different, covering all phases of physical fitness. I took the captaincy away from him when I got the manager's job. I said, we won't have any captains. He was the captain of the club. I said, we're gonna have one chief and the rest are Indians. And some guys, it was a country club. I saw it. I saw it firsthand because I was there in '63 and '64.

Carl Yastrzemski

You had freewheeling. Nobody cared about advancing runners. They had that short left-field fence and everybody was trying to jerk it out of there. And the front office didn't back up Johnny Pesky, or the other previous managers, at all. So it was a big joke there. But I learned from that. That was a good experience for me, taking over the club two years later.

Yaz thanked me. He said, thank you, sir. I don't need that thing pinned on me. He says, I'll give you 100 percent. He was all for it. And we got along well. We got along real well. He's a class person.

He had power to all fields, especially in Fenway Park. But it was a long way to right center. It's a long way unless you hit it down the line to right field. He was disciplined. He could hit any pitch, fastball, changeup, breaking ball. He just had one phenomenal year to win the Triple Crown. He tied with Harmon Killebrew for home runs. And I put the blame on myself for that because I pitched to Killebrew one time late in the ballgame, nobody on. He hit a home run and tied Carl with 44 home runs. But Carl was the outright Triple Crown winner. He was so grooved on facing the pitcher. We knew he was gonna come through.

In the 1967 World Series, I pitched Lonborg with two days' rest. I know that you look back at that, especially now, and say that's impossible. But he did it twice for me. I pitched him twice on two days' rest. He had a no-decision and won the other one. So I didn't feel bad about pitching him in that game.

But he faced the best right-hander I've ever watched pitch in Bob Gibson. Gibby is the best right-hander I ever saw. The best left-hander might be Carlton or Ford or Koufax. Now, Koufax only pitched five great years in his career. I was one of his guinea pigs when they had him throw, so he could find home plate. But once he found it, he was the best. The only time I faced Koufax, I hit a ball off a palm tree for a double. The only time I ever faced him. And I keep telling him that every time I see him. What a class person. He's a great guy.

Bob Gibson had the best intimidation factor. He'd stare at you.

He didn't want his teammates to talk to him the day he pitched. But I don't think he needed it. I thought he was just fabulous. He beat me three times in '67 with ease.

Drysdale, I saw him as a baby. I was on that ball club when he first joined us. And he'd knock you down. Bob Lemon was the same way. When I went over to Cleveland, I was taking batting practice the second day, and I hit a ground ball through the middle. The next pitch I'm flat on my back. We don't do that here, kid. Yes, sir.

I had three Hall of Famers in Oakland. I would put the whole club in the Hall of Fame at Oakland. That was a great ball club. And it was an easy, easy job. Charlie Finley's ballclub, believe it or not, the players were 100 percent. You're gonna have some guys that don't like the manager and all that. My players disliked Finley so much that they liked me.

I had Reggie [Jackson], who's like a son to me, and we still are very close. And Catfish [Hunter], same way, and Rollie Fingers. Rollie was a pitcher that couldn't start. The closer it got for him to start—and they went every fourth day, not every fifth day, every fourth day—the more nervous and hyper he'd get. He'd last maybe one inning or at the most two or three. Bill Posedel was our pitching coach.

We finally stuck him in the bullpen. Vern Hoscheit was our bullpen coach, and he made sure the reliever, whoever it was, knew who he was going to face. And he pumped that into Rollie. Then when Rollie got to the mound, I'd ask him, what did Vern say? He said, well, I'm gonna face so and so. I said, how are you going to pitch him?

He said, Vern told me this way. Okay, as long as you know. He put him in some games that didn't mean anything, as the score indicated. He did well. Put him in a little tougher situation, he did well. Put him in a save situation—what they call a save situation now—and he did well. So that's how he became a relief pitcher. And he got better as he went along.

Reggie Jackson

One time, Reggie hit a rope to right center in Oakland Coliseum and went into a strut. The ball hit off the fence and he had to slide into second, just barely made it. I used to correct them as they came in. I didn't have to say a word. He came up and he said, Skippy, I'm sorry.

He said, it will never happen again. And he said, I'll run hard all the way. And from that day on, he did. He played hard for me. He played very hard.

Catfish in spring training would get lit up like a Christmas tree, because he was working on something. The modern equivalent is Greg Maddux. That was Cat. Cat didn't overpower anybody. He used the finger thing, moving the ball here and there. I'd say Maddux is the closest to what I saw in Catfish. He would get lit up in the spring. Once the season started, they didn't light him up. He knew how to pitch. He knew what to do. Had command of all his pitches and was a winner. And he proved that, after he left Oakland, he's a winner there and threw the perfect game there. Went over to the Yankees and did the same thing.

In Oakland the scouting director was Ray Swallow. I don't know if you ever heard the name before. He got Jackson, he got Sal Bando, he got Rick Monday, he got Vida Blue. He was in charge of the scouting talent. They had talent just coming out of their nose, at all different levels. Bill Posedel was their minor league pitching instructor; eventually brought him up to the major leagues. He was at Pittsburgh. He never had won anything.

He got his first World Championship his final year with me in

Charlie Finley

'72 when we beat Cincinnati. Charlie [Finley] was the owner. So that was his team. Charlie and I got along well. But I hated calls at three in the morning with his speakerphone on so all the cronies could hear him at his office in Chicago, I didn't like those.

One day, Norma [Williams's wife] had a friend of ours in from Missouri staying with us. And I just got through to talking to him on the phone in the office. The phone usually rang when the game was over. And it was Charlie with the squawk pipe. So, yeah, Charlie, yeah. He said, well, if you had done this in the fifth inning, you would've won 5–2 instead of winning 4–2. Okay, Charlie. And he is listening to what we call the spy in the sky. Monte Moore was our announcer, and he had a line. And Charlie is listening to the play-by-play. I talked to him after every game, win or loss. It was bad when you lost because you screwed up here or screwed up there. When you win he's happy but if you'd done this, you would've won it easier. Now, I drive twenty-five minutes down the road to Fremont, where I live. And we have a houseguest and we're going to have a cocktail and have dinner. The phone rings. It's Charlie, and you can tell when the squawk box is on. He said, let's talk some baseball. I said, Charlie, I have a houseguest here, we're just sitting down, getting ready to eat. He says, what's more important, your houseguest or talking to the owner of your club? I said, Charlie, right now, it's my houseguest, and I hung up the phone. I didn't hear one word about it. Not one word. They probably got the biggest kick out of that but he never mentioned it again.

When the Mike Andrews thing came up, that was the icing on the cake. I mean, he's treating the player very, very badly. And two of those plays in the '73 World Series, one of them shouldn't have been an error because Gene Tenace was the first baseman, who was no first baseman, which leads to another story I got in trouble with.

But Mike made the throw after he made the error that went through his legs, two runs scored. Next ball was a topper over the mound, Mike came in and got it and threw to first, but Ken Holtzman, who was covering, got his feet messed up and didn't touch the bag, and they gave an error to Andrews on that play that shouldn't have been his. So anyway, Finley pulls him into my office, he has a doctor there, and he wants to say that Andrews is unfit to play. And I said, he's fit to play. He's all right.

And I said, Mike, I have nothing to do with this, and I left the office. Pretty soon you saw Mike getting his suitcase off the truck, taking his suitcase to go to the airport. He said, he has let me go; I'm not going to be with you. I said, that isn't right. And he didn't make the trip with us. He went back home to Boston, where he lived. He didn't make the trip to New York. And the commissioner found out about it and forced Charlie Finley to bring Andrews back. Now he's activated for the next game and the first chance I got to use a pinch-hitter, I was going to put Andrews in.

So, it was early in the game but in the third inning we were behind and I was pinch-hitting and he got a standing ovation, Mike Andrews did. Everybody stood up except Charlie. We were the visiting club, their ballpark. He swung at the first pitch and grounded to the shortstop and he got a big hand standing up and Charlie stood up at the end. I said, you're the dumbest son of a gun I've ever seen. I said, if I had to take strike three, I was going to see at least three pitches, you know, because they're clapping all the way, they're rooting for Andrews. He was a good kid, good kid.

In the 1972 World Series we had seven games with Cincinnati. We won four games, all by a run. And they won two games by a run and wiped us out in Game Six. In Game Seven I used about all my pitchers except my regular guys. They had us by a run, men on first and third. One out, Morgan's on third, Tony Perez on first, Bench is at bat. On a 2-1 pitch, Perez ran. But I had a catcher that could throw anybody out, and he was the MVP in the Series, Gene Tenace. He's my backup catcher, but he had a hot bat. Dave Duncan was my regular catcher. So we didn't throw through. The pitch was called a ball.

And I told Posedel, I said, if this next pitch is a strike, I'm going to go out and raise some Cain here about not putting him on the pitch before. And the next pitch is a strike, it's now 3-2.

First base was open, one out, you got to walk Bench. So I went on out there. I wanted him put on first base. But all the time I was telling them, Gino [Tenace], kind of stay out like you're going to intentionally walk him, put your glove out. And Rollie, who's the pitcher, I said, go to the end of your stretch. But as you're ready to unload, Tenace is going to get behind the plate. And Rollie is going like this. I said, this has to be a breaking ball. Tenace got behind the plate a little too quick and Morgan started yelling at third. And I think Tony Kubek was the announcer, and he said, he's pitching to him. Well, they froze Bench, and Rollie made a perfect pitch right on the black on the outside part of the plate. And later on, Bench said, why me? That was his comment, you know? But we saved a run there. It was strike three and we got the next guy out.

We had to throw a breaking ball because you can recover from a fastball. If you're there and you think you're walking, if the ball is straight, you've got a better chance of hitting it than if it isn't straight. One guy that I know and I read about that did this when he was managing the Braves—he went in the Hall of Fame with me in '08—was Billy Southworth. He had pulled it one time during the season. It had never been done in the World Series.

So now the press came in. They talked to Tenace. He said, I didn't know what Dick was talking about. He said, he had to explain it to me again. And he said, I may have gotten behind there a little too quick. I explained what I was doing to the press. They went to Rollie and asked him about it. He said, Oh, I knew exactly what he was talking about. We used to do that in Little League.

Game Four in that series. Cincinnati scored in the top of the eighth on four straight singles. I've got a picture of me and Holtzman when I'm asking for the ball. And he's got this expression on his face like, you're out of your mind, or something, I have a picture of that at home. I took a lot of heat on that. But I had a reason for doing it. Even though they're both [Holtzman and Blue] left-handed, Kenny was a finesse pitcher. And his breaking stuff, once he got it on, he was great. But Vida Blue was a power pitcher and Vida was in the process of having some pretty fabulous years for me. I needed a strikeout so I brought him in. It didn't work out but we came back and got some runs, and we won the game. We won it by one run.

Kenny Holtzman used to play pepper with Rollie Fingers and take his money. He used to play golf with him and take his money. They'd go bowling and Kenny would take his money. He taught Rollie how to be street smart. Plus being an outstanding pitcher on his own. Holtzman held the key. He joined our club, our player rep was a pitcher named Chuck Dobson. And he had an elbow operation. He won 15 ballgames for me with the bad elbow.

We got Holtzman and he just brought that whole pitching staff together. He was a smart son of a gun. And they all could handle the bat, too. We didn't have the DH when we went to the National League to play. They held their own as far as hitting. But Kenny Holtzman was very instrumental in our pitching staff.

Once I also sent in three pinch-hitters in the same inning in that World Series. That set a record, didn't it? And they were all prepared. First, it was Gonzalo Marquez. He was an instant base hit. He led off the inning. Then I had Don Mincher, who couldn't run any, but he was a good first baseman for a number of years with Minnesota and he made two trips to Oakland, a good fellow to have on a ball club. He lined to right center. Should have been a double, he only got a single. We had a runner for Gonzalo, I think he scored on the play. And then I had Angel Mangual. He's a guy who thought the world was against him.

He said to me, Dick, you make me nervous, me playing for you. I said, Angel, the next time I make out the lineup that you're in it, you come and see how shaky my handwriting is when I write your name down. But he had about a thirty-hopper between first and second, a little roller that just barely got out and died on the grass from malnutrition. And it was the big hit of the ballgame. But the three pinch-hits, that was amazing. I didn't realize it until after the game but they were all ready, they all had bats in their hands and knew exactly what they had to do.

When you win four games by one run, you've got a hell of a bullpen. And Cincinnati won two of their three games by one run. They had a heck of a bullpen.

As a manager, I wanted guys to give me 100 percent at all times. I didn't want them to make many mistakes. I hate the fourth and fifth out in an inning. My players do that, and bust their tail for me. I never had one guy dog it on me that was an everyday player. I've had players very unhappy because they didn't get to play. I like that. I want a guy to want to play.

We had a situation one time in Montreal where I think Tony Perez got on base in the bottom of the ninth inning, and I put a runner in for him. It might have been the tenth or eleventh inning. I put a runner in for him because I've got the chance to win the game.

I think the runner stole second, we advanced him to third and got him in, the game was over. John McHale, the GM—McHale was a first baseman in Detroit, backup first baseman—asked me after the game, Dick, who would have played first? First of all, John, I said, I got the chance to win the game, and I'm gonna try to win it. And if I don't win it this inning, I've got a chance at the next inning to win it. I'm the home club. He said, but who would play first? I said, well, John, you played first. I said, I played first. If we could play first, anybody can play first. He didn't like that. But he's a fine man. I like John very, very much, even though he fired me in 1981.

In my induction speech, I praised Jack McKeon quite a bit, because he's an older man, I'm an older man. I said he took over the Cincinnati club and got them stabilized. Then he went down and won a World Series with the Marlins. I said, so age doesn't have to be a factor. When I was there [at San Diego], Jack wanted to get back on the field. Jack is a good baseball man, a good baseball man. But Jack wanted to get on the field and eventually he did, as I had talked about. But he didn't do it as manager of the San Diego ball club, he didn't do well. They had Larry Bowa in there, he didn't do well. When we won in '84, that was the first time they had ever won anything. And I think we finished third the next year and then they didn't want me around. Joan Kroc was wonderful, a wonderful lady. Ray Kroc was just super. Unfortunately, he died in January, in '84. Joan was gonna sell that club except we won it; then I guess she was forced to keep it.

But when I signed my contract there, we're up in Ray's office and behind him, he looked out the window, there's one of those McDonald's restaurants. So to celebrate, I have a quarter-pounder with cheese, Jack had one also, he had a Coke and I had a malt, and he sent Ballard Smith, his son-in-law, over to get them.

I left there and then Seattle came after me. It was either gonna be Billy Martin or me to manage that ball club when Chuck Cottier was the manager there. They were letting Chuck go and I was doing something for the Miller Brewing Company. I was one of their Lite All-Stars, doing those commercials. I made about nine commercials with the group, Whitey Herzog and myself.

I signed with the Yankees, a three-year contract for $100,000 a year, in 1973. I was the first one to get that, and Gabe Paul handled all this stuff, and I'd never met George, didn't know what George Steinbrenner looked like. So now, we have the press conference in New York and I'm going out to Shea Stadium because that's where we're going to be playing the next two years while they refurbish Yankee Stadium. I see Weeb Eubanks; he's the head coach for the Jets. I see Namath. We have our pictures taken.

I get home, in Florida. I'm living in Riviera Beach. And about seven days later, I get a call from Gabe. He says, well, Charlie Finley is questioning, he wants compensation for you. At first, he wished me well, he wouldn't stand in my way after we won the 1973 World

Series. But he was told that he could get compensation, so we had a hearing up in Boston. Joe Cronin is the league president and Gabe says, don't talk to anyone. So I bring my own attorney with me. The only thing is they didn't know he was a real estate attorney. He didn't know anything about baseball.

But I hear a *psst*, Dick, Dick. I looked over, I see a guy behind the pillar over there. I ignore him; I'm registering and checking in. Dick, Dick. I don't say anything again. Pretty soon, there's a tap on my shoulder. I say I can't talk and he says, I'm George Steinbrenner. That was my first meeting with him and it didn't work out. They got Bill Virdon in after Cronin ruled against us. And I was laid off for half a year and went to work for John D. MacArthur, who was one of the richest men in the United States. He had a hotel just about half a mile down the road on Singer Island called the Colonnades Beach Hotel, and that's where he was headquartered, where he had Bankers Life and Casualty out of Chicago.

And when Getty and Hughes were out of town, he was the richest man in town. A wonderful gentleman. I worked for him half a year; he paid me more than Charlie was paying me. And then when the Angels called me, he worked my contract for me. I had three and a half years at $100,000 a year. The first man to go into six figures. Everybody has gone by that tenfold since then. But I stayed in touch with MacArthur quite a bit until he passed away.

Once I was through managing, I enjoyed my association with the Yankees. I was down there every spring with them. I did a lot of things that George wanted me to do. I went over to Japan. He sent me over to Japan—and I'm one of the bad guys in this—both me and our international scout, we're over there at different times, and our report on Hideki Irabu was outstanding. I saw him pitch three times over there and he just blew the league out. He was in shape, though. He was in good shape. He just came right after hitters. He didn't pick here or pick there. And I saw a young kid breaking in that year that I made a report on, too, his name was Ichiro. And he was the MVP of the league that year. But Irabu was just fantastic.

We got films of him, we showed the films, and we couldn't get him, San Diego got him. They had the rights, and then they sold the rights to the Yankees. He was in shape then.

Harry Dalton, the general manager with Anaheim, called me. He was told to call me by the owner, Gene Autry. I told him exactly what I needed. I went to see John D. MacArthur, and he said, I'll handle it. Got everything I asked for. So I went ahead and signed with him. I joined their club. I was supposed to be there July 1, but I had a commitment up in Hartford. I was with Casey Stengel and Joe Namath. Now I'm name-dropping. We were putting on a charity softball game. Casey was going to manage the one club and I was managing the other, and Namath was the commissioner. And Mike Andrews even came over to Hartford from Boston to see it.

But then, I have to catch a plane down to Kennedy, and then Kennedy into Anaheim, or into L.A. And I take over the club and I'm watching, just looking at these guys. All I know is I've been away from the game for six months. I don't know a lot of these players. I know of them. Whitey Herzog is the coach there. He managed three of the games before I got there for my turn to manage and he won one and lost two. It was not a good ball club. We had a pretty good pitcher over there named Nolan Ryan and a would-be good pitcher in Frank Tanana. Dave Chalk was a first-year player and the number one draft choice.

He was playing shortstop and eventually went over to third, but we really didn't have a good ball club. And I'm watching, I proceed to lose the first ten games I manage. And Gene Autry came in and went to Whitey, he said, goddamn, Whitey, I think I hired the wrong manager. Gene was great, Gene was super. But I didn't fare too well there. And in '76, they let me go. And right away, John McHale and I got together the last couple of days of the season in Chicago and I'm going to be the manager and Charlie Fox is going to be the general manager in Montreal. And we turned the franchise around.

* * *

You know, that pitch count they have now. . . . Nolan Ryan used to throw a lot of pitches because he'd strike out a lot. He threw 160 pitches without batting an eye and he'd be out playing catch with my players the next day, throwing long-distance tosses. No problem with pitch count or anything. I think that's so absurd. And then they have a five-man rotation now. He went on a four-man rotation. Fergie Jenkins and Bob Boone both still believe now—and I'm sure there's some more—four-man rotation, you're a lot better off. The pitchers are coddled now. But here again, we go back to the agents, they don't want their pitchers overworked so they won't last as long and they won't make as much money.

They're groomed now as middle relief, long relief, short relief. That's why they're brought up now from the minor leagues, which I think is totally ridiculous. I'd go, well, Boone and Fergie have come out and said a four-man rotation is much better than a five-man rotation.

A complete game is unheard of now. If a pitcher on your staff has three or four complete games, that's amazing. I'd have at least 15, 20, 25 complete games. You see, a four-man rotation, you got 37, 38 starts during the course of the year in a 154-game schedule. And they'd throw their 250 and some of them would throw 300 innings. They were stronger. The more you throw, the stronger you are. I'm a firm believer in that. I think it's a bunch of hogwash, the pitch count. And oh, I'm a reliever and I'm the stopper and I pitch one inning. I can't pitch for two days now. That's ridiculous.

On my all-time starting team, I would put Willie Mays in center. And Hank Aaron in left. I'd put Reggie Jackson in right. Third base I've got to do the Philly third baseman, Mike Schmidt. I had a catcher that became my number one catcher because the other guy had contract problems, and that was Gary Carter. He became my catcher. And he was basically a rookie although he played some outfield. But he played hard for me and was a team leader.

At shortstop, we both are the same age, I'd take Luis Aparicio with a drop of the hat. My gosh, I was a little kid watching him play, but Jimmie Foxx was a pretty good player. So was Tony Perez as far as RBIs go. I know I'm skipping over a lot of names, but let me put the right-hander, Bob Gibson, and the left-hander, Whitey Ford. And I'll take Rollie Fingers out of the bullpen any day of the week, but Dennis Eckersley could help him. Oh, Johnny Bench, how can I forget Johnny Bench? He's got to be my number one catcher.

All Whitey did every time he went out to the mound was win. He's got a fabulous World Series win-loss record. That's the key to everything.

I had the pleasure of playing in the spring and into the second game of the season for Joe Gordon at Kansas City. And he was a player's manager through and through. I could remember him playing. And like Bobby Doerr said, he couldn't say enough about Joe Gordon. They alternated as starting All-Stars for over a decade.

I saw him play, but I was younger and I really didn't know that much about it. But I followed his record quite a bit. Once he became our manager, I wanted to know all about him. And he was a delight to work for. And of course, Bobby was, too. I brought Bobby back to the major leagues. He was a minor league hitting instructor in Boston, and he helped me when I started out managing Triple-A at Toronto. He made four or five trips up there, talking to my hitters and that. And luckily, he came back and was the coach with me when we won that thing in '67. I just swear by him.

My last year was '64 as a player for the Red Sox. Johnny Pesky was the manager. We had two young kids coming up, Tony Conigliaro and Rico Petrocelli. So, Johnny wanted me to talk baseball with Tony and room with him. Well, I was unhappy because usually I roomed with Russ Nixon and we were real close. So, first half of the year, I roomed with his luggage. He was single, good-looking guy, his hometown. We never hit it off. I recognized he was gonna be a hell of a ballplayer, but we never hit it off; wasn't on my part. Now, I come back two years later, I'm the manager.

Tony Conigliaro

And of course, he's established and he's done a heck of a job, and he's a Hall of Famer in my book if he continues to play and play well. And then he got hit. I saw the films the other day on Major League Baseball TV, showed when he got it. And the first guy there was Rico Petrocelli. Next guy coming in was me, along with the trainer. We're out there right away. Tom Yawkey said, I don't want anybody going there to see him. I inquired each day and let it be known that I was asking about him.

Tony got very upset with me; I never went to the hospital to see him. I said, well, I was just doing what Yawkey wanted. No big deal, but Tony and I never did really get along. And his name was in the lineup every day and it was a shame what happened to him. Young-est player ever to hit 100 home runs. He could do everything. He was the right fielder like Carl Yastrzemski was the left fielder. That's how good a ballplayer he could have been. And he had the world made, and that was unfortunate.

He was aggressive, Tony was. And he was on top of that plate. This ball just sailed and it got him, and it got him good. By the time we got there, like Rico said, by the time he got there, it was out like a balloon. And it was really a shame what happened.

I was on deck when George Kell got hit twice, once by [Steve] Gromek, and I don't know who the other guy was, can't remember. That was his last year when we were at Baltimore, got beaned twice that same year. I've had my cap spun—and we didn't wear helmets. But if you're up there that many times, you're gonna have pitches come close to you. I used to have a thing, the pitch got close to me, knocked me down. As I went down, I just squeezed the heck out of my hand and showed the umpire it hit me there, and I'd go to first.

I really enjoyed working for George Steinbrenner for ten years. I babysat Darryl Strawberry, both myself and Arthur Richman.

Arthur and I were assigned to watch him. When he had to go to his hotel room, we had a police guard out there. He could go from his hotel room to the ballpark, had a police guard there. When he was through there and he'd showered, right back to the hotel room. He ate in his room. We had rooms on either side of him. He was gonna make one of his many comebacks. He was going over to Puerto Rico. Oh, and then from there, he started playing A ball. But before the Puerto Rico thing, he started playing in the Florida State League, no, Florida Rookie League and then the Florida State League, and we were with him all the time. And then he went to Columbus, and Arthur and I got on a plane, we went to Columbus with him.

Now, in Columbus, we went on a road trip. We went there, but we were on either side of the room, his room, and watched him all the time. And he worked hard. He walked around with a little Bible he had in his hand. And now, another comeback and he was gonna play in Puerto Rico. And they call me, this is a week before Thanksgiving, I'm gonna make the tour. And George is letting me take Norma, my wife, with me.

We're going to Columbus and we're going up to the Double-A team and I'm gonna spend a little time in Boston, and so it's like a vacation. Well, no sooner do I get those tickets, I get a call from Bill Lindsay. He says, you got to change those tickets. He says, George wants us, this is on a Sunday; he says, he wants you down here by Tuesday. And that's when I was with Strawberry for five weeks. Now I go to Puerto Rico. George wants to see how he is physically, if they're gonna bring him to the Yankees. He's playing the winter ball in the Puerto Rican winter league, and they want to see if he can hit any left-handed pitching.

So I get down there and two days later, Strawberry comes down and he works out a couple of days, and I've got Thanksgiving prepared for our whole family down in Orange County. So I see him play three games, he hits five home runs, all against left-handers, and I call and I talk to Joe Malloy.

I talk to him and he says, well, how's his defense? I say, he's not playing any defense. You got him down here to see how he's hitting left-handers. And I say, my report is he's handling them without any problem, and in comes Gene Michael. I'm leaving and in he comes.

He comes down and he sees him hit three more home runs in three games, so he leaves. So that's when he came back up to the Yankees the next spring and made the ball club. But I did a lot of things for George and thoroughly enjoyed it. And Arthur and I were together quite a bit. That's a great organization, except the ones in Tampa didn't agree with the ones in New York. They used to go back and forth.

I was one of only two managers to take three teams to the World Series. Bill McKechnie is the other one.

In Boston, I wasn't one of Mr. Yawkey's people. I was Dick O'Connell's guy, and Neil Mahoney and Ed Kenney. But I wasn't one of Yawkey's. Yawkey didn't particularly care for me. And after I won that first year, I got a new contract. I didn't do any big holding out or anything. We signed, two days after the World Series was over, I signed a three-year contract. I thought, maybe some security. I guess Yawkey didn't care for that, so I wasn't one of his favorites, except we turned the franchise around there. That's when the impossible dream here became Red Sox Nation.

I had a year to go on the contract, but I went to work as a coach for Gene Mauch up in Montreal, and I learned more baseball from him. I had already won an American League pennant and Gene hadn't won anything. But I learned more from him and I used a lot of his thoughts and maneuvers and ideas that helped me. And I left there—I was coming back with Gene, except Charlie Finley called me in the next-to-last day of the season, in 1970. And I imagine he called a bunch of guys that turned him down, but I said I'd be happy to manage your ball club.

It was a good experience. I inherited a great ball club. They finished a distant second to Minnesota the two previous years, and he changed managers and all that. We won 101 ballgames my first year there, but Baltimore beat us three straight in the playoffs. And there were rumors that I wasn't gonna be retained, you know, after winning our 101st ballgame. But I came back and then we won back-to-back. So that was great. I got along well with Charlie.

I had time with my family, so I had the Yankee thing I was working on. And that's when I left. So now I can't manage and I go to the Angels. We weren't successful there and, bingo, I'm gone. Montreal picks me up right away. That franchise lost 107 games, I think, in 1976. I think they lost 107 ballgames. Three years later, we won 95. It wasn't good enough to finish first, we finished second. The next year we won 90. It wasn't good enough to finish first, we finished second. And then we were right there. I had five years with them and enjoyed it. John McHale was a fine man, but he didn't think I could do it. So that's part of the game.

San Diego, they had never won. We ended up winning there. I

had two .500 seasons with a ballclub that never had a .500 season before except ones under Roger Craig, and we won it my third year, the National League. And by that time, you know, the most I was ever at one place was five years. So I rubbed a lot of people the wrong way, but my job was to win ballgames on the field. I'm not going out to dinner with the owner every night.

I didn't know I had enough ability to play professional baseball, let alone play in the major leagues. But things worked out well for me through thick and thin, through injuries, and all that. And I was able to play for thirteen years in the major leagues and manage for twenty-one, was successful, winning a couple of World Series, winning with three different organizations. I moved around a lot, but somebody was always there ready to offer me a job because I had success. As it turned out, it was enough success to reach the pinnacle of my profession, and that's being inducted into the Hall of Fame. It's been my whole life.

I follow it very, very closely now. I get the baseball package on TV. And now, we have Major League Baseball Network, I'm constantly watching. Norma puts me in a room and closes the door because she can hear me yelling at the TV. I was talking to Art Ditmar just yesterday. He's got the same situation. He's got a little room that she sends him in. And then he'll walk out, and he said, I can't stand it anymore, and she says, then I'm left to watch the game.

But it's a great game. Faces change. Naturally, players change. I try to keep up with it as close as I can.

I broke down and cried when Jane Forbes Clark called me from Cooperstown about the Hall of Fame, as did Norma.

EARL WEAVER

Nicknamed the Earl of Baltimore, Earl Weaver spent his entire major league managing career guiding the city's beloved Orioles to baseball prominence from the 1960s to the 1980s. Spending the first decade of his coaching career in the minor leagues, Weaver honed an outstanding knowledge of baseball strategy and player psychology while developing a comprehension of the role that statistics play in the game that was decades ahead its time. In the days preceding desktop computers, Weaver used three- by five-inch index cards to maintain data that would rival today's digital productions.

He made his debut as skipper of the Orioles in 1968, and captured his first American League pennant in 1969. Weaver's philosophy was based on three basics, "pitching, defense, and the three-run homer." As he often said, "If you play for one run, that's all you will get." He eschewed the bunt, steal, and hit-and-run style offense for the big inning, where his dominating hitters could bring in multiple runs. He also developed a field demeanor that was based on intimidating the umpires, earning him an American League record of ninety-seven ejections, one of which involved his being tossed while turning in the pregame lineup card.

"Earl Weaver is so good," George Steinbrenner said. "He is ahead of *everyone on the field. He is a great manager and a master intimidator of umpires. The last thing they want to see coming from the dugout in front of a home crowd is Weaver. He just plain scared them. In 1980, Reggie Jackson batted just .120 in the big series in Baltimore because Earl neutralized him. If that isn't taking the tank, I don't know what is. But a big part of it was Weaver."*

Weaver's players were also aware of his talents. Said second baseman Davey Johnson, "Earl is a master of psychology. He can get the most out of anybody. He used to be a used-car salesman and he can sell anybody anything, I believe." Fellow Hall of Famer and Orioles pitcher Jim Palmer observed, "Nobody's been more surprised than me that this team has averaged ninety wins the last four years without great overall talent. . . . So it had to be Earl's doing. The only thing is, I don't know why."

Retiring after the 1986 season, Weaver had managed seventeen seasons, entirely with the Orioles, winning four American League pennants and one World Series championship. He accumulated 1,480 wins against 1,060 losses. His teams surpassed the 100-wins-in-a-season mark on five occasions and his .583 win percentage is the ninth highest in major league history.

New York Yankees executive Gabe Paul may have summed it up best when he said, "I don't know if Earl Weaver is the greatest manager of all-time, but he is close. . . . He certainly is the best around now. He is fearless. He uses his twenty-five players better than any manager I have ever seen. He knows the statistics and he runs the game as well as anyone." Earl Weaver earned the highest honor for any manager when he was elected to the National Baseball Hall of Fame in 1996.

My father owned a cleaning plant and he did the uniforms for both the St. Louis Browns and the St. Louis Cardinals. By six years old, around 1936 and 1937, when the Gashouse Gang was doing their

Earl Weaver

thing in St. Louis with Dizzy Dean and Joe Medwick and Leo Duro-cher, and Frankie Frisch was the manager, I was fortunate enough to go into the clubhouse with my father while he got the uniforms and loaded them in the truck, and I got to look up and see their lockers with their name on the locker and their shirts hanging in there.

Later on as I was growing up in St. Louis, I had an uncle who had tickets for all night games and weekend games, and he would bring me out to see that. That was both the Cardinals and the Browns, too. So it was almost every weekend I got to see major league base-ball. As I got a little bit older, you get what they used to call the Knothole Gang. You bought a little ticket through school for a dol-lar, and Sportsman's Park was roped off way down the left-field line where I could get in the park with that card anytime I wanted. As I grew older, more or less, I was seeing maybe about a hundred major league games a year.

My favorite teams I guess were Billy Southworth's '42, '43, '44 St. Louis Cardinals. They're one of the two teams that won a hundred games three years in a row. And I think the Baltimore Orioles when I was there was the other team that won a hundred games three years in a row.

As I was growing up, there was no Little League at the time and there was none of this Tee baseball, but there were always enough kids in the neighborhood where you could get a game together when you were eight, nine, ten years old. Two of the parks that I used to go to to play were O'Fallon Park in St. Louis and Fairground Park in St. Louis. And we'd always, during the summer, you'd always be able to get a makeup game and go out and play.

As I got older, around eleven and twelve years old, there was Corey League that was just getting started in St. Louis. And I knew George Corey, the founder of that league, very well. And we got into a twelve- to sixteen-year-old league. We needed a sponsor. I asked my dad, look, you know anybody who would like to buy us some T-shirts, you know, that we could look halfway like a baseball team? And he found a fellow that he knew real well who was a jeweler. His name was Waldman. And I'm, today, I'm not sure how you'd spell it, but the team became the Waldman Jewelers. And my father, more or less, coached us and made sure that everything was right.

I went out for the varsity baseball team my first year in high school, and I made the varsity baseball team. First of all, I sat on the bench for the first three or four games, but, and I don't know really what happened, so that I got in there and played as a regular as a freshman. I guess this was the first time that I realized that, oh, I made this team as a freshman, and the other kids that I played with and everything else weren't going to make it. So, I guess you got to figure, well, my ability was a little bit better than theirs.

But as a freshman at Beaumont High School in St. Louis, we had a fellow who I played with on the same high school team, became the Rookie of the Year in the American League. His name is Roy Sievers. He led the American League in home runs one year. Also on the same team was a fellow by the name of Bobby Hoffman who played for the New York Giants. Also a pitcher that pitched briefly for the White Sox on that same team by the name of Jim Goodwin. So, really, we got four people that went to the major leagues off of a high school team.

I don't believe that the scouts were allowed to talk to a high school player. I had gone and received letters from both the St. Louis Cardinals and Browns to attend their tryout camps, which I did. And the Browns also gave me an invitation to come over to Sportsman's Park and work out with them before a ballgame. That was in my senior year in high school. But I think it was six organizations that I had received offers from, the Yankees, the Red Sox, the Cardinals, the Browns. There were two others. It seems like I should be able to remember, but right now I don't.

But I went over and I talked to Bill DeWitt, who was then the owner of the Browns, and he said to me, Earl, he said, you're kind of small, you know, for major league baseball and you're not the fastest runner in the world. You're a great glove man. We don't know if you'll ever hit or not, you know. But I had hit .400 or .500 in high school, and I'm thinking, well, what do you mean you don't know if I'm going to hit? You know, everybody thinks that they're going in there and wear everything out. But anyway, I left there and we walked right over to the Cardinals' offices, which were, you know, in the same building right there at Sportsman's Park.

And a fellow by the name of Walter Shannon, a great scout for the St. Louis Cardinals, took me over and made me look out a window and he said, look here, Earl. He said, see out there at second base? And I said, yeah. He said, well, that's going to be yours a couple of years from now. Now, that's scout talk, you know, but that's going to be your position a few years from now. Well, that's all it took. The minute he told me that and I could look out and see second base at Sportsman's Park, I wanted the pen [to sign the contract] right then and there.

I signed for $2,000 for the year. I could take what I wanted in bonus and the rest in salaries. I opted to take $175 a month in salary and the rest in bonus, which amounted to $800 or something around there.

There were only eight teams then in each league and it was pretty tough to get to the major leagues. So I'm kind of proud of the fact that I did get on the roster in 1952. I played a lot of spring training games.

I was a singles hitter. Single, double. Defense was the best part of my game, you know. I hated to make an error. And bases on balls, on-base percentage was always good, always. I'd hit about .280, .285 in the minor leagues up to Double-A level. Triple-A was a little tough for me as far as carrying an average. But the on-base percentage and defense were, I guess, the two best parts in my game.

When I signed and I had a Lynchburg contract, that was a Class B contract at that time, of course, I knew I wasn't going to play Class B, but where I'd wind up, nobody knew. You even maybe got sent home, like 80 percent of the people that were in that camp were. If I remember, and I don't remember exactly, but my number was something like 580 something. The Cardinals had, they had thirteen teams at Albany, Georgia, from Class A down. And the truth was, if I could have found my way home, if I had a ticket to get back on the train and go back to St. Louis, when I walked out on the field and saw all of those people and reported to the Lynchburg club, there were five second basemen standing there on the Lynchburg club. Now, remember, there's thirteen Class A down, so, it was traumatic. And all you can do is say, well, I love to play baseball. Let's play baseball.

There was a catcher, a major league catcher, roomed with Ruth at one time or another. His name was Freddie Hofmann and he was a coach with the St. Louis Browns. And I told you that the Browns invited me over to work out before the ballgames and everything. Freddie had hit me ground balls. He'd watch me take batting practice. And he was a real good friend with my dad, because my dad was still doing the uniforms. And Dad would be in that clubhouse and they'd talk to each other. So when the time came that I signed a professional contract, my dad went up to Freddie and said, Now, tell me the truth. I really want to know. What do you think of my son?

And Freddie said, Double-A tops, and my dad never talked to him for another year or two. But Freddie gave him the good scoop. Freddie was a very astute baseball man, and worked in the Baltimore organization later as a scout that they really relied on. And more or less, it came out to be true. The most successful years I had were at Double-A level.

In 1952, in spring training, you know what a thrill it must have been to me, I think I was twenty-one years old, to get out there and play second base with Enos Slaughter in right and Stan Musial in the lineup and all the other players. In fact, I played one game with Red Schoendienst at shortstop. I guess the reason for Red going over to shortstop was that Eddie Stanky was going to make himself a player-manager. But, really, there weren't that many big thoughts in my mind about making the major leagues that particular year, and I thought I'd go back to Triple-A or Double-A, and I thought I'd eat up that league like I did, you know, the other leagues that I had played in, and that's where I got my shot down there in the Texas League.

But that spring was just fantastic for me to play against the Yankees that in 1952 won the World Championship. And the box scores that I have with Phil Rizzuto and all their stars, Hank Bauer and Gene Woodling and the team that won the American League Championship. We played a lot of games. I must have played five or six games against the Yankees that spring.

Maybe in 1952, where the Texas League was so strong and they had so many former major league players plus former major league pitchers in there that that league ate me alive. And I went back to

Omaha and again had good years. Then the Cardinals traded me to Denver. I had a very good year at Denver. I had a very good year at New Orleans in Double-A. But by that time, I had been in professional baseball around six or seven years, and I was smart enough to realize that I was playing with people that were passing me up and doing well. And I could see that, well, you know, they've got things that I don't have, and I measured myself against the fellows that were going to the big leagues.

And about that time, I decided, well, I'm going to start looking for some jobs that are permanent in St. Louis during the winter. I had three children at that time and decided this isn't going to work. I'm not going to go to the big leagues. I think after having a good year in New Orleans, going back to New Orleans and getting sold to a lower league, I knew that was it, that that was going to be my baseball career.

In 1957, after I had been sold back to the Sally League from New Orleans, I was working and I was taking some tests to become a manager. And, you know, evidently I did pretty good in that business because they took me back every winter and were offering me this manager's situation as soon as I wanted to take the test and try to do the job. So, it looked like I was going to be set as far as having work or doing something and earning a living.

But then I got the call from Baltimore. Jim McLaughlin, who was the farm director, said, Earl, would you like to go away as a playing manager? Now, I don't know what I would have said if he'd said, would you like to go and manage a Class D club? Because you have no idea how bad those ballparks were in Class D and everything else, but he said the magic word "playing," playing manager. So, I could continue to play baseball, you know, and be a manager at the same time.

Well, I went away and I guess the rest is history. Fitzgerald, Georgia; Dublin, Georgia; Aberdeen, South Dakota; Appleton, Wisconsin; Elmira, New York; and Rochester. A couple of years in some places, four years in Elmira, and on to Puerto Rico in the winter-time, which was very beneficial financially. And then on to the major leagues.

Jim McLaughlin was the farm director of the St. Louis Browns when DeWitt tried to sign me. And Jim had sat in on that conversation about, Earl, you're a little bit too small and, you know, you might not run fast enough, but we'll give you a chance to play. And Jim sat in on that and never said a word. It was between myself, DeWitt, and my father. But evidently he must have followed my career and liked what he saw.

In Class D we had 300 people in camp, probably 280 people in camp and naturally we were the lowest. Class A was the highest. We might have brought in 50 players for each team. So, 300, it was six teams down there that were going to be formed. I had a fellow that was looking out for me by the name of George Stoller, who became my first-base coach. He was managing an A club there.

And George kind of took a liking to me and would give me a little advice, but he also, as the players were going to be cut and George had been there a year or two before, was letting me know maybe who to look for. And then, well, you know, I know baseball. I'm going to do my own picking. I'm going to do my own selecting. What I'm going to do is win.

So, that was my first year and when it came time, there were, I think, three D teams, maybe just two D teams. Let's just assume there were two D teams. A fellow by the name of Barney Lutz, a dedicated baseball man, he's now passed, but he was the manager of the other Class D club, and now we got to pick one, he'd get one pick, I'd get one pick. He'd get one pick, I'd get one pick. These are players that are available that were still there from D and ones that were sent down from C, some that were sent down from B.

You know, it's a chain reaction. When A cut, they went to B, B is cut, they went to C, C cut, and they were available to us. So, we formed our teams and there were two guys that year I think that went on and pitched a little major league baseball that I let get by, because at that time one of them couldn't get the ball over the plate. I'd watched him pitch in spring training. And I don't want no part of this guy. Well, it was Steve Barber, who eventually pitched a no-hitter in the major leagues.

I was happy to have the job in baseball and supplement my income in the winter. And do just a little traveling even though it was Fitzgerald, Georgia, or Dublin, Georgia, and then all of a sudden about the second year saying to yourself, boy, maybe one of these guys that I pick and manage and teach will go on to be a good major league ballplayer. It started about the second year that I managed.

The first year I did care about the ballplayers that played for me. But whether they went to the major leagues, that was up to them. You know, you do that on your own. The second year was the fact that maybe I can help this guy, these kids get to the major leagues, and we were in charge of cutting the players, too, sending them back home in spring training.

You know, saying, son, you just can't make a Class D club here, you can forget about going to the major leagues, what you have to do now is go get some meal money so that you can get home to your parents who have just given you a big party, a send-away party and they're going to welcome you back. So, just tell them you hurt your arm and that's it or something.

You learn the heartbreak of it right from the start, when you start sending the high school kids that can't make a club back home without a chance at playing a year in the minor leagues. They'd do anything just to stay: I'll pay my own rent, just let me stay here, let me play, let me try to make a team. No, the consensus of all these scouts that we have in here is that you're not going to make the major leagues, so we're going to let you go home and get started in another profession. And I can remember those words and, oh, boy, watching them cry. I know I would have. I would have if they told me we're going to send you back home.

The following year was just unreal with the ball club that I had in Class B. They were all babies. And the thing is we got off to such a horrible start that the general manager was on the phone every day calling Baltimore, saying get some ballplayers in here, get some ballplayers in here, but the ballplayers we had, number one was Cal Ripken Sr., caught for me, you know. He got to Triple-A and the smell of the major leagues.

But as we go on, Boog Powell was there. Pete Ward was there, Bobby Saverine. Now that's most of my infield. Paul Blair was there for a while, we had Pat Gillick, who, you know, a story about Pat Gillick, I still think today if he hadn't taken a job as assistant farm director he might have gotten some innings in the big leagues. But Dave McNally was there. Dean Chance was on that team.

So, I was a successful minor league manager, because I worked for the Baltimore Orioles, who had a great scouting staff, and made good decisions in signing ballplayers.

Harry Dalton and Jim McLaughlin together made me—a camp director is what they called it. And everybody hated the camp director because the camp director was making you do a lot of things. I was talking to the staff a lot; you'd be out, you know, playing golf or something, but it wasn't that strenuous, it wasn't that hard, and we got a lot of work in the shortest period of time. Paul Richards would just have us all in, you know, in the spring training camp.

Okay, I'm still the minor league manager and I'm the camp director. So, he wants to put a lot of his stuff into this program that I specifically wrote but a lot of it was, you know, some of it was Paul's, Paul Richards's. And everything good that I saw Paul do in spring training we incorporated as the years went on. I think I only did it three years, but it was the program now, it's Orioles, it's Paul's, part of that. And then along came [Billy] Hitchcock, and then Hank [Bauer], and I was no longer the camp director at that time, but I was a minor league manager at the Double-A club in Elmira and the Triple-A club as the years went on. Well, I put these things into my spring training programs. Paul's, Hitchcock's, whatever Hitchcock contributed, and Hank. So, the Orioles' way is a lot of theirs, some of theirs as much as mine.

Paul Richards

So, when I got the major league job, in spring training I said to myself, well, there's a lot of fundamentals that we're not getting to here. We were lacking the fundamentals that I had put into the minor league program. But there were some things that were lacking in this major league camp. So, when I got there I had the experience of knowing what extra I could put in.

And again I wrote my program so that if the writers came in and said, what's going on today, Earl? I could hand them a sheet of paper. And if they wanted to see the catchers work out they could go at 10:10 in the morning or whenever the catchers worked out and see whatever they wanted. They wanted to see the baserunning drills that were written down there and what time, they could see the baserunning drills.

If they wanted to see cutoffs and relays, it was down, if they wanted to see what was happening. And the other thing it was for was the boss. The boss could come out and see whatever he wanted any time that he wanted, or the general manager or the owner or whatever, and it was all written down on a piece of paper. It kept me from answering a lot of questions. And everybody knew exactly what they should do at any one time.

I never thought that I'd go and be a major league manager, or maybe I wasn't capable, but I never thought of it. I'm an organization man and I'm saying to myself, you know, I'm moving up the ladder here. And there's going to come a time when something goes wrong. How high can you go? You keep climbing up, but you're going to have to go back down, maybe work your way back down, you know, so make sure that you leave a nice taste in Elmira or a nice taste in Aberdeen so that you can have a job.

But my thoughts probably were, if I ran out of towns to manage in—with the success I've had with my reports to Baltimore on not only our organization, but who we should draft and everything else—that if the same regime stays in there I'm going to be a scout, an advice man, or whatever they want me to do.

Now, all my guys were moving up to the big leagues. Paul Blair was there, Hitchy, all of them that I had managed, you know, a lot of them.

Davey Johnson, Blair, that was our team up there. And I thought, well, I've managed all of these guys, how hard would it be to go up there and manage them? You know, so, with no desire really to be a major league manager, I'm thinking this might happen, but now here's the deal about this, when they named me as the coach, that was it, that's all I wanted, nothing else, because the life of a major league manager, the average life with one city was two and a half years.

Now, if I could get in, it took five years to be vested in the pension plan. If I could get in five years in that pension plan I'd be the happiest guy that ever lived. A major league life, yeah, that's nice;

big cities were scaring me at that time, you know. I had no desire to go to New York. I had no desire to go to Chicago, but that was what the job called for so that's where my job was going to take me.

I had Lou Piniella at Elmira. There was no calming Lou down at that time. I mean, Lou, another door is going to cost you $250, you know, Lou. I don't care, and there went the door. I think he was on his fifth helmet and the general manager told me that's all I'm paying for the helmets. From now on each helmet Lou breaks, we're taking it out of his salary.

You always thought that being that way would disturb his chances of being a good ballplayer, but it never did. That was a fact. But he had a temper like no other ballplayer I ever had and where it came from, I just don't know.

I got thrown out a lot. I got suspended in the minor leagues. I couldn't accept the fact that an umpire would miss a play that would hurt me and cost me a ballgame. He could miss a play, because he's human. But each and every win was what kept me getting a job for the next year is the way I felt.

You always wanted to win the pennant, no matter what league you were in or wherever you were, and you wanted your ballplayers to be winning ballplayers. But in the dugout, yeah, exactly the same, not exactly the same because in the minor leagues, believe this or not, I think you had to demand more respect from your minor league ballplayers than you might have to from your major league ballplayers because, maybe it was because I had such a great team.

And we had the kangaroo court. But I could laugh at myself a little bit more in the major leagues. Or kid just the least bit more with a ballplayer in the dugout in the major leagues. Don't ask me why. I don't know if the relationships were closer or not, or if you were more of a father image in the minor leagues. In the major leagues, some of my ballplayers were only six, eight, ten years younger; you know, when I first got there, probably Frank Robinson and Brooks Robinson were maybe eight years, ten years younger, so I was like a big brother more or less.

And these are all grown men that have been there and that have made it in the major leagues. So, how much do they have to be guided? Yeah, playing on the field they have to do their job, they have to be instructed as to what you want done. But as far as life-style, they are in the major leagues and if they don't know how to take care of themselves or what to do in the major leagues, then there's something wrong. They wouldn't be there if they didn't know how.

One time when I was managing Elmira, we were on the road. There was a line drive that I thought, and I don't remember the circumstances, I remember picking up third base, but it was a line drive that the umpire either called fair or foul, but anyway it went against my ball club. And I just went out and I just said, look, if we're not going to use the base, we don't need it. And bang, I picked it up; I'm thrown out of the game. So, I just carried it right in front of the clubhouse, right in front of the door in the clubhouse, and I left it there, because, I don't know, in the minor leagues, they might have had to stop the game. But, you know, those are just situations that happened impromptu. I understand Lou Piniella has done it a couple of times, taken that base out.

In 1968, the first day of the All-Star break, Marianna [Weaver's wife] and I were lying at the pool enjoying ourselves and from the front office of this complex, they came out and said you got to go home, you have a very important phone call. And, you know, it could be anything, a relative died, your mother died, your father died, it could have been anything.

So, bang, I went home and Harry Dalton told me, tonight, you go check in to some hotel or motel, get out of your apartment, take Marianna with you, and register as Earl Sidney, because you're going to be my major league manager. And I said, what? He said, I'm on my way to fire Hank Bauer right now. He said, I'm going to Kansas City. He said, you check into that motel and wait to hear from me.

And then I said, well, Harry, I don't know about this. And the story a little bit later is whether I'm going to take the job or not, believe it or not.

Marianna said, well, is this good? I said, I don't know whether this is going to be good or not. And then I told her about the two-and-a-half-year average life of a major league manager. But, anyway, we checked in to the motel, but getting back there, Harry wanted me to meet him the next night. I guess he talked to Hank and then he wanted me to meet him at a certain spot.

I forget where the spot was. But at any rate we went over there and he said, you're going to be the major league manager. Okay, Harry, you know this, what am I going to make? What's the deal? Well, he was going up a certain amount of money, which didn't seem fair to me. And then I heard that he didn't want me to manage in Puerto Rico, where I really supplemented my pay by managing in Puerto Rico.

He didn't want me to do that. So, I said, Harry, come on now, we got to have something here. You know, and it's interim, I figure I'm just going to finish this year out and they're going to look for an experienced major league manager. So, Harry was fair finally, and we came to the agreement. And we did win more games than anybody in baseball the second half of that season. And there was a reason for that.

Well, Frank Robinson had been out half a year the year before, that's one of the reasons that they finished tied for sixth, or tied for seventh, whichever way you want to call it. But also Frank had caught the mumps earlier in the year and had lost a lot of strength, and he wasn't really himself during the first half of that season. And things just fell in place.

I didn't think anything about it that we won 109 games [in 1969] and had to win three out of five to get to the World Series. I thought, what a bummer this is now. Two divisions, you know, didn't seem to mean anything until you've won, and now you've got to put it on the line for three out of five games. Traumatic.

First two were one-run ballgames, extra innings. They could have gone either way. We blew them out in the third game.

In the 1969 World Series we had a better team than the Mets. So let me just say we should have beat them. But Tom Seaver is going to beat you, and then that Nolan Ryan. And I don't know about this Gary Gentry. We got a report that, well, he's just average, throws average. Now here's where you needed the radar gun; nobody had one.

Son of a gun, if we had known Gentry threw as hard as Seaver, it might have been a different story, but we were unprepared. They said Gentry was just average. He threw the heck out of the ball in that Series.

But you're thinking we're getting outplayed here. You know, they're doing some things right. That's what it was. We were awful anxious to show the world how good we were at 109, and we chased some pitches that we didn't swing at during the course of the year, you know. We were up there swinging at balls we shouldn't swing at. We just couldn't get it settled.

But we came back in 1970 and played a magnificent Series against Cincinnati. I don't think anybody could ever have had the chances that Brooks Robinson had in that Series. We had left-handed pitchers, Dave McNally and Mike Cuellar. Man, they're making batters hit that ball down to Brooks or Mark Belanger. Brooks made every play there was to be made. And we'd see him all through the course of the year. Man, one after another in that Series with those strong right-handed hitters, Bench, Perez, Lee May. You know, they're pounding that ball down at him. It was phenomenal.

In '71, we had four 20-game winners. I don't think we're going to see that again. Never. Two of them were artists, McNally and Cuellar were artists. Jim Palmer was a good pitcher, but mostly a fastball pitcher, an overpowering pitcher. Pat Dobson learned how to throw

Jim Palmer

a curveball over when he was behind. That's all you have to do in baseball. Learn to throw a breaking pitch or an off-speed pitch or anything other than the fastball when you're behind. Palmer didn't have to do that. Palmer went right straight over the top. He had that little jump on the fastball that might go or jump half an inch, sometimes maybe an inch and a half. He got more pop ups and flies to center. Of course, he's pitching away at that time, but more pop ups and flies to center on the two-ball-and-no-strike count than anybody I've ever seen.

Now, Ryan, Roger Clemens, they can do that, you know. He got a little hop on it. But the other thing about Ryan, he could get a curveball over when he wanted, and he used all his pitches in a game, too. He pitched a no-hitter against us. The last out of the game was Bobby Grich. He threw him a 2-2 changeup. Nolan Ryan struck out Bobby Grich, the last out of a no-hitter with the 2-2 changeup. So, you know, if you can pitch, you can pitch. But Cuellar and McNally knew how to pitch, and Palmer knew what he was doing. He pitched away from a hitter's strength. And Dobson used that curveball and manipulated it.

Three of the pitchers used that defense that we had. Palmer struck out a lot but not like Ryan or any of those people. He got a lot of strikeouts, but he also kept the ball away from people. And Palmer was a very intelligent pitcher along with great stuff. Well, so were Cuellar and McNally. But along with breaks, he didn't have the breaking balls that those two guys had. He had a little slider. He had a curveball, but it was tough for him as much as it broke to throw it for a strike. But he was an intelligent pitcher and he knew what he was doing.

I had two ballplayers hated me, because they got to bunt so much, and that was Paul Blair and Belanger. You know, everybody wants to hit. And if you're giving yourself up and giving up an out, well, number one, like myself, I don't like to give up the out unless it strictly calls for it in a situation. But Mark, that was his forte. That's what he had to do. He had to move runners over and he had to bunt them over. That's part of the game. But the other part is you got men on first and second, and I got Frank Robinson hitting third, and I bunt with Frank Robinson coming up to get them over to second and third. That gives him one out. They walk Boog, who is hitting behind him, and get Brooks, who leads the league in hitting into double plays every year, because he's slow. They can get it out on one pitch. Not that Brooks didn't drive in a lot of runs, but I'm not going to sacrifice those two guys that can both hit the ball out of the ballpark. They both drive in a hundred runs every year. That's what they're paid for. We used the bunt, but it had to be the right situation.

There's no place in the game for the hit-and-run as far as I'm concerned. Run and hit is what I had assigned; go if you get the jump. If you don't know you can steal, don't go. And the hitter could do whatever he wanted at home plate. He didn't have to protect that runner, because that runner is going with a good chance to steal the base. So that's all right. If the hitter wants to take the pitch, fine. If he wants to swing, there's your hit-and-run. But I've seen, oh, Jesus, I've seen it so many times against me. I got a man on first base, just a fair runner. The count is 2-0 on the hitter. All right, a perfect time to put the play on. You hear the television announcers, a good time to put on the hit-and-run.

Well, if the pitcher could throw a strike, number one, he wouldn't be 2-0. So, all right, here comes the ball, way over the hitter's head. The poor guy at first doesn't get a jump, but you know. Or the guy swings at a bad pitch, you know, to try to protect the runner. Well, maybe he does and maybe he doesn't, but there's one thing sure. That runner is going to get thrown out. And there's nothing that says that hitter is going to get the bat on the ball, either. You know, he can miss the ball.

I didn't have a sign for the hit-and-run. I'd touch my button, the player could go when he wanted to. And they couldn't steal a sign, because a player might not go on that pitch. He could pick his pitch.

Not everybody has four tools. Yeah, I learned it in the minor leagues watching people of certain abilities go to the big leagues. Certain guys are not going to steal bases. Don't ask them to steal, and don't use them in a hit-and-run, because the hitter might miss the pitch, so the heck with the hit-and-run. Players fit in certain situations. Don Buford was not the best outfielder. He had speed, and he could outrun a fly ball, but he'd misjudge one or two. But for his .420 on-base percentage, I'm going to let him play. One mistake every fifty-two games is not going to kill you, or one mistake every forty games is not going to kill you.

If it's a mistake every other game, you don't want the guy. There are players that are going to make mistakes, and you've got to accept that. There are players you can't ask to do certain things, because they just can't do it. I would not ask Paul Blair to go to bat against Nolan Ryan because it was useless. And I play a little guy by the name of Tommy Shopay, who I know was going to walk twice and steal once, and there you go. Tommy couldn't go out there and play every day as a regular, but there were a lot of spots for him, to pinch-run, do this, do that.

When I took over the Orioles I knew from minor league experience, and from listening to major leaguers talk, "Oh, he's pitching today. I hate to go to the ballpark." Now, that's a heck of an attitude to go to the ballpark with. And it shows up in black and white, and I asked a fellow in our office by the name of Bob Brown, who was in charge of our publicity. I said, look, can you tell me what Boog is hitting against Mickey Lolich? He said, certainly. And I said, can you go back through the '68 season? This is in the start of the 1969 season. He said, yeah. He said, I can do that with all the players.

So I said, well, I'd like to know what my players are hitting against the starting pitcher that day. So he devised just a simple set by going back into the books. Now, he didn't have computer help at that time, but going back into the books, he would hand me, we'll say, Nolan Ryan, and their pitching staff, of course, Nolan pitched for a lot of teams, you know. But I get the eight or ten or twelve pitchers on the staff and there'd be a sheet: Nolan Ryan, Mickey Lolich—no, I know they're not on it—Roger Clemens, you know. Say, that's one team, and then my players would be listed alphabetically on the other side. Well, Belanger against Ryan. Believe this or not, he was a .300 hitter off of Nolan Ryan. He was the best hitter on my club, yet he's hitting .180, but he's going to play against Nolan Ryan. That's a cinch.

And Boog was not going to play against Mickey Lolich, but unfortunately, one time Lolich opened against us, and you can't sit Boog down for a rest on Opening Day, you know, so Boog played against him. But over the course of the years, I think in those years, he was one for sixty something. Now, when there were only eight teams in the league, the manager knew who could hit who. But with all the teams in the league, I needed a little help. But I knew who was going to be my best hitter that day against, you know, certain pitchers. And I knew who couldn't hit them. That information helped me tremendously, especially when it came time to pinch-hit.

So I used those stats as well as I could use them. And not many people had them at that time. Well, from that point on I think I used them about a year or two years, and then they were computerized and almost everybody had them.

Winning is fun and we won a lot, and you could have fun in the dugout. Laugh at yourself, laugh at some of the things that happen, pretend that you didn't hear some of the jokes about yourself, you know, from the other end, but it was all enjoyable. And comfortable? Never, because if I got comfortable, I wouldn't have hollered at those umpires like that. I was always worried about my next win, always, because if you didn't have enough of them, you were going to get fired, and I did not want to get fired, not after five years, not after ten years, not after fifteen years. So I was proud of the fact that that never happened to me, and that we averaged whatever we averaged, 95 wins or 94 wins a season.

I don't think that we could have won that amount of games if the umpires were not completely honest and full of integrity. They were just fantastic people. For me and some of them to argue, and for them to go out the next day and give you the type of game that they gave you is just amazing. So, yeah, I should have changed. I shouldn't have gotten thrown out of that many games. But again, I was so intense in trying to win so hard each and every game that we were out there that if a play went against me, I instructed my players, Belanger, Brooks, and whoever was out there, that if the umpire got the play right to give me the high sign on the way out or something, you know, so I could just get out there and say a couple of words and get out of there. You know, I thought you missed it or something. And sometimes they did, sometimes they didn't. Maybe the umpire had missed the play, and he's human. And if it was a tight ballgame, while I could accept that he's human and he did miss the thing, I just had to have a say and let him know how much he hurt me in other things. And yeah, the worst part was wanting to get the last word in. That was the worst part. That's why I got so many ejections.

Ron Luciano got me nine times, so did Marty Springstead, but it was a different nine times, because Luciano made a statement on California radio one time that he didn't care who won as long as it wasn't Weaver or [Billy] Martin. And now, Lee MacPhail was the president. He should have let it ride. He should have said something to Luciano. He made Luciano make a public apology in front of the press to me and Martin, which I didn't want. You know, it just made matters worse. And he was dishonest. He definitely would make calls that were against us.

In 1971 against Pittsburgh, Clemente had a great Series and we lost in seven. We were down 3–2 in that one. I mean, that was theirs to win. Frank Robinson, you know, made that heck of a slide, I think it was to get us back, with that run on a short sacrifice fly. But then we got more or less shut out in the seventh game. '79 was the heart-breaker. We were up 3–1 with Mike Flanagan, Palmer, and Scott McGregor all in order, all on proper rest, and we quit hitting. We couldn't get any runs. Eddie Murray, I think, went 0-21 in the last few games or something like that, no fault of his. The team just quit hitting, and it was a tremendous turnaround. That's one of my biggest disappointments.

All the players have to be treated the same. And most of the players, 99.5 percent of them, accepted that. There'd always be one guy that might not accept that, but I was blessed. Frank Robinson, he'd do what he had to do as far as being a team guy. If he didn't want to hit in July, I said, Frank, then you're going to have to come and get permission. Frank, if he didn't hit, he would come in and say, Earl, is it all right if I don't hit today? Naturally, it's all right, but he did come into the manager's office, you know. Somebody else comes in, well, do you think that you should take the day off or whatever? Well, whatever. And then you figure it out. But I was blessed with the superstars that just loved to play baseball and went along with the flow. We had a good time.

I don't think I knew the game better than the umpires, but I could have a rule book right on that bench, open it to anything that I wanted to know. They couldn't pull theirs out on the field. So, that's another thing that worked in my favor against them. And they knew I had the rule book. So, if you did question a rule, you got a little respect most of the time. Not all of the time, but if you did question something that went on, you got respect. If you want a story, we're in Cleveland. We're winning by two runs. Cleveland in the bottom of the ninth has men on first and second. So a ball is hit to Richie Dauer, takes a hop, bounces off his chest, he picks it up, throws it to first base, but the ball goes into the dugout. Now, naturally, the rule is, and the umpires know it, it's two bases from the pitch.

But as the play developed, I'm looking there and I'm seeing one run scores, two runs score, three runs score, and I say that ain't right. That ain't right. And everybody is running off the field, you know. It was the end of the game, bottom of the ninth.

I caught Marty Springstead. Marty, I said, let's review the play here. Let's do this. I said, three runs can't score. Now, because I got the rule book in the dugout, I think I gained some respect, you know. But at any rate, Marty, we went over the play. I said, it's two bases from the pitch. I said, the guy had never reached first base. He hadn't rounded first base. Marty says, you're right, and Marty started to walk away from me.

And I say, where are you going? He said, I'm going to get the umpires. You get your team and we'll get the other team back on the field. Well, they were starting to put the tarp on the field already. By the time all of us got out there, our television, in fact, radio and television had signed off and nobody in Baltimore knew that we had won the game until the paper came out the next day.

Everybody went to bed thinking we had lost. We all got back on the field. We won the game in the eleventh inning. The two runs scored and tied, and we got the next guy out. We won the game in the eleventh inning.

I know Larry Barnett got one wrong, and that was in the World Series. I forget what year. But Ed Armbrister bunted the ball and ran into Carlton Fisk, who was throwing the ball to second base. It went out into center field. Barnett let the play stand. The same thing happened the next year in Cleveland. This was when I tore up the rule book. The same play happened and the rule, to quote the rule, as a batter-runner, he was a batter when he bunted the ball. The minute the ball is bunted, he became a runner and he ran into the catcher.

A batter-runner is out when he interferes with a fielder fielding the ball. Armbrister did not try to avoid him. Armbrister should have been out. The man should have gone back to first base. The play stood in the World Series. Sure enough, the same play happened, I don't know who bunted the ball in Cleveland, but he ran into my catcher. Larry didn't call it again. I said, you got it messed up in the World Series.

I was going to quote; I said, I'll go get the rule book and show it to you, Larry. He said, you get the rule book, you're out of here. And already [Billy] Hunter was coming out with the rule book. I went over and got the rule book. He says, you're out of here. I said, are we going to play by the rules? He said, we're playing by the rules. I said, well, then, we don't need these rules, and I tore up the rule book and left.

Almost every time I got thrown out I deserved it, except for Ron Luciano and Bill Haller, but almost every time. The umpires were good, and, you know, they're going to miss some. That's why they have all these replays in football now. They certainly should have replays in the World Series.

But the umpires were so good, it's almost impossible that I could disagree with them that many times. I really respect them and I respected how they handled it. I respected how they handled me. And in almost all cases, you know, they were right.

Over seventeen years, it happened a few times that I got thrown out because of the ballplayer. If a ballplayer was arguing with an umpire, I went after the player and tried to get him out of there. Once I started arguing with the umpire, the ballplayer usually walked away. And sometimes I got thrown out, sometimes I didn't. But you better get out there to make sure your player doesn't get suspended, and lose a good ballplayer for three or five days because he bumps an umpire. Yeah, you got to watch out for that.

Jim Palmer and I had arguments, but we didn't have any problems. Either starting or not starting or who to pitch to, calling a pitch, maybe. They were just arguments. And one of the biggies was the year Flanagan was the Cy Young Award winner. I guess it was '79. We won the playoffs. I mean, we were going into the playoffs. The minute we clinched, I said Palmer is going to be the starting pitcher.

He comes to me, "I'm not going to start." "What do you mean you're not going to start?" "Flanagan is going to be the Cy Young winner. He's won more games than me. He should be the starter." "Mike Flanagan has never pitched in a playoff game. You've pitched in the World Series and you're going to be the starting pitcher. Now just go ahead." "No, I'm not doing it." "Yes, you are, Jim. You're going to start the thing. If you're not going to start"—you know, and he'd give me the sore arm stuff—"if you're not going to start, don't come to the ballpark anymore. It's as simple as that. Then I can start Flanagan. But I don't want you at the ballpark. You just leave the team."

Well, he went up to the general manager's office, and the general manager said—yeah, they have to stand by you or you'll have no success as a manager—well, you go down and whatever Earl said, you're going to have to do. So he started.

There were a lot of changes with free agency. I think we could have signed Reggie Jackson if we'd only, if Hank [Peters] had only known what was in the future, because Reggie was going to set the standard for everybody and he happened to belong to us at the time. And Hank would fly out to Arizona to try to sign him.

Now, Reggie didn't report to us till mid-May in 1976. If we had Reggie all year, there would have been no contest. But Hank would fly out there and come back with figures that were mind-boggling. Mind-boggling, because nobody in baseball ever had the audacity to ask for what Reggie was going to ask for. Well, as time passed we finally got Reggie in on the rest of the one-year contract.

Reggie wouldn't sign for two years. Number one, he was asking for so much that he didn't know what to ask for, you know, what would be fair and what wouldn't be fair. So, Reggie was there to play out his contract. Now, Reggie played as hard as he could. When he

Reggie Jackson

got there, he had had no spring training. It was May. We'd leave the lights on after a night game and the coaches would throw him batting practice, trying to get Reggie in shape.

He worked his fanny off, Reggie did, trying to get in shape. He just couldn't do anything. I don't think he was hitting .220 at All-Star break time. But this is Reggie. Skip, don't worry about it, I'll take this league over the second half of the season. And he did. Oh, my God, I think he hit all 27 homers in half the season. Yeah, he hit home runs and he did everything.

I don't know what his final stats were. He earned what he got. Now, let me tell you about the mind-boggling figures that nobody knew was going to happen. Sometime during the year, Kansas City, and I don't know who the owner was at that time, signed a first baseman, a young first baseman by the name of John Mayberry. He did not want to lose him.

And he signed a contract for $200,000 a year for I don't know how many years, but it would have boiled down to this $200,000. Nobody was making $200,000. I think it was a $2 million contract. And, naturally, when we heard that happened, we went to Reggie. I think Hank went to Reggie, and Reggie says, no, wait a minute, I heard what that kid over in Kansas City is getting. So it was definite that he was going to play it out.

But here's something about Reggie. He signed over there in New York, where he wanted to go in the first place I guess, you know, all the endorsements, but I think it was $400,000 and something a year for I don't know how many years, but the one thing about Reggie, everybody in baseball was passing him up, and not once did he ask, renegotiate, or anything. He played his contract out the way it should be done.

You hated to lose the ballplayers, but there, again, you can go out and get a Cy Young Award winner for half the price, like Steve Stone. Just good baseball judgment. Make the right decisions. I don't know if Stone made $300,000 a year. I don't know what he made, but he was a .500 pitcher when we got him. And George Bamberger and I said there ain't no reason why this guy isn't winning if he'd only quit bouncing the curveball on the plate and throw it for a strike.

So Bamberger cut his curveball down, as far as I know. I told Bamberger, well, we got to get him to throw a breaking ball over the plate. And he did, and he is a Cy Young Award winner. So, they're out there. You lose, but yet sometimes you gain.

Well, we had a good scouting staff. There's no doubt about that. But I had good baseball judgment, and that came from the minor leagues, watching guys pass me up and wondering why are they going to the big leagues and I'm not, you know, what can they do at a big league club that I can't, and as the years went on being able to, through the minor leagues as a manager now, saying that this guy can go to the big leagues, this guy can't go to the big leagues, and this guy could help you in a certain situation, turning those reports in to Baltimore from Class C, Class B, Double-A. I thought I had pretty good baseball judgment.

I started Cal Ripken Jr. in 1982 because the team was losing and the shortstop that I was playing was making errors in the eighth and ninth inning, costing us games. Cal Junior was a rookie and he wasn't hitting. And the shortstop that was making the errors was hitting even less. So I said, we're already eight or nine games out, and I said, something has to be done here. We've got to win a few ballgames. I went to Cal Senior, I said, look, I'm going to play the kid at shortstop tomorrow.

I knew that he could play the position, or at least felt like he could. And what was going on with our team dictated that I had to make some kind of move, an offensive move like Donny Buford when I first took over the club. So I put in a second-string catcher to play third base who was a good infielder, Floyd Rayford.

I put him in at third base, moved Cal to short. Magically, for some reason, Rayford was going to hit a little bit, but Cal started hitting. And now I said, oh, the organization didn't want me to do it

Cal Ripken Jr.

and they flew in a few scouts to talk to me and everything else. And I said, well, I'm going to do this. You can fire me if you want. It's my last year, anyway. I was retiring. And I said, but I'm going to play this kid at short until I'm satisfied that he can't do the job. Well, all of a sudden, he started playing shortstop. He started hitting, for some reason. We started winning ballgames. We wound up losing the division on the last day of the season, but Cal stayed there for a long, long time.

But he led the league in putouts and assists and made three errors at shortstop in a whole year. That has got to be the most fantastic thing that has ever happened in baseball. And that will never happen again, either. Junior, he's a natural-born. Now, everybody—

Ernie Banks, Rico Petrocelli, Junior—these were all shortstops that had to be moved sooner or later. Whether Cal stayed there a year or two too long, I'll never know. But there's one thing for sure, he had great hands and he wasn't going to make that error in the eighth or ninth inning that cost you the ballgame. He was a steady ballplayer.

I retired after 1982. I had promised Edward Bennett Williams that if he ever thought he needed me that I would be there. And when he called me [in 1985], I didn't even want to talk to him, because the man was very persuasive. He was very, very persuasive. And I felt obligated to him, I guess. I don't know, because we lost that last game in 1982. Maybe if we had gone on to win the World Series that year I might have said, I'm not coming back. But it wasn't the fact that I thought I could do something. You know, the team was there. I wasn't familiar with some of the players. I hadn't seen the league. I knew I wasn't going to be quite as good a manager as I was the years before.

I relied on my coaching staff and they were great. But I wasn't doing this myself and I hadn't seen the players and I didn't know exactly before the game to tell the pitchers what to pitch to certain hitters. But he was so persuasive, he said, Earl, we're losing attendance. You know, attendance? And if you sign, the fans will come back. That's what he thought. And I did sign and the fans did come back and he sold a lot of extra season tickets, I think, in '85 because of my going to manage them. I told him it would only be for a year and a half. That's all, he wouldn't sign me to a longer contract. I said it's only going to be for a year and a half, yet when I retired again, he was very disappointed.

You know, there're so many Manager of the Year Awards, then you didn't know which you were winning. I got them from here, I got them from there. Boston gave me their thing. You're going all over the country accepting awards.

Probably the most fun I ever had in my life was when I sold cars in Elmira. My goodness, you couldn't stop a person from wanting to buy a car. I've never seen anything like it.

I found out about the Hall of Fame from Marianna. I was playing golf and she got a golf cart and caught me on the ninth hole. And I knew what happened. The first year I was eligible. Baltimore sent two writers down to cover me the whole day.

When I saw her coming on the cart, I said, oh boy, I guess I got voted in. You still know as a manager that you're in there because of your players. It's not like I hit .400, you know, or .380, even, or was Most Valuable Player. But it's still a thrill to be recognized, and to know that you did something that somebody, as I said, recognized.

TOM SEAVER

"He's so good that blind people came to the park just to listen to him pitch," said Reggie Jackson about Tom Seaver, the most highly regarded of the outstanding crop of pitchers who entered the major leagues in the mid-1960s.

The Southern Cal graduate earned Rookie of the Year honors in 1967 by winning 16 games for the hapless Mets. "There are only two places in the league," he said, "first place and no place," providing a winning attitude that was new to the team. Just two years later, he led the franchise to its first World Series title, winning 25 games to earn the first of three Cy Young Awards with the Mets.

During his decade with the Mets he became known as "The Franchise," before being traded to Cincinnati in 1977. He continued to pile up victories and accolades, notching his 300th win for the White Sox in 1985 and finishing his career with a 311–205 record, a 2.86 ERA, and 3,640 strikeouts. Among his records are the most Opening Day starts (16) and most consecutive strikeouts (10).

"My idea of managing is giving the ball to Tom Seaver and sitting down and watching him work," said Sparky Anderson, who managed him in Cincinnati. A power pitcher with pinpoint control, Seaver relied mainly on two pitches, the fastball and slider. His credo was that "my job isn't to strike guys out, it's to get them out, sometimes by striking them out." Make that striking them out often. Seaver is the only pitcher to strike out more than two hundred batters nine seasons in a row, including five seasons leading the National League.

Seaver was a team leader on and off the field wherever he went, described by famed sportswriter Red Smith as "his own man, thoughtful, perceptive, and unafraid to speak his mind." A disciple of Mets manager Gil Hodges, he was a consummate pro who put the team's success ahead of all other considerations. He believed that "the concentration and dedication—the intangibles—are the deciding factors between who won and who lost."

"A lot of people think of Tom as being larger than life," said his Mets roommate, shortstop Bud Harrelson. "Especially those ballplayers who have to bat against him." Seaver combined his outstanding stuff with an intelligent approach to conquering an opposing lineup, and later wrote books titled How I Would Pitch to Babe Ruth and The Art of Pitching, among others.

Former opponent and fellow announcer Tim McCarver called Seaver "the consummate professional. He always figured out some way to beat you. When you were quick enough to catch up to his fastball, he used his intelligence. He figured out when to challenge you and when to finesse you. He had overwhelming confidence on the mound."

"My theory is to strive for consistency, not to worry about the numbers," Seaver maintained. "If you dwell on statistics you get shortsighted. If you aim for consistency, the numbers will be there at the end." No wonder he finished his career with numbers that made him a shoo-in first-ballot Hall of Famer in 1992.

Baseball became a part of my life at a very early age. In Fresno, where I was born, I went through all the youth leagues, and they had a very

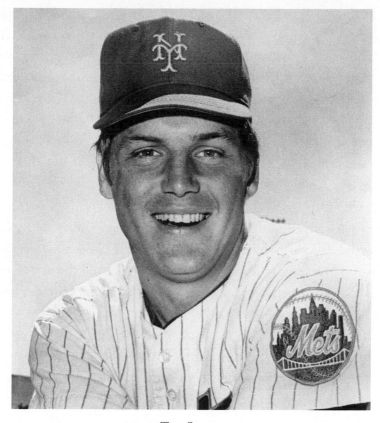

Tom Seaver

good youth league program. And I can remember one time, I think my first memory about baseball was I was eight years old and trying out for Little League in Fresno, and I lied about my age because you had to be nine.

But I was good enough to play. And I went to the tryouts. And I was on a par with the kids that were nine and ten years old, as far as ability went. They found out my age and they cut me from whatever the program was. They said, no, you can't play, you're not old enough. And I can remember going home and climbing into bed, it was a Saturday morning. This is what, forty-nine years ago. I climbed into bed, it was a Saturday morning, I climbed into bed with my mother and I was absolutely heartbroken that I had been cut from Little League and I just didn't think it was fair.

The next year, I started into the Little League system. I played for Rotary International at nine years old, and I played in that league for four years, and I wore number 13 for four years. I remember that. Another thing I remember about it is that I rolled up the sleeves on my uniform because I had seen on some baseball card or some picture in the magazine or whatever, some big leaguer had rolled up his sleeves. So, I figured that's what big leaguers do so I'm gonna do it, obviously, and show these guys that I'm a big leaguer.

I was fairly successful in youth programs in Fresno, California. I played all the positions. I played shortstop and third base. I could throw the ball very well. I pitched, et cetera. I had a good average. I was a good hitter, and that lasted until they started throwing curveballs, and then I began to focus on the one position that was left for me to do, and that was pitching.

But when I was eleven years old, I led the league in hitting and I led the league in home runs. And I remember I must have been about ten. I was ten years old, I got hit in the head by a pitch, I remember this. My father was at the game, and he came to home plate and told me to get up and get on to first base. That's the direction that he had in his life, was get up and get on with it. He was sure I was okay, I presume. You went up and went to first base. A couple of other things that happened that I remember about Little League. I threw a perfect game in Little League when I was twelve years old.

It was the sixth inning and I had retired seventeen hitters in a row. I went to 3-2 on the last hitter. I threw the pitch way up here and the umpire called a strike. That was a perfect game. I still have the baseball, too, as a matter of fact. With all the baseballs that I collected over the years for twenty years in the big leagues, I still have that baseball.

We didn't have a fence in this league. We had a chalk line in the outfield for the home run line, and my father would come to the game with our dog. He was literally my dog, my constant companion, slept on my bed and everything.

And I'd look around, I'd be pitching or whatever position I was playing, I'd look around in the outfield, and beyond the white line, it would be my father and my dog. And that's where they watched the game from. Those are some very fond memories that I have.

We won the championship of the Babe Ruth League in Fresno when I was fifteen years old. And that was the time that they started, you know, throwing curveballs and my average went from .500 to .250. I mean, it was cut absolutely in half.

I started pitching on a regular basis at that time, and one of the good things was that I had a coach on that team who had pitched in the minor leagues. He began to teach me certain kinds of pitches, teach me the slider, teach me the changeup, et cetera, which was very difficult in my professional career to learn. But I began to learn about the quote unquote art of pitching at a very young age. It began to be instilled in my mind. I'll digress for a second to go back to Little League. In that same league was Dick Selma, who I was a teammate with in New York, and he threw the ball extremely hard at a very young age. I was not one of those individuals. Physically, I developed late. And it was actually a blessing in disguise because I had to learn about control and learn about movement and learn about pitching on both sides of the plate.

I understood excellence. My two heroes when I was a kid were Henry Aaron and Sandy Koufax. So, I wasn't going for the .250 hitter. I was going for the big boys, you know? I probably knew when I was at USC, which is a good story. I was the last of four children. A sister went to Stanford and a brother to Berkeley and another sister to UCLA. I paid for my own education with a scholarship. It's one of the proudest achievements of my life. Taking the onus of that off my father after he had put the other three through school.

After high school, I went into the Marine Corps, which was another step of tremendous maturity for me. I was going, oh, wow, this is real stuff. And I blossomed physically as well. I came into high school five-seven, 165 pounds. When I came out of the Marine

Corps, I was six-one, I weighed about 205. So, in that eighteen-month period, I just, I blossomed. The physical discipline, the mental discipline, the perseverance, everything that you have to have, that was really a help to me in my career. It was one of the major steps for me in my career.

Discipline is the word that I think of when I think of the Marine Corps. I was always a very disciplined athlete, and I learned that way from the Marine Corps. The other part of the Marine Corps is that I came out of high school and I was not a good student. I was a B-minus, C-plus student. I didn't care. I didn't care about academics. I cared about baseball or basketball or football or whatever it was, golf, or whatever. Sports was it.

Then I went to junior college for a year. I got a full scholarship to USC and played there for a year. When do you realize, finally, I am gonna be able to play in the big leagues? Is it more than a dream now? Is it a possibility? We played an exhibition game at USC against the Triple-A team from, I forget who it was—maybe the Angels or somebody—they were on their way to Spokane or Seattle or something like that. And I pitched against that team, the Triple-A baseball team. And I think after five or six innings, I had pitched two-hit baseball against them. All of a sudden, the dream, I said, oh, now it's possible.

I said, maybe I can do this. Maybe this becomes a possibility for me. And the next year, I ended up playing Triple-A baseball. I went right from college to Triple-A baseball. And then the year after that, I was pitching in the big leagues. When I was at USC, my uncle had seats right behind the Dodger dugout. I would call him and say, Uncle Ben, are you using your tickets tonight? Or he would call me. Tom, do you want to go? So I would go, I'd watch Koufax pitch or Drysdale or watch Clemente play or Aaron play, or whatever, when I should have been studying at the library, but I was doing other homework, okay?

When I was at USC, baseball instituted the draft. It was obviously for economic reasons. And the very first draft, I remember, Rick Monday was drafted. I was drafted by the Los Angeles Dodgers in about the fifth round. I was drafted by the Dodgers and did not sign with them. They never made me an offer because, what I'm told, they were going through the holdout, with Koufax and Drysdale holding out, at the same time, so that focus came off of me, obviously, and went to their big boys.

And then, subsequently, in the secondary phase of the draft, I was drafted by the Atlanta Braves. I signed a contract for $50,000, $52,000.

The contract was never ratified, never signed off on by Major League Baseball. Then, because of my intent to sign, Walter Byers, who was then head of the NCAA (my father wrote him a scathing letter), declared me a professional and I lost my scholarship. So by the professionals, I was an amateur, by the amateurs I was a professional, so I never received any money, and I lost my scholarship.

My father called the commissioner's office, William Eckert was the commissioner, and he said—I'm sure the word "lawsuit" came up in the conversation—this is unfair to my son, et cetera, and we have to find a way in which this can be rectified. And what happened was that Major League Baseball or professional baseball went to each team, excluding the Atlanta Braves, and said that if they wished to match this $50,000 bonus that I got, their names would go into a hat and one name would be pulled up. And the New York Mets got drawn, which is how I ended up in New York. It's a little twist of things, just quirks that have a tremendous effect on your life.

I knew I had my money for college. Marriage was on my mind, et cetera. I was off to Jacksonville, I was off to Homestead, Florida, for spring training. And, ultimately I'm twenty-one years old, and made the Triple-A team out of spring training. Now, this is in the day when guys played Triple-A baseball for a living. So if you're a green rookie coming out or whatever young puppy coming out of college or high school and you go to Triple-A, you're taking somebody's job, you're taking somebody's livelihood. The system was different then than it is today.

I begin to get little snips from some of these older Triple-A players in batting practice. Here comes the bonus baby, you know. Okay, I can play the game, too. I know how to move the ball. So I started breaking a few bats, and that made me even more unpopular. I began to be accepted. They want to see how you're going to hold up. And that little bit of Marine Corps comes out of me and all that stuff. I ended up playing on the same team with those guys. I ended up getting married in Jacksonville, Florida.

Coming to the ballpark after my one-day honeymoon with my wife—we went to St. Augustine—I walk into the clubhouse and it's totally filled with gifts from my teammates, wedding gifts. Those are little parts of your life you'll never forget. I had a good year there and I never missed a start. I pitched a lot of innings and I began to throw harder. I was gonna go to the big leagues. They were gonna call me up at the end of the year.

I was on the team with Tug McGraw, who was heading to the big leagues, and he was up and down. Buddy Harrelson, who ended up being my roommate, was on that ball club. He went up to the big leagues. I was gonna go, and then they call a week later, and I was actually upset because that was gonna prohibit me from going back to get a semester of college at USC.

Wes Westrum was the manager of the Mets, and he wanted me to pitch the Opening Day as a rookie. And we had Don Cardwell, Jack Fisher, a number of veteran pitchers. He wanted me to pitch Opening Day at Shea and we're playing the Pirates. Somebody talked about it. I think it was Sheriff Robinson or somebody; Harvey Haddix was the pitching coach. They talked to him about it and I pitched the second day. I started the second game of the season against the Pittsburgh Pirates, pitching against Clemente and Stargell and [Donn] Clendenon and all these guys that I've been watching at Dodger Stadium, sitting in Uncle Ben's seats. No-

Hank Aaron

decision, got my first base hit in the big leagues, infield single—I beat the pitcher to first base. The pitcher was Woodie Fryman. No matter what you do, you always had butterflies. I had butterflies when I was forty years old. If you don't have them, something's wrong. You learn how to deal with that. It's an energy that you make a positive energy as opposed to working against you.

Coming out of USC, I went to the minor leagues and played for a year. And a year and a half later, I was pitching at Dodger Stadium. A year and a half later, I was pitching in the big leagues. A year and a half later, I was pitching in the All-Star game in 1967 in Anaheim, California. And my locker at the All-Star game was next to Henry Aaron's. Yes, I was very nervous. I was extremely nervous.

I have two favorite stories about Henry Aaron. I spent a year in

Triple-A and made the big league club the next year. I was in spring training and started the second game of the season and didn't miss a start for ten years or whatever it was. And I knew where Atlanta was on the schedule. I knew the potential of pitching to Henry Aaron, which was gonna be a big deal for me.

We were in Fulton County Stadium and he came up in the first inning, must have been the first inning, the first time I faced him. I knew every mannerism that he had. I knew how he came to the plate. I knew how he put the bat against his upper thigh, he put his helmet on. I knew everything. I knew every move that he made. And here I am, the green-nosed kid, and I threw a sinker on the inside part of the plate, he hits a ground ball at shortstop for a double play. I just got my hero out.

Three innings later, Henry came up and I threw the same pitch in there. But instead of Henry Aaron stepping at me, Henry Aaron was like this, stepped over here. So that ball that first time up was in on him now became a ball that was really, literally, in the middle of the plate for him and he hit a home run to left field. And he stopped being my hero that very moment.

It was a great lesson. Why are these people great? They're not just doing rote things there. There is a constant adjustment. There is a constant learning process. And it was a huge lesson for me. And I went, oh, this is how they play here. So learning from your mistakes is one of the best things that you could ever pass along to some younger athlete. Learn from your mistakes. Everybody makes mistakes. That's how you learn. Just don't make them twice. And try to get rid of those mistakes as quickly as you possibly can.

That home run by Henry Aaron was a piece of education for me. That was the year I went to the All-Star game. He's in the locker next to me, and I was just absolutely beside myself.

The other Henry Aaron story that I've got to tell you that made me so proud. Henry had come out with a book, written by Furman Bisher, who wrote for the *Atlanta Constitution*.

And by that time I was mature enough to be able to walk up

and speak the English language to Henry and introduce myself, et cetera. I felt that confident about myself. We were in Atlanta, it must have been Atlanta, and I asked him if he would autograph a book for me because I'd love to have it. And I figured that'll be thrown in the trash bin mentally for him as soon as he walks away from it.

Atlanta Braves came to New York to play the Mets at Shea Stadium. Before game one, Henry Aaron walks into our clubhouse with an autographed book for me that he gave me, which is on the bookshelf in my office at home, and always will be. You know, To Tom, et cetera, and a very nice inscription to it, Henry Aaron. Absolutely. I can remember him walking into the clubhouse like it was yesterday. Fabulous. Absolutely fabulous.

I'm in the All-Star game, selected from the Mets as their member to go to the All-Star game. And deservedly so. I pitched, I think my record was 8–5 or whatever, and I pitched very well as a rookie. I wound up winning Rookie of the Year in 1967. I was so nervous. As I talked earlier about being late to mature, they said I looked like I was about sixteen or seventeen years old. I mean, I looked like an absolute baby.

And I got to the ballpark in Anaheim with my bag and I went to whatever gate it was and told them I was on the team, and they laughed at me. And I said, wait a minute; I said, I'm on the National League team here. It was like an hour before anybody else got there. Oh, I was so excited. It was unbelievable.

And so I got in there, and I got halfway dressed, got my shorts on and whatever. I was walking around the clubhouse, and by that time, players begin to filter in, Aaron and Mays and Drysdale, I'm going, please help me here, what am I doing, because somehow there's one thing wrong with this picture and it happens to be me. And so, one of the great moments that happened to me in that game, before the game, in the clubhouse, Lou Brock came in and he looked over at me. I was walking around doing something, trying to hide, probably.

He said, hey, kid, get me a Coke. He thought I was a clubhouse kid. He thought I was the clubhouse boy. And I said, what? He said, get me a Coke, will you? And I can't tell you what I said to him, right? I can't tell you because it's not polite. But the gist of it was that I'm on this team, too, you know. To this day, now, obviously, Lou Brock, Hall of Famer, to this day we go to the Hall of Fame and the first time that I see him in the lobby of the Otesaga Hotel, what do you think he says to me? Hey, kid, get me a Coke. And we both laugh and roar.

There's a great story I'll tell you about pitching in the All-Star game in 1967. We talked about going to the clubhouse and being introduced, et cetera, and, you know, along with Willie Mays and Aaron and the rest of them and all the way down the line playing the American League for a few hours and it was like, what in the world am I doing here? And sitting in the bullpen, and the game went into extra innings and so the National League won 2–1 in the fifteenth inning, I think it was, the fifteenth inning, Tony Perez hit a home run off Catfish to right-center field and we went ahead 2–1.

And there were two pitchers left at that point in the ballgame to pitch the bottom of the inning, Claude Osteen, who had pitched the previous Sunday for the Dodgers, and me. The home run was hit, the phone rang, and they said, get Seaver up a notch, and I was gonna pitch the last inning for the National League. Nervous, butterflies, you wonder if you're gonna throw up. All that stuff. And I marched across the outfield, coming in, it was top of the fifteenth, and I walked across that outfield and I looked around and it was either Mays, Aaron, or Clemente in the outfield, something at that level, I'm starting to feel a little bit better.

And I got to second base, and Pete Rose is playing second base. He said, you look a little nervous. You want me to pitch, kid, and you can play second base? So he's trying to settle me down, right? And—talking about confidence and about how butterflies manifest themselves and how you control them—and I marched across the infield, I got to the grass, and when I got to that mound, I said, I know how to do this. This is my area. This is my spot. You know, I'm twenty-two years old, a year and a half removed from USC, but when I got to that mound, on that rubber, I said, I know how to do this. I can do this. I wasn't confident coming out there, but once I got to my office, I said, I know how to do this.

I had two right-handers, I knew who the hitters were, who they had on the bench, et cetera. And I got them out on fly balls to the outfield, ran the slider, ran the sinker in, or whatever it was. Yastrzemski is the third hitter, 2–1 ballgame, two outs, bottom of the fifteenth. Ball one, two, three, four, in the on-deck circle, the right-hand hitter, the last hitter they have. I know that. I do my homework. I want to get, that's my out over there, not this guy, not Carl Yastrzemski. Ball one, two, three, four, go to first base so I know exactly where you are. Go stand right over there. Now, I'm a rookie, I'm a half year in the big leagues.

A difference between pitching and throwing, I said, there's no way. I'm not pitching to this guy. Three pitches, Ken Berry, he's the hitter over there, strikes out on three pitches and we win the game, 2–1. I'm coming off, the likes of Henry Aaron and Clemente and Timmy McCarver patting me on the back saying, congratulations.

I went from a guy that was basically sinker-slider, and the workload that I took on, the more work that I did, the stronger I was. All of a sudden, as opposed to being a sinkerball pitcher, I began to ride the ball through the four-seam fastball that would take off. I never lost that. I know how to do that. That was the wonderful thing about it. I could, now, all of a sudden, I could do both. I could do this and I could do that, both. And because when I was kid I didn't have them, so I didn't throw it by people, but I could do it over there.

I was sitting on the bench one time with Joe Torre when he was a teammate of mine. He said, how many strikeouts did you have last year? I said, 235. He said, how many did you walk? I said, 77, I think. And you know what he said to me? You're disgusting. You're disgusting. Learning how to throw hard was really more understanding the mechanics and refining, mentally, the understanding of the mechanics of throwing the ball, and with the physical workload, I just kept getting stronger and stronger and stronger.

You're self-taught to a degree, but you learn from everybody. You learn from Frank Lary in Jacksonville, Florida. You learn from Harvey Haddix. You learn from Rube Walker. You learn from Wes Westrum. You learn from Gil Hodges. Across the board, physically, mentally.

The strikeouts were part of the game. And they were part of pitching. There are certain people you want to strike out. There are certain games, times of the game, when you want to strike somebody out. You'll learn how to do that after a while. The objective is not really to strike everybody out. If I went into the ballgame and I said, well, I'm gonna strike Matty Alou out, well, you're not gonna do it. You're gonna waste your mental and physical energies trying to strike out Alou. You're not gonna do it. It's not gonna happen.

You have to try to make him hit the ball to a certain part of the infield. To get him out, you're not gonna strike him out. There are certain hitters, certain situations I tried to strike out. There's 2–1 ballgames when you try to strike people out, depending on an individual, depending on who they are, certain hitters that can't hit the ball out of the ballpark. You may not try to strike them out, you try to just make them hit the ball on the ground. It's conserving your pitch count, if you know what your pitch count is.

And my pitch count, through the course of my career, was somewhere where I was effective; it would be between 125 and 135 pitches. Now, that would vary, obviously. But as a general rule, that's about where I was. If I got to 135, my tank, as a general rule, was empty. You begin to learn after a while how not to throw seven pitches to one hitter. You'll learn how to get him out on the third pitch. You'll learn how to get him out on the fourth pitch. You'll learn how to get the double play. That's learning the art of pitching.

*   *   *

The game in which I had nineteen strikeouts was the most at one time. Clemens has since gone by that. It was a 2–1 ballgame. And there are certain days when the best weapon that I had was a strikeout. Now, if that had been a 9–1 ballgame or a 5–1 ballgame, I may have pitched differently. I had given a home run up early in the ballgame, I think. But it was a one-run ballgame, and the conditions were such, it was, strike these people out. Go get them. So, it was, boom, boom, boom, the last ten in a row, bingo, win the ballgame. That's the bottom line, we still won the ballgame.

I pitched a game in Chicago one time. I was playing for the White Sox, and Ken Harrelson was doing the announcing upstairs. And I threw a pitch to Dwight Evans and struck him out. And Ken Harrelson came down the next day, and he was a good guy, we're good friends and all, and he said, geez, you got away with that pitch last night in the eighth inning or whatever to Dwight Evans. And I said, what do you mean? Well, how you threw that slider up here. I said, it's exactly where I wanted to throw the ball.

He said, what? I said, that's exactly where I want to throw the ball. I said, with his swing, this Charley Lau swing where you hit with the bottom hand and you go from the bottom to the top, that's where you attack that ball, it's up here. If you're a top-hand hitter, you don't want to throw the ball here. But when you start at the bottom, there is only one place to make contact with the ball—up here. And I told him, that's exactly where I wanted to throw the ball. I was thirty-nine years old at the time and I wasn't throwing the ball by people. You trick them once in a while, but you don't throw by them. It's not like Nolan Ryan. I wasn't like Nolan Ryan when he was thirty-nine, throwing fastballs by everybody.

It is my contention that the era in which I played, right before and through that era, was the best era of pitching ever in the history of baseball because there were more top-flight pitchers in that era, Ferguson Jenkins and Don Sutton and Steve Carlton and Jim Palmer and Bob Gibson. I mean, there's numbers of them. I give you one story.

Every year at the Hall of Fame, Sunday night after the induction, there's a Hall of Fame dinner, and it's only Hall of Famers. You pinch yourself a little bit when you're in there with this group. There's a group for the last two or three years that had been sitting at a certain table, which I will, for want of another word, call my table, right? My table consists of, last year, on my left, Don Sutton; to his left was Bob Gibson; to his left was Sandy Koufax; to his left was Rollie Fingers; to his left was Steve Carlton; and me. Now, that's a pretty good table right there.

And then Carlton Fisk got inducted. He was my catcher in Chicago when I won my 300th game, and I insisted that he come sit with us. He was at the table. This was about two years ago, last two years. Phenomenal. That's as good as it gets. Everybody has the understanding of the pitching. Everybody understood it. Everybody knows what it was about. We don't talk too much about pitching. We talk about wine and other things.

Nineteen sixty-nine was a dream come true for me as an individual, for a franchise, for teammates, for a city, in the middle of the Vietnam War and all that was going on at the time in New York City. It was a monumental period, in many respects, for a lot of people. We had the making of a very good pitching staff. And we had finished last, or next to last, the year before, I forget. But Jerry Koosman was there, and I had two years under my belt.

I came in '67, Koosman '68. We went to spring training [in 1969] and Jerry Grote, who was an outstanding defensive catcher, said that we're gonna win this year, and everybody looked at him like he was nuts. I said, what planet is this guy on? Well, he was the catcher, think about it. He saw Seaver and he saw Koosman and he saw Ryan and he saw Gentry and he saw McGraw, and he saw what the pitching was gonna be like for the entire year.

He said, we're gonna win this thing, and everyone, through the course of the season, one by one, everybody began to go, we're gonna win this thing. He was the first one, and one by one, we said, we're gonna win this thing. We had a chance to win every game we played. Every at-bat became important, every ground ball became important. We were never out of ballgames. You're at bat in the eighth inning, you're hitting, and the score is 3–2 as opposed to 8–2.

So, it elevated everybody's play. We had a great manager, who was a marine, by the way. We had a common bond, Gil Hodges and I, immediate common bond. And he set the rules for a very young ball club about how to play the game, how to go about your business, the same kind of stuff that I've talked about learning in the Marine Corps, the dedication and the concentration and discipline and all that stuff. That's the way you play the game. He taught me how to be a professional player. That's what he did for me. And that's what he really did for the entire team. And one by one, we just knew we're gonna win. We lost the first game to the Orioles in the World Series, and I pitched poorly in that game, relatively poorly. Donn Clendenon looked at me and said, we're gonna beat these guys. And this is one of the dominant teams of that era, you know? Frank Robinson, Brooks Robinson, Palmer, McNally, et cetera, et cetera. Boog Powell and, I mean, they had a tremendous team. And Clendenon, Clen looked at me and said, we're gonna win. We're gonna beat these guys. Now, they just beat Seaver, right? Cy Young Award winner, beat him. Three more games they are gonna be World Champions. He looked at us, said, you know, Tom pitched poorly today. We get a couple of base hits here or there, we win this ballgame. And you know what? They get Jerry Koosman tomorrow. That was at the back of our mind. And Koosman went up the next day and pitched a no-hitter to the seventh inning. And then they get Gary Gentry. We had a good pitching staff that threw very hard and could dominate people, could strike you out when we needed to strike you out. Gil Hodges, his fingerprints were all over that ball club. Boom, we won four in a row. And we weren't surprised. Loved it.

The so-called perfect game, the near-perfect game, you know, the ninth inning that I had against the Cubs, '69. And it's funny, now, there were 55,000 or 59,000, whatever it was, at Shea Stadium, middle of a pennant race, Leo Durocher managing the Chicago Cubs. And it's just one of those moments in your life that people will focus on because it was an effort which is beyond reality, in that sense.

The game started and it was one of those games when every pitch that I threw, the ball would get there and get around the hitting area and just explode, boom, explode. I mean, absolutely precise stuff. They had a good-hitting ball club. Ron Santo, Billy Williams, et cetera, et cetera. Middle of the pennant race in Shea Stadium, huge, massive crowd, and they are a veteran club, so that didn't make any difference to them. And you go into the ninth inning and the one guy in the lineup that I didn't know anything about was Jimmy Qualls, and he hit the ball hard to right field, he hit the ball hard to the first baseman, ninth inning with one out, and I went away from him and he hit the ball hard to left-center field.

I didn't know him. I was still pitching without information that I needed on how to get him out, other than just overpowering him, which I tried to do. He hit the ball to the warning track in right field. You have to know how you're gonna do it. I could say this guy is a high-ball hitter. That's what he does against me. I'm not talking about everybody, but certain individuals. And the next pitcher might be, you know, he likes the ball down and in off of me. Scouting reports are good to a degree, but he was a guy who I just knew very little about and ended up giving a base hit to in the ninth inning.

My wife was crying after the game. I said, my God, I just pitched a one-hit shutout and won, 4–0, and struck out ten against the Cubs. One thing that I'd never thought about is, I was probably still too naive about what it meant, the psychological aspect of pitching against major league hitters and teams. The effect that it had on that Chicago Cubs ballclub when they went back to their clubhouse after that game, they're in first place, they come to Shea Stadium, and some young pitcher, it's my third year, we got one hit off this guy, one hit, in the ninth inning.

We went to Chicago in '69, and they were throwing at our guys. I'm pitching the first game of a Sunday doubleheader. Well, I threw one right between Ron Santo's helmet and his head, and I came up and they hit me, and I hit their pitcher. It was part of the deal and then it was over. That was it. That's just the way the game was played. We ended up winning both games of the doubleheader, 3–2, by the way, after we lost Friday and Saturday. So you try that tactic if you want and, you know, we can play the game, too. I never tried to hurt anybody. I tried to hit some people sometimes, but it wasn't a large part of my game plan.

I pitched pretty well in Game Four [of the 1969 World Series], yeah, pretty well. Ten innings in that game. Gil Hodges and I talked about

Gil Hodges

it. I talk about it all the time when I'm broadcasting. The way the game is played today, managers look for reasons to take pitchers out. You should look for reasons to leave your pitcher in there. If you're a starting pitcher, as I was twenty-five or twenty-four, twenty-five, twenty-six years old, I was at the peak of my physical career and Gil's like, why am I taking him out?

I mean, this is all in hindsight. You know, he's going, I got this. This guy is pitching. Why am I gonna take him out? I'm not gonna take him out. He's still throwing well. Leave him in there, you know? He didn't, he never looked at me. Gil, I didn't have to look at him and say, am I still in there? If I was out of the game, he would've told me. I'd be out. And I didn't look at him, you know, and say, sometimes I go out, I wouldn't look at him, period, because I didn't want to come out of the game. I went back out in the tenth. We won 2–1 in the bottom of the tenth inning.

But it's the catch by Ron Swoboda. When the ball was hit to right field by Brooks Robinson, I think it was. They started it with Frank Robinson as the hitter. And the scouting reports were, this is interesting, the scouting report was Robinson likes the ball middle in, keep the sliders and stuff away from him. We're late in the ballgame and it's 1–0. I think it was 1–0, and I'm going, I can pitch inside on anybody. I'm right-handed and I can get in on anybody. I went in there and he hit a rocket to left field, Frank Robinson, and I said, and that's the eighth inning or whatever it was, well, maybe I shouldn't have done that. Boog Powell was the next hitter, and I made a good pitch on him and he bounced it in the dirt in front of home plate or whatever, and it bounced over Ed Kranepool's head. I was trying to get a double play.

I made a good pitch, he got a base hit. So now I got first and third and the ball hit by Brooks Robinson to right-center field. And Swoboda comes in and says, you know, a dumb play, the ball gets by him, now Boog Powell is on third base with a go-ahead run, it didn't happen that way, you know? If he doesn't make that catch and if Tommie Agee doesn't make those two catches, arguably, the Baltimore Orioles win the World Series, maybe, maybe. So says Earl Weaver, by the way.

I'm not saying that I agree with him. But what did happen, I mean, if the ball would've gotten by him, there'd have been nobody out, I think there was nobody out. The ball would've gotten by him, and they'd have been on first and third, et cetera, so I get the same situation all over again. He made the catch. Robinson, heads-up ballplayer, standing on third base, waiting for the ball to land or be caught, boom, tags up and goes in, you know, with the tying run, get out of the inning, get out of the inning. And we didn't score, and then I pitched in the tenth and we won in the bottom of the tenth.

You know, winning the World Series is probably, for anybody that's ever played with their imaginary friends in their backyard, the dream. It's what you're looking for. It's the goal that you're trying to reach. It was fabulous. I mean, you pinch yourself. My wife and I afterward, we were off to the Caribbean for a week and we rented a house. The Cy Young Award was announced and I won it, nobody knew where I was. Yeah, I was gone. We were just by ourselves down there. And it was crazy.

To me it became an art form. It wasn't a game anymore, it became an art form, pitching became an art form, the game became an art form. You identify what's the most important, right? It's between the lines. That's where the love is. That's where the desire really comes from. The rest, everything else is on the periphery.

I was walking in New York City—you can do anything you want, there are enough big cheeses in this town where it's not a big deal. I can remember one time we came in, my wife and I came into the city, and we were walking around shopping or whatever we were doing that day. And I was on Fifth Avenue and Fifty-fifth or whatever it was, someplace in Midtown, and we're getting ready to cross the street, and I looked across the street and there was John Lennon over there, waiting to cross the street going this way. And you know what? Nobody was bothering him, either, and nobody was bothering me. And I didn't say hello, I was scared to death. I came around the corner in Manhattan one time. Went around the corner, there was construction. There was a wooden wall, and I came around the corner and boom, Paul Simon bumps right into me. Do you know what he said? Hey, Tom, how are you doing? I want you to know you guys are doing great. Thanks, Paul. Nice to see you. And then he walked down the street and I went my way. And it wasn't that big a deal.

I was with the Cincinnati Reds the time of the Paul Simon encounter and I was running in the outfield and I looked in the dugout and Richard Burton walked into the dugout. He was doing *Camelot*. And I've always been a big fan of his for his professional work. And I said, I'm not passing this up. I'm going to go in there and say hello to him. So, I had it all set up about whatever I was going to say. Hello, I'm Tom Seaver. I'm a very big fan of yours. I just want to take a second and say hello, et cetera, yada, yada, yada. And I ran in from the outfield and I kind of pushed my way through the wall of reporters who were around him and I put my hand out to shake his hand and introduce myself. And I went, hello, my name, and he said, Tom, how are you doing? He says, how is your shoulder? I've been reading about your arm. And I went, this is not how I was supposed to do it.

He said, I read that you had some trouble, shoulder trouble in the last couple of strikes. So, how are you doing? And I said, oh, things are better, Rich, you know? So, we sat there and yakked for ten or fifteen minutes or whatever. He's a big baseball fan. He says, I just began to learn the game, I love it, et cetera, and I read about you all the time. He says, come to Broadway while I'm doing *Camelot*. I say, well, I'm going on the road. He says, where are you going on the road? And making a long story short, we ended up in Chicago at the same time. He said, call me, I'll leave you tickets. So I called him and he left me tickets and I took one of the young kids on the team.

Two seats in the very front row. He comes up, knows right where I am, and he kind of gave me a little wink and went on with his business. And this is like father and son in the sense of I'm taking a young kid, trying to expose him to something else. You know, I'm the crusty veteran, take these young kids coming out of college. We're going to start learning from all of these experiences.

One of the great lessons I got from Gil Hodges, maybe the most important lesson, I got in 1968. It was in a game in which I was ahead of the Giants 7–0. And I turned around at Shea Stadium and the score is 7–6. They have Mays, McCovey, Jim Ray Hart, Jesus Alou, and they can put points on the board real fast. It was 7–6. I end up winning the game 7–6. Gil called me into the office. He said, I don't care if it's five thousand people or fifty thousand. I don't care if it's Chicago at Wrigley Field on Tuesday, or Dodger Stadium on Saturday. I don't care if it's the first inning or the seventh inning. I don't care. Your approach as a professional never changes. I don't care if it's 75 degrees or 35 degrees. It doesn't make any difference.

I never forgot it. I benefited from that lesson for seventeen and a half, eighteen and a half years. It was one of the most important parts of my education about being a professional athlete, if not the most. That was the beginning of understanding my art, my trade. And once you begin to understand that, it doesn't make a difference where it takes place. It doesn't make any difference if it's five thousand people at Candlestick on a freezing night, or if it's fifty thousand people at Dodger Stadium or in New York. It doesn't make any difference. It's what happens in between those lines and on that mound, that's what becomes important.

It doesn't make a difference if nobody is watching, doesn't make one hoot of a difference. It doesn't make a difference if the score is 10–1 or 1–1. That's when you finally realize that everything on the periphery has an effect on how you go about your business. What am I gonna do—am I going to pitch better in front of fifty thousand than I am five thousand? So, then, you're at the whim of the call, whim of the call of weather. Tuesday night or Saturday, how many people show up and buy tickets? Is that what you think about your art or your profession or your trade or whatever? It can't happen that way. So, again, and that, from that standpoint, Gil took me to a different level.

That year in my life [1976–77], that part of my life was very difficult because I was a guy that gave my heart and soul. Gil Hodges had died, and the franchise began to go to hell in a handbasket. And I worked for a guy that was not a nice man, Mr. Donald Grant. He called me a communist one day. I said, excuse me? We just, he didn't like me and I didn't like him. It was time to get out. And that's really all I want to say about it. It's just, it was not pretty. The man took some of the love I had for the game. There's no question about it, but I left. I left and went to Cincinnati. I got to play with Johnny Bench and Pete Rose and Ken Griffey and Dave Concepcion and Joe Morgan. That was pretty good duty over there.

Gibson pitched every fifth day. He didn't care who it was. He didn't care if it was Fergie Jenkins or if it was the fifth pitcher on the Chicago Cubs. It didn't make any difference. His theory was that you're going to win with your team. And you're pitching every fifth day. Carlton and I pitched against each other a lot. Gibson and I pitched against each other a lot. We all did, you know? There were a lot of Hall of Fame pitchers in that period of time and we pitched against each other a lot.

It wasn't a matter of it becoming a marquee thing. You're not pitching against Carlton, you're not pitching against Gibson, you're pitching against the Phillies or the Cardinals or the Cubs. If you're pitching against Gibson or you're pitching against Carlton, you know you're not going to get many runs. So that has an effect.

In the 1968 All-Star game, it was my second year in the big leagues so I really started to throw the ball pretty good. I pitched against Mickey Mantle in that game, only time I ever faced Mickey, struck him out on three pitches. Kenny Harrelson came up and I think I struck him out on three pitches, three high fastballs right here. Just let her fly. I was really throwing hard. I didn't know Kenny.

I'd never met him, really, but we became good friends and played golf together in Chicago.

He said when he was going back to the dugout after he'd struck out, he went by Boog Powell in the on-deck circle and he told Boog Powell, remember the old thing about hitting, about wait and be quick? Forget the first part. He says, that's the way you were pitching that day. And I said, kind of looked like it to me, too.

My favorite park to pitch in was Fenway Park. At the end of my career, yeah. At one time obviously [my favorite] had to be Dodger Stadium, because that's where I was as a kid, a college kid. And then it became Shea Stadium, and it just grows. It grows, it just grows and grows. I hated pitching in St. Louis. You want to know why? The very simple answer is Lou Brock.

Think about it. You got a big outfield. You got a place for the ball to run and it wasn't a hitter's ballpark, home run ballpark. He would hit the ball in the gap. He made it not a fun place to play. I'm being a bit facetious but you're getting the drift of what I'm talking about. And then, at one point, you know, pitching in Boston was very, very special. I never went into Fenway Park until I was a player in my eighteenth year when I went to play for the White Sox.

My sister used to live in Boston and we used to drive by it going to her house when we lived in Connecticut. And I could see the wall, I could see it from the Mass Pike. It's a piece of history. I had a pretty good sense of history of the game of baseball, but as you go through it, you begin to learn. Going into Fenway Park as a member of the Chicago White Sox, I didn't go through the dugout, I went through up the ramp, where the fans would go. And here was this canvas in front of me. It was just mind-blowing. From a physical standpoint, from an emotional standpoint, historical standpoint, it's a piece of art, absolutely a piece of art.

Going to Yankee Stadium the first time was a huge thrill, going out to see the monuments and stuff. But the difference between Yankee Stadium and Fenway Park, Yankee Stadium was cavernous, an absolute huge monstrous cavern. Fenway Park is this beautiful field, this beautiful field with lots of light coming in. That was just the ultimate place for me to pitch. I adored it.

When I was going for win number 300 at Yankee Stadium, George Steinbrenner decided to run me off the field while they were doing the ceremonies, pregame ceremonies, with Phil Rizzuto. The game was supposed to start at a certain time and they got past, and as a creature of habit, I knew exactly what I had to do. It was time for me to get up and start running if the game was going to start on time. He had one of the security guys come in and tell me that Mr. Steinbrenner wants you to leave the field, because stuff is going on at home plate and I'm out running in the outfield, and I was a disturbance.

Well, I can really make an issue out of this, you know? But I said, all right, I'll play, and I went back to sit down. If I make an issue of this, I'm going to take that to the mound. Right? Just go back, sit down, whenever, I'd rock and roll, you can get up and start your shtick, start running. They got done, boom, and I went to work.

That's an example of what part you play, who you're pitching against. Where's the ultimate focus? Am I going to take this instance, that George Steinbrenner ran me off of the field, and let it become a negative against what I'm trying to achieve today? Well, then you're shooting yourself in the foot if you do. Okay, fine. I can understand that. Go sit down. You go to that mound, you're totally focused and totally centered on what you want to do.

I won 300 on my first try. Because my daddy came, he's from California, and I didn't want him trucking all the way around the East Coast waiting for me. I didn't know if he was going to stay or not. He said, well, let's get this done, I got a golf game next Saturday.

I won number 299 at Fenway. Okay, now, in five days I'm pitching in Yankee Stadium, win number 300. We were living in Connecticut at the time, and got in the car. My two children in the back, I had my wife in the front seat of the car, I'm driving back to our home in

Connecticut, down the Mass Turnpike, out in the middle of Mass. It's one in the morning or twelve midnight, or whatever it was, after the game in Boston. And I say, okay, now, in five days I'm pitching against the Yankees, what are you gonna do to beat the Yankees? Keep Bobby Murcer and Dave Winfield in the ballpark. Two biggest things; how are you gonna get them out?

Don Mattingly hits a home run, he's gonna have to hit the home run to left field. You know, they're gonna get their hits. Maybe they'll hit it at somebody and get an out, whatever. But I was past the point of being a strikeout pitcher, a so-called strikeout pitcher. Still, the operative word is "pitcher." Keep them in the ballpark. How are you gonna get Winfield out? Use his aggressiveness against him. He's a spotlight player, great athlete in three sports. At zero hour, like Reggie, he wants the spotlight on him and he wants to perform. That's what makes great players. He is gonna be aggressive; use that aggressiveness against him. Get the count to 3-2 and we change up. Okay? If the situation comes up in the last nine outs in the ballgame. So the game comes, bottom of the eighth inning, score's 4–1. Men on first and on third, and the hitter is Dave Winfield, tying run, last nine outs of the ballgame. How are you gonna get him out? Get the count to 3-2, use the changeup. Now, there's a little something to do there, too. Fisk called for a curveball, which I never would've thrown in that situation.

It's a perfect call and boom, I threw a curveball. It was maybe my third- or fourth-best, fourth-best pitch, actually. Totally fooled Winfield. It's a great call. Mattingly was a great call, too. The rest of the time I threw nothing but fastballs. I mean, I pounded everything I had right in here. Three and two, runner at first has taken off, spotlights on, fifty thousand people, twenty-five people in that dugout. What's he gonna do? What's he gonna throw in this situation? It's a game, you know?

I made that decision five days before on the Mass Turnpike. This is what pitching is about, right? I already made that decision. I've already done the homework on this. I've already decided what this situation is. Very creepy. Now, the eerie part about this is, I walked one man in that game. I walked him in that inning, which set up the situation that I'm talking about. So, it's your psyche, gives me chills thinking about it.

So, I got all these people, the announcers or whatever they do, whatever they're doing for the business, saying, oh, my God, what is he doing? And I'm going, I already decided what to do. So, one time, I'm in the stretch, 3-2, two outs, tying run at the plate, runner at first base, means nothing. Step off the rubber, checking the runner at first, means nothing. I did it solely for Dave Winfield because I'm throwing a changeup. I want him, right? All I have to do is execute, physically execute. I'm trying to make him as hungry as I possibly can; he had 3-2, he's definitely looking fastball.

I threw him no changeup, nothing, until I threw him that first off-speed pitch. Nothing but hard stuff and so, because he's got to protect here, and that's what I want, I can throw him a changeup, so then he'll be early. He's got to be out front. Three-two, changeup, boom, way out front, strike three. And you walk off and you go, nobody, nobody announced, nobody. You're the only one. See, that's the wonderful thing about pitching. All of a sudden, in that situation, they know, fifty thousand people and twenty-five there know after the fact what happened. I knew before the fact. I knew five days before the fact what was gonna happen.

I went to spring training, and I went through with the White Sox, winning it for the White Sox. Fisk says, Tom, what kind of signals you want to use? I said, one, two, three, four. One, two, three, and a wiggle, for fastball, curveball, slider, and a wiggle for a change. And I said, I also throw my changeup off the fastball. He said, what? I said, you put the fastball down, I can throw either, I can throw a two-seam, four-seam, or a changeup.

He never heard of that. And he was kind of hesitant to accept it. I said, Pudge, try it, just try it. If it doesn't work, we'll figure out something else. I've been doing it this way because I don't want there to be a delay in the timing of delivering two different pitches.

Carlton Fisk

It's pretty simple when you think about it. I want the tempo of the fastball to be exactly the same as the tempo of the changeup or vice versa. Or, if I don't want the tempo to be the same, I want to be able to control it. I want to make it longer or shorter, and what the hitter reads, because everything he reads, I want to program for him. There are certain things I want him to know, certain things that I don't want him to know.

So I said, if it works, fine. Let's see. If it doesn't work, we'll figure something else out. There was never another word said. And when he put down that fastball on that pitch to Dave Winfield, he knew I was throwing a changeup. He knew that because we worked together all year long. Now he knows exactly how I pitch.

The communication between the catcher and the pitcher, the

relationship between the two is very special. There are times when you want that catcher to know that you need a kick in the rear end. There are times—and I called my own pitches through my entire career—there are times when you go to that catcher and say, here is the range. I've got enough to worry about today for I don't know how many innings; I'm controlling my physical body, just controlling the physical aspect of it. I'm taking this off my shoulders and giving it to you. I may take it back later, whatever, but this is it. All I can do is worry about me. That's all I can do.

There are certain days that's all you're capable of doing. You got to recognize that. But I always called my own pitches. And I had great catchers. I had Jerry Grote, who's a terrific catcher, Johnny Bench, Hall of Famer, right? Carlton Fisk, great. If you don't call your own pitches, which is so simple to me, and Johnny Bench or Jerry Grote shows up today and the manager is gonna use this catcher because of a pitcher or give him the day off or whatever, now you've got another set of gray matter in the decision-making process, which is totally different than what you've been using. Now, how can you control any of that? Just call your own pitches.

What we're talking about on the mound just depends on situations, and I'll give you the perfect example. I love Johnny Bench as a catcher, arguably the best catcher of all time. I had started a game in Cincinnati, and for whatever reason, emotionally, I was very uptight, and I just gave up a double and a single and another double, and I'd probably thrown maybe five pitches or something and the score is 2–0, man on second and nobody out.

And John came out to the mound, didn't take his mask off, and I know he must've done it before sometime. And he came to the mound and he got about that far from my face, mask still on, he goes, are you trying? That's all he said, turned and walked away. I laughed so goddamn hard. He knew exactly what I needed. Let all the air out, this hot air, whatever it was, you know? And after I stopped laughing and I went back, we ended up winning 5–2, or whatever it was. The vibrations that go back and forth, it is a very special rela-

Johnny Bench

tionship. And they really begin to understand you and you begin to understand them, and all of a sudden it becomes like two minds that really work as one.

You reach the big leagues and it's not a flat line at that point. That's when graduate school begins. That's when you really start to learn what your business is all about. You may not learn and have enough of an education by the time you first get there.

Some ballplayers do. Some kids listen, some don't. Some kids get it, some don't. But when you get there, hopefully you'll have Gil Hodges, hopefully you'll have Rube Walker or Bill Fischer, or whoever it is that passes these things along to you, to try to open your eyes. Think about this, think about that, you know, what about that situation? What about the 50 degrees or 35 degrees or 75 degrees in L.A. on Saturday, and five thousand people and fifty-five thousand people? Is there a difference?

Is there a difference in your effort because of the five thousand people, fifty-five thousand? Is there? If there is, then it's wrong. If that makes a difference, then you don't understand what you're doing is an art form. If it is a Tuesday game, there's nobody here, or it's a Saturday TV game, so you're gonna give extra effort on Saturday. I suddenly began to realize those things.

You kind of have your own system for preparing for games. After a while you learn how much you have to throw. I think if I had to do it over again, I probably would throw a little bit more. I'd probably throw more, just play catch. A lot of times I didn't do much. If I had worked two days afterward and thrown on the side, maybe I would've played a little bit more, just soft-toss catch is what I would have done.

Stretch out, I used to do that, absolutely. I did. And I would throw from the right-field line to center field. Get your pitching coach to throw it back. Just stretch it out, get to where you're reaching out, not cutting everything off.

I started lifting weights in college for triceps and lats and all these muscles in the back. I think that's one reason why, from the acceleration standpoint, my career really blossomed, because I started lifting weights at the time and I was physically developed and I got a lot stronger as I went along. In the winter, I lifted weights.

Physically, for me, I had to drop and drive and generate. I suffered because I didn't have a great curveball. I had a very good slider, but I had pinpoint control, too, and lots of stamina. You stand up, you're not gonna be able to pitch, no, you're not gonna be able to throw as many pitches if you are taller. That's my theory. Where is the biggest muscle mass of the body? Thighs and your rear end. That's where the large muscles are. You have to incorporate those muscles. Baseball today seems to be very happy with five, six, and sometimes seven. But you have pitchers that are pitching five and a third innings, or five and two-thirds innings, and they're throwing seventy-five pitches, and you're gonna take them out of the game? It doesn't make sense to me.

I have certain pet peeves about the game. It's a place where you, it's an escape from all the noise that you have. It's a place to go and listen and smell and look at the beautiful things that a ballpark has to offer.

You have ballparks these days where sometimes, nobody takes batting practice, nobody takes infield anymore, and you put something on a screen for the fans to watch. It's some sort of video high-tech stuff with this godawful noise all the time, just noise. What's wrong with, let's have silence? Isn't it beautiful to be silent here? Isn't it beautiful to see why you're doing this and watch Roberto Alomar take infield? It's one of the spectacular things in the game of baseball.

And when you get two balls going on the infield, I mean, it's like a piece of art, and the crack of the bat, batting practice, fabulous. Mike Piazza taking batting practice, crack, crack, you can't hear it because of the stupid noise coming out of the loudspeakers in center field. Well, I guess I'm a purist from that standpoint and maybe I get that these guys are smart. They did research and they said, now we have to have all this stuff. Maybe you do. Maybe you don't.

Amphetamines were something that was, and still is, I imagine, part of the industry, and it was part of the industry when I played. And I never took amphetamines and stuff. Never did. I took one of them when I was a student at USC, and I got so dizzy I said, I'm never taking this stuff again. For me, my body, it didn't work. I always took aspirin. So, yes, I'm taking something obviously legal, and you're buying it; it was part of the deal, is still part of the deal in clubhouses today.

The ball, they changed the ball. Ownership changed the ball. They went from a Spalding baseball to a Rawlings baseball. They changed the core of the ball. They changed the center of the ball. They changed the yarn that is wound to make the ball. They changed the thickness of the yarn that's wound when they make the baseball.

They fiddled with the baseball. I used to take a baseball apart every year and kept them at the bottom of my locker. And I put the year in, and put it in a plastic bag, and put it down in the bottom of my locker. Like an idiot, when I was traded from the New York Mets I threw all that stuff away. It was stupid. I mean, you can still cut up baseballs to find out, but the core has changed, the way it went from a cork center to cushion cork and all that stuff.

Definitely, baseball changed. As far as the steroids and all the enhancements that the individuals can take, they got to control this as far as I'm concerned. Every other sport does it. It's unfair to the people who played before. It's unfair to the fans, and it's unfair to the athletes themselves to feel that they have to do this. Whether it's in the long term, what it's going to do to their life.

The no-hitter came in Chicago on a day that wasn't one of the best days I had. I had great defensive players behind me, Ray Knight, Joe Morgan, Concepcion in the infield. It's kind of like if you pitch for twenty years and have a level of ability, somewhere you're going to get a no-hitter. That's kind of what happened that day. When I retired, Jack Lang, who was around in the New York press area most of, if not all of, my career asked me, you want to do a column of the top ten games of your career? The no-hitter wasn't in the top ten.

Why did I have Henry Aaron as a hero? It was just this model of consistency year after year after year after year. It's the same level of excellence year after year. I look back on it, and say, well, I won 311 games and I lost 205. The other side, the same side, the continuum of that is what did you do for the guys you played with and the team you played for? How much did you help them get above that .500 mark over the course of the year? That's not one statistic. It's not 3,000 strikeouts. To me that far exceeds 3,640 strikeouts.

Best piece of advice I ever got: I was in Triple-A, a coach said, listen to everybody. Listen to everybody, listen to what everybody has to say, walk away, and digest it. It works for me, it doesn't work for me. It may work for me in ten years. It may never work for me. But don't ever exclude it when somebody gives you a piece of advice. Don't say, well, I don't have to listen to you. You don't know what you're talking about. There's something in there, it might be something you'll learn from everybody and you make the decisions after you hear it.

The toughest hitters for me were low-fastball hitters, Billy Williams, Willie Stargell, Willie McCovey, Ted Simmons, left-hand hitters. I came up in an organization with the leadership of Hodges and Rube Walker. There's two theories of pitching, in one vein. You pitch with your strengths or you pitch to a hitter's weakness. Rube's and Gil's theory was you've got Seaver and Koosman and Ryan and Gentry on the Mets, forget the scouting reports, make them beat you. Let's go with your strengths. That meant, okay, low-fastball hitter, you've got to prove to me you can hit it first before I'm going to do something else.

And that was kind of my theory. That was their theory and I adopted it and I agreed with that. The farther that you go along, the more you learn about your trade, the more that changes, the more you begin to pitch a little bit differently. But if you can beat somebody and somebody says, well, he's a high-fastball hitter, I'll say, well, let's find out how good a high-fastball hitter. You don't say, well, I can't throw my fastballs. You see, you have to learn. You have to learn where everybody fits in the scale but, the toughest outs for me, McCovey, Stargell, Billy Williams, Simmons. I mean, there's more, but those are the ones that come off of the top of my head.

What I did for twenty years, I loved what I did. I absolutely adored what I did, and I put my heart and soul into it. When I started, it was a dream. And because of the people that I had along the way, and then becoming a professional, from Rube Walker to Gil Hodges to Harvey Haddix to John McNamara et cetera, mostly Gil Hodges. It became an art form, and I adored it for twenty years and it always was a challenge, a rewarding challenge to continue to do it, time and time and time again, to figure it out. You certainly are not the same pitcher you were when you were eighteen as you are when you are in your forties, physically. You're certainly different mentally. You certainly have a much better understanding of what pitching is about even though you're a pitcher to begin with. But the whole trip, the whole journey, was fabulous, loved it, and I was lucky to be able to do it for twenty years.

.

DON BAYLOR

Don Baylor has an impressive baseball résumé, with four decades in the big leagues as a player, coach, and manager. His suitcase carries a lot of stickers, as he played for six big league teams: the Orioles, Athletics, Angels, Yankees, Red Sox, and Twins. He's also managed the Rockies and the Cubs and coached the Brewers, Cardinals, Braves, Mets, and Mariners. A power-hitting outfielder, designated hitter, and first baseman, Baylor is one of only two players to play in the World Series three consecutive years—with different teams.

"He does a lot of things on and off the field that you're supposed to do to win," noted Red Sox teammate Jim Rice. "I didn't know much about him before he got here, except that he was a good hitter and a nice guy, although I don't think I'd like to be on his bad side."

Baylor grew up in Austin, Texas, and integrated his junior high school. He was a star football, basketball, and baseball player in high school, and signed with the Baltimore Orioles out of junior college in 1967. That year he was Appalachian League Player of the Year, the first of many professional baseball honors. In 1970, he was Minor League Player of the Year and broke in with the Orioles. He became an every-day player in 1972 and made his first postseason appearances with the O's in

1973 and '74. In 1976, he was traded to the Oakland Athletics, and that November, was one of baseball's early free agents, signing with the California Angels.

He had his greatest season in 1979 for the Angels, leading the league in RBIs and runs, belting 36 homers, and leading the team to the first of his two playoff appearances there. He won the American League Most Valuable Player Award that season and made the All-Star team for the only time. He was signed by the New York Yankees following the 1982 season and played there until they traded him to Boston in early 1986.

"I've played with a lot of great people; he's one of the best," said Red Sox teammate Dwight Evans. With the Red Sox, Baylor began his unprecedented string of reaching the World Series three years in a row—with three different teams. He won a ring with the Minnesota Twins in 1987, and reached the series again with Oakland in 1988, when he played his last game.

A natural leader, Baylor was quickly back in the majors as a hitting coach with the Milwaukee Brewers from 1990–91 and with the St. Louis Cardinals in 1992.

"Don was rock-solid, he conducted his affairs with dignity and class while at the same time being a fierce competitor. I can't say enough good things about him," said Rockies team owner Jerry McMorris in 1999, after Baylor's six years at the helm of the Rockies came to an end. The highlight there was a 1995 playoff appearance as a wild-card team, the first of three consecutive winning seasons with the Rockies. He was the Sporting News and the BBWAA Manager of the Year in 1995. Don Baylor remains active today, as he still coaches for the Colorado Rockies.

The earliest that I can recall, just a picture that my mom had, that's a precious picture to me today. I was about two years old. It's a black-and-white picture, I'm holding on to a ball down on Congress

Don Baylor

Avenue, in Austin, Texas. I believe my grandmother, my mother, were probably Dodger fans because of Jackie Robinson. So I grew up just enjoying the game itself, baseball.

But we lived in a neighborhood that was a very poor area. There were no paved streets, so that's probably how I learned how to throw, because of the rocks there in the street. Because Clarksville, which was a community in Austin, was developed as maids' quarters for all the butlers and maids around some of the mansions that were there in West Austin.

First glove—looking through magazines, you know, my mom would get Sears and Roebuck. And seeing how expensive gloves were, you couldn't go to your mom and dad and say, "Buy me a glove." I had to save for it, so I delivered newspapers just to order a glove mail-order. Probably took too long for me, so I wanted to see it. I wanted to hold it, go down to a place called Davis Hardware. They did sporting goods, they did all the hardware and things, so you go in there in their sporting goods section and kind of feel the glove for $14.95. Ted Williams was endorsing Sears at that time. So it was something I kind of saved up for. I loved the six-fingered glove when it first came out. I liked that. So that's probably the first glove I had, was a six-fingered glove. Because I played shortstop and played center field, and pitched.

Hitting the ball was pretty much easy, as far as making hand-to-eye contact. I think I was good in doing that. Just anything with the ball competition, because I always played with older guys, so that made you become very competitive. So I always looked forward to that challenge. I was always the one who stepped in first with the older guys, playing basketball or football. I wasn't the bully, but I was not going to be bullied, to put it that way.

In 1961, two other African-American kids and I were all the same age, going to the seventh grade. So it was three African-Americans going into an all-white school in 1961. I transferred to get to a school that I could walk to in ten minutes.

The first day, wow, not knowing what to expect, are we going to be accepted, because I grew up in this town. It was difficult, a lot of pressure that I felt, you know, that everyone's looking at you differently. You go down to downtown Austin where you had separate water fountains, blacks only and whites only. But going to school, it was a reality check. It was very difficult just to get from class to class. Some kids said hello, some kids looked at you like you were some evil person. The teachers were not ready for it.

We had our own community baseball team. Not until later did I play with white kids. This was our community. We had our own team. We were the lower end, you know, so we always competed hard. It was my brother, Doug; my cousin Ronnie, he was a catcher, third baseman. And the three of us kind of ran the team.

There was a Double-A team, the Austin Senators, which was

the Braves organization. It was a Double-A team that we followed. You know, I remember Bill Lucas played on that team, Rico Carty, Frank Howard came through with the Dodgers and things. So we saw a lot of those young guys early. And it was right there on the Colorado River, we could walk down to the games, get in and watch the games. But we were interested in baseballs, that's what we needed, baseballs.

So I was standing in one exit. My brother would be in another exit and my cousin would be in another exit. And they hired people there to retrieve baseballs that were hit, foul balls or whatever. And once a foul ball left the stadium, it was all-out war.

It didn't come back. That's how we got baseballs to play with. They were precious baseballs to us. Sometimes we would hit them into someone else's yard. One lady that was related to me, she would keep the baseballs. But she forgot that I was the person who delivered newspapers, too. So on Sunday, the heaviest paper of the week, I'd make sure her screen door was dented with those newspapers. But she would always keep the baseballs on the back area, so we found a way to retrieve our balls.

Mays was the guy we all looked up to. And Mantle. Everybody tried to walk with a limp like he did. In the sixties, it was those two guys.

Back when I was fifteen years old, Paul Richards was there, kind of looking at some older guys at Austin High School. He was the first person, professionally, that I can recall. He walked up and introduced himself to me. So my sophomore year, when I was fifteen, sixteen years old, they started looking at me seriously. Paul Richards at that time, he was the general manager of the Houston Astros.

I was one of the first black ballplayers on my high school team. Alvin Matthews, who was a pretty good football player, played for the Green Bay Packers. We were on the same team, you know. I was a sophomore and he was a junior. So, we were the first two blacks on that team. We played for a very tough coach, Travis Raven. He didn't like black players at all. It was difficult. I sat at the bench for a long time, hit .345, and never forgot. So, I was one of the two sopho-mores on the team. So, sophomores had to kind of sit and wait, but I played enough, not every day or every inning, but I played enough that he couldn't keep me on the bench. I was not going to be de-terred in any way, because that's what I really wanted to do, was play baseball. And Travis Raven left, went to the University of Texas as an assistant football coach. That was a great sigh of relief seeing him go. Then entered Frank Siegel, who was just the complete opposite. I had to try to enjoy his sense of humor because he went to Texas A&M, you know. But he was a person that really gave me the lead-ership just, you know, as your baseball team, you just kind of take over, made me captain of the team my junior year.

So he was just a great baseball coach, so it really left me feeling that anything I wanted to do in baseball I could do it, because you finally had somebody there that didn't look at color; he just looked at winning baseball teams in high school.

I remember jumping onstage in junior high when someone called me nigger. That word was never in my vocabulary. Someone called me that in seventh grade and I ran after him across the stage and got into a fight there. So the leadership part, I just defended what I thought was right. I didn't worry about anyone else following me. But that's just probably how it got started. I was going to defend what I thought was right.

I was coming along about the time that Darrell Royal and the University of Texas were not ready for the black athlete to come along. What I wanted to do at Texas is to play football, baseball, bas-ketball. And pretty much their out was, they wanted me to play football only. And I decided against that, because I wanted to play baseball and do all three, really. And I know I could have done all three. There was another player there at the same time, James Street was the quarterback. He was a pitcher on the baseball team. Randy Peschel, a guy that I played against all through high school, he was a tight end on that team. He played baseball. So I could see the handwriting on the wall that I was not going to be given a scholarship over the other two. So the Orioles came along, drafted me number two. I signed for 7,500 bucks. I thought that was a lot of money.

The Orioles scout was Dee Phillips. He signed Davey Johnson, the second baseman from Texas A&M. So he was a scout that followed me. I really thought I was going to be the number one draft pick with the Houston Astros. But I dislocated my shoulder playing football and I dropped out of the number one with Houston. They took John Mayberry instead. And so, he didn't have to convince me, you know, too much about signing, but I wanted to do it the best way I could. So to this day I'm the only player who, probably, in the history of the state, ever signed a professional contract at the state capitol.

My dad knew a guy named Bill Bowers, he was the assistant secretary of the state of Texas. Dee Phillips came in, I believe Frank Siegel was there, and my dad was there, because I was not old enough to sign a contract. So the legal part of it was taken care of, the signing actually happened at the state capitol. It was probably two and a half weeks after I graduated from high school, in 1967. I was seventeen years old.

The Orioles, let's see, they were in the World Series in 1966, I believe, they had just swept the Dodgers four straight in 1966; they beat Koufax and Drysdale and Osteen. So the Orioles were my team. I was drafted by them. You felt like you were going to be with that team forever. That was your team. And the $7,500-plus they paid for college education, which was important because the Vietnam War was going on at that time. And you had to stay in school, maintain eighteen hours of classes. So I went to Miami Dade North and went to spring training and worked out and then went to school at night.

My first minor league assignment was Bluefield, West Virginia, which was what in those days was called a redneck place, very tough, difficult to find a place to stay. We were making $500 a month, $250 every two weeks. So it was three players, three black players on this team with Joe Altobelli, our manager, who was a great baseball guy. The three of us shared a room in downtown Bluefield, because we could not find housing outside the area at all. It was $100 a month, and we split that, two nice beds and one bed that they provided that was not so good. What we decided to do—the other players were an outfielder and a pitcher—we're going to give the pitcher the best bed and whoever got the most hits was going to sleep in the other best bed.

I led the league hitting that year, so I got that bed a lot, but a hundred bucks a month, we split that, and I probably spent that on phone calls calling home.

I thought I grew up poor until . . . When you go to some of the areas in Bluefield, you find black families willing to share with some of the young players that are playing in that city. You'd get invited to their homes for a nice home-cooked meal, after a ballgame. And they were poor. In the areas that we were in, where the train tracks were, there was the coal mine, and the coal would be transferred back and forth, that was the front of their house. I thought growing up in Clarksville was tough, but they had it a lot tougher.

My first game as a professional, I was 0-5 with two strikeouts. I said, welcome to pro ball. I was hitting third in the lineup. I tried to bunt for a base hit with a man on third. Altobelli grabbed me and said, you're hitting third to drive in that run, not to bunt him in. So he was another figure that came along, like Frank Siegel, at the right time. Bobby Grich was on that team with me, one of my closest friends. He came from Long Beach and we just kind of hit it off, playing together throughout the minors. Ron Shelton, the guy who wrote *Bull Durham* and things, he was on that team, and Johnny Oates was on that team.

So we had a few older guys that took care of the younger guys on that team. We got through it as young baseball players. I felt no prejudice on that team at all. We were all trying to survive. First day I walk in, there's four guys just got released, and I didn't know what a release was, where some guys that signed for $500, just a chance to play, were released. I believe I came in the first day with a brown bag, it was a brown paper bag. I didn't have a duffel bag. I had a brown paper bag. And now it was about survival, to get all the work you could. We played twenty-five games in high school. Now we're looking at seventy games as a minor league player.

I was playing center field. I could go get them in the outfield. I remember one of my greatest catches. I overran a ball, lost it in the lights, just reacted and caught it barehanded.

My first spring training was 1969. It was a great feeling to walk into that spring training. I'd see Dave McNally, Frank Robinson, Boog Powell, Jim Palmer, Mike Cuellar, Brooks Robinson. There were great people on that team.

You had to earn your way to an invitation to spring training. And Earl Weaver was the manager of that club and you just had to go in, with your mouth shut, eyes open, you know, ears open, and just take it all in. We always played B games, which was guys who needed extra work or whatever early in the morning. Dew was still on the ground and we played those games with no batting practice, just get loose and let's go play.

And certain guys had to stay over for the A game and I was one of those guys. Pick up Frank Robinson, extra at-bat, he would get two at-bats, I'd be glad to go out to right, never played right before. You know, if Don Buford needed relieving in left, go play left. And that's what spring training was.

A writer asked me, how are you going to break into the outfield here? You know, Mervin Rettenmund was the extra outfielder. Buford, Blair, Frank Robinson. And somehow I just told him, if I get in the groove, I really didn't care who was in the outfield. I was nineteen years old. And the team was on the road that day and when the newspaper came out, Frank Robinson got a copy of that. So he called a little clubhouse meeting the next day. I had no idea what he was doing because he was pretty much the leader, he was the leader of that team. And he was the judge in the kangaroo court. And when he called a meeting, everyone was at attention.

Frank Robinson

So he's reading this article to the entire team. And he says, when I get into the groove, it didn't really matter if Frank Robinson, Blair, or Buford, or whoever, is in the outfield. So somehow that "groove" stuck. And to this day, pretty much everybody in the league, that's what they call me.

I got called up in 1970. The Orioles had participated in the World Series in '69, '70, and '71. My first callup in 1970, it was probably three, four players that were called up. And I remember Earl Weaver said, "You guys sit over here. We're up by seventeen games, we want to win by twenty." So I understood what winning was all about at that time at the major league level. My first full-time season was 1972.

In 1970, I was the Minor League Player of the Year. Hit .327, drove in 107, and scored 127 runs, 15 triples, 34 doubles, had to go back to the same league the next year, 1971, where Bobby Grich had a great year that year. He hit 32 home runs as a shortstop, hit .336. It was probably the most difficult time for me as a young player. I was one of the last ones cut in spring training. Earl Weaver said, "You need to play every day." He said you can only probably get about 250 at-bats; I said, "I'll take them." And then he said, "Nope, I want you to play every day in the minor leagues."

So I wanted to go home and think about it. Harry Dalton was the general manager. He came down to Daytona Beach and talked me out of going home. So baseballwise, executivewise, he was one I respected tremendously; he just told me, you know, in time you'll get your shot to play in the big leagues. So that was 1971, and by 1972, I was in the major leagues full-time.

Joe Altobelli was probably assigned to two players, Grich and Baylor; you get them to the big leagues, because he was our first manager, then he was at Stockton, which was Class A. Let's see, Double-A was Altobelli again; at Dallas–Fort Worth, Cal Ripken Sr. was there, the Triple-A manager, and Altobelli followed him to Triple-A in '71. So I had Joe pretty much every year. And they were baseball guys, you know, they'd talk baseball all the time. I learned how to use flip-down sunglasses from Cal Ripken Sr. In the instructional league, I mean, day after day after day, you know, just get your glasses down. You know, play the day game, do not come into that dugout looking for sunglasses after you dropped a fly ball. So, he always had those flip-downs in day games. So I think of Cal Ripken Sr. all the time as a young guy. He was a drill sergeant as far as instruction. You were not going to step on the field with the Orioles unless you knew every aspect of the game.

Play it the right way, understand giving up yourself for the team. We had an incident in 1973 where they had a string of '69, '70, '71 World Series appearances; 1972, not so good. That was a struggling year. But '73 and '74, you know, we won the Eastern Division. Earl was a manager that loved the three-run homer. A couple of times, we were hitting into double plays and Earl would say, "Can you guys ever strike out?"

We had a meeting after the game, just the players, a players-only meeting, at Brooks Robinson's house. And we all had to get on the same page. Earl was kind of living in that three-run-homer mode, and we just decided that—Billy Hunter was the third-base coach, you know. He didn't give a sign for the man on second base, get the runner over, we'd do it ourselves. And we all agreed that we were going to get the guy over ourselves and just do what we had to do to win ballgames. From that point on, to the end of the season, we were 22–5. But I think Earl caught on probably after about the first five games. You know, we were, because we all agreed that when the guy comes back to the dugout, we are all going to congratulate him for getting the guy over, a bunt for a base hit, whatever, and Earl just kind of looked around and said, "Something's going on here."

We all understood how to play the game, we all wanted to win, not about egos, but it's just about winning baseball. That's what Frank Robinson brought to that organization; that after he departed, it continued, win the Oriole way, this is how we're going to win. And I believe that lesson really kind of taught me and some of the other young players what it was to do it the Oriole way.

The Orioles were just loaded with good young talent. Go to first base and look at Jim Gentile, Boog Powell, his successor, Eddie Murray, for a long period of time. You go to second base, you're going to do the same thing with Davey Johnson, Grich, Rich Dauer. You go to shortstop, Aparicio, Belanger, Ripken. Third base, there's only one there for almost twenty-five years. And then to left field, do the same thing. To center field, Blair. Right field. So, young guys really never moved up. You know, the talent was there.

We all know Brooks Robinson was a great player, a great fielder, great competitor. He was my lockermate for six years. I don't know how I got the assignment, but his locker was right next to mine. And Blair was on my other side. Brooks once made three errors in one inning. I remember coming in after the game and he said, "Yeah, they tell me I'm the greatest third baseman that ever lived." So he had a great sense of humor. He was just very professional. He taught me how to be a professional in every way.

Brooks, he was the quiet leader of that team, just by his play. Frank Robinson was more of a vocal guy that everybody went to. If you needed good bats, you let Frank order them for you, because they would always send Frank the best wood, always. I started using R161, because I picked up one of his bats in spring training. I liked it, I liked the balance. I asked him what the R161 was. We knew what MC44 was, that was McCovey 44. You know, he was 4-4, his first day in the big league. R161 was Robinson number 1 and 61. You know, M110 was Mickey Mantle's model. So as young players, you use someone else's bat. Frank was the guy that kind of taught even the older players the toughness. I recall he had a bum wrist, couldn't swing the bat, but the Red Sox didn't know that. Man on third, he drops down a bunt and wins the ballgame for us. So any way to beat you, that was Frank. Breaking up double plays at second base, he went in hard. It was one of those things that everyone else picked up on, just that toughness.

After a win, everyone would get a soft drink or whatever and the press had to wait. It wasn't ten minutes after, just a quick kangaroo court. Frank was in charge. It was an award for the longest home run; if somebody gave up a home run, the award was a shredded baseball. McNally got it sometimes, Palmer got it sometimes. Base-running award was an old beat-up shoe if somebody didn't run the bases correctly. The weak swing award.

Frank was the judge. You could always bring up someone on charges for fraternizing. I believe you got two minutes to say hello to a friend on another team. If you went over that, you were fined a dollar a minute. So there was none of that fraternizing going on. It was about baseball. Not moving runners cost you money, not getting guys in from third base, that'd cost you money.

I was asked to bring in the kangaroo court in 1986 with the Boston Red Sox. It was heard from the news media that the Red Sox were twenty-five players with twenty-five cabs. They would go in different directions. So when I got there in spring training, I remember, Tommy Harper was talking about the white players were going to the Elks Club to eat for free and the black players could not go there.

Right away, I knew the Boston Red Sox were separate in a lot of ways just because of race. We were picked fifth in our division. Roger Clemens was on that team, Bruce Hurst. I knew Clemens from Texas, and I knew he was probably not a part of that racist idea that they had with the Elks Club and things. I took Dwight Evans's suggestion that we create a kangaroo court where players came together. They had a lot of fun. That's probably the most fun I've had on a team, you know, where Bill Buckner, Marty Barrett, Wade Boggs— Wade coming from Florida, where, you know, that was probably difficult for him as far as being on the team with a strong black player like myself.

Jim Rice had been there. And Jim was kind of outnumbered. Oil Can Boyd, Rich Gedman. So they were looking for something different, someone to take charge, and I did. And we had fun doing it.

No one played center field like Paul Blair. We're playing in Minnesota one day and Earl wanted him to play deeper. So Blair moved back. Dave McNally's pitching, Steve Braun hit a ground ball up the middle. Braun never stopped. Ended up with a double. After the inning was over, Dave McNally went to him, he said, "You play anywhere you want to play. Earl, he's playing center field." And that was the end of that. He was the best center fielder that I saw until Andruw Jones, but Blair was the best. To me, he's better than Andruw Jones.

Earl was an intimidating manager. You had to show him, just show him. Bobby Grich was playing, Orioles were ahead by fifteen, sixteen games toward the end of the season and Bobby's on his way to the plate and he hears his famous whistle that when Earl's whistling, you know it's him. And he gives you the whistle and Bobby turns around and Brooks Robinson's coming out of the dugout to pinch-hit for him. Bobby gets back to the dugout, he grabs Weaver right by the throat here. He says, how do you expect me to hit? You keep pinch-hitting for me.

They traded Davey Johnson the next year; Bobby played second base. So he liked guys that had some fire about them.

Players today could not play for Earl Weaver. They'd be calling their agents all the time. But he was a great motivator in his own way, very critical of the players. That was just to get you wild enough that you'd do it the correct way. He was always a manager that, if you made a mistake on the field, he'd be the first one on the step to tell you about it, now correct it.

We always had meetings before each series: how we're going to pitch certain guys, how we're going to play them. Then it became the Jim Palmer meeting; that's what we called it, the Jim Palmer meeting. Jim always knew how he wanted to pitch certain guys or where he wanted everyone to play. He was standing on the mound; move guys this way, move them here and bring them in, after we talked in a meeting, how we're going to play; but you couldn't dispute Jim's success at all, because that was just Palmer. You just had to live with that.

Earl calls me into his office one day after a game. He says, you know, you're going to have to curtail your temper. I say, what do you mean? He says, let me tell you what happened to me and my temper. He says, they always called me Mickey Rooney, because he's five-four, five-five. So one day, he says, he got hit by a pitch. He's running to first and everybody on the other team says, hey, Mickey Rooney. He made a right turn; he jumped in their dugout. They beat him up in the worst way, dislocated his right shoulder, broke his left arm, kicked him, stomped him, and threw him back out on the field. The next year, he tried to play. He couldn't play. So he started managing at age twenty-five. He says, I don't want that to happen to you.

Then he says, within the next seven or eight years, you're going to win the Most Valuable Player in this league here.

The worst day of my professional career was being traded from that club. I was running in the outfield after a spring training game. Earl summoned me to his office and told me I'd been traded to the Oakland Athletics and Reggie Jackson was coming to Baltimore. I cried in his office. Leaving a team that you had all your friends on that team, going to another clubhouse that they had beat us in the playoffs a couple of times, you know.

I already had gone through the Frank Robinson deal; just now it's a Reggie Jackson deal, going to another locker room. How you're going to be perceived by Sal Bando, Joe Rudi, Gene Tenace, Rollie Fingers, it was very difficult, because it happened late in spring training, right before the season started. Chuck Tanner was the manager, but he made the transition a lot easier than I did, because Chuck was positive, positive all the time. Third day of the season, Dick Drago hits me in the hand, breaks my hand. I was going to be a free agent that year and that's probably, that's the real reason that I was going to get traded, because of the upcoming free agency for the very first time.

We had nine guys on that team that were going to be free agents after the season. Bando, Tenace, Bert Campaneris, Fingers, Rudi, Vida Blue . . .

A lot of things happened in 1976. The Yankees had just moved back into a refurbished Yankee Stadium, but I think a lot of things were on players' minds, as far as what are we going to do now that we are free agents. Now you needed an agent to negotiate a contract for you. Jerry Kapstein came along and represented a lot of those young free agents at that particular time. Goose Gossage and Freddie Lynn, Rick Burleson, Carlton Fisk—and we were all just young players— and Charlie Finley wanted to keep Gene Tenace, Campaneris, and myself. We were all represented by Jerry Kapstein.

Mr. Finley came to Austin—we had a place there in Austin called the Headliners Club—and he had dinner with us and wanted to really get us in the fold. He asked Jerry to write down on a piece of paper what our contract should be, and it was $1 million. I remember Jerry wrote $1 million. He took that and put it in his shirt pocket and we never heard from him again. I think if we would have stayed at 900. I mean, I didn't want to move around at all. It was going to be $250,000 a year for four years. That was 1976. So I ended up signing with the Angels; Harry Dalton, $1.6 million, $580,000 as a bonus. I had a provision in there if I won the Most Valuable Player in those six years, which I did in 1979. We won our division in 1979, first one for the Angels under Gene Autry.

In 1972, we were on strike for eight days. Brooks Robinson was the league rep at that time and then the things that we were fighting over, the health care and just four years, I think, in four years you become a free agent. We voted on a strike in the old hotel in Miami, the McAllister Hotel. We had players vote, everyone raising their hand for a vote. And here, I'm a young player, finally made the team, gonna play my first full year in the big leagues, and they're going on strike. So I really didn't know what I was voting for. Majority rules.

So that's when I promised myself that I was going to find out about the union, what it was for the players and what it stood for and what it represented. So that was my introduction into the union. You know, I had to find out what I was voting for.

Marvin Miller was the person that every player looked up to. Whatever Marvin said, this is what we're going to get out of the owners. They will crack first, before the players crack. It's going to take hard work, sacrifice by the players to get it done. And Marvin was the person that got teams together in spring training. And that's when, say, we were in Bradenton one time and the meeting just happened. The Orioles and the Pirates in a meeting, and Roberto Clemente, my early recollection is that it was the spring of 1970 or so, before his death, 1972, you know, and he was translating for all the Latin players, so that they also understood what was going on.

But whatever Marvin said, that's what the players were going to do. The union was much stronger with his leadership.

Joe Torre was the National League player rep and Brooks Robinson was the American League rep, for ten years each. Didn't come with a car, didn't come with any perks whatsoever. You had to notify all the players about certain decisions to get their votes. Not only the star players, the fringe players—they all wanted to know their rights and what they were entitled to. Finally, they had someone speaking on their behalf. I would go to the union meetings and see Dave Parker, Dave Winfield, Gossage, and Catfish Hunter, just at union meetings. So American League and National League guys sat down and discussed things with Marvin, the future of the game, the license and the revenue. So those were the real early stages of the Players' Association being as strong as it is today.

Players really didn't know what other players were making. That was kind of kept from players, and guys really never divulged what they were making. The pension was always something that you couldn't really understand when you were a young player. The pension now, you need one day of service. Before you maxed out at twenty years, you had to be a player or coach for twenty years to get the maximum. Now, guys are maxed out after ten years and what the government allows is $120,000 a year. And you're vested after one day. It might buy you a tank of gas but, you know, you're vested as a player.

In L.A., I'm playing for Harry Dalton, who drafted me when I was a young Oriole player, then he left. He became general manager again in California, so I had a chance to go back to the Angels and play for him and Gene Autry. It was difficult the first year, because Joe Rudi signed, Bobby Grich signed on that team, so the three of us go to the Angels, which already had Nolan Ryan, Frank Tanana on the team. Offensively, they didn't have a very good team, so the three free agents come in, now all the Angel fans thought that was going to be an instant winning team for them, because Mr. Autry opened up the saddlebags and brought in three players.

After the first month, Joe Rudi was hit with a pitch by Nelson Briles. Grich hurt himself lifting an air conditioner at home; he has a back operation. So I'm the lone soldier out there, I'm getting booed every day. That wasn't a good feeling. But I got through that first year; the second year, I hit 34 homers, so I then got the fans back on my side a little bit. And '79 was just an unbelievable year offensively for the entire team. Rod Carew came over and I just instantly became a good friend of Rod's. He hit third, I hit fourth. He got me off to a great start because he was the best bunter in the game. He would always get guys in scoring position for me, and I said, you know, I'm going to drive these guys in.

So it was a good team and the fans started the slogan "Yes, we can," and we were the "Yes, we can" Angels. But I believe the Angels became a team when the Yankees came to town. Weekend series in June, it was probably the most fun I had playing. They were renovating the Angels' stadium, because the Rams were going to play in our stadium the next year, so it was only forty-five thousand seats and there were probably five thousand people outside trying to get in for the Yankee series on a Friday night. The Yankees were up, Goose Gossage on the mound, someone hit a three-run homer that hit the foul pole. Tied the game; we won it in extra innings. Saturday, we won another miraculous game somehow.

Grich drove in 5 against Ron Guidry in Sunday's game, so we swept the Yankees. So the Angels felt like they could finally compete and we won our division that year, and it was a lot of fun.

In 1979, Jimmy Reese, one of our coaches, said, you hit the ball better in '78, but they were line drives in '79. They didn't catch them. It started to roll in April. I had 28 RBIs in April; one month I had 34, played on the All-Star team. I had 85 RBIs at the All-Star break. Pete Rose came up to me at the All-Star game in Seattle and said, eighty-five RBIs, that's a season for most guys, you know. I knew, I wanted to drive myself to 100 RBIs, because that was kind of etched in my brain from the year before, because in '78, I drove in

99. The next-to-last day of the season, I hit a bases-loaded ground-rule double, where the ball bounced over the wall. If it hadn't, that would've given me 100 RBIs.

Last day of that season, you're swinging for the fences, which is a no-no, so I finished the season with 99. That August of '79, I got to 100 RBIs. I said, okay, now what am I going to do? So I finished that season with 139. It was an unbelievable run for the team. We had two guys on the team who hit over 30 homers and drove in 100 runs. Bobby Grich hit 30 homers and drove in 101. He hit eighth.

So we went into Baltimore in the playoffs and Nolan Ryan was the starting pitcher. We lost the first two games there. We won game three in Anaheim and eventually lost to Baltimore in the playoffs.

Hitting is a physical skill and it's also a thinking man's game. The pitchers are always the ones that, they have their little tricks. Gaylord Perry always used K-Y Jelly all over his body. He'd go to his head, find someplace to get it. Don Sutton would find it from his belt buckle, a little scratch here and there and make the ball move.

I knew certain pitches that guys were going to throw at me, especially with runners in scoring position. You can tell if you look at the outfield positioning. When Sparky Lyle was throwing to me, I could always look out of the corner of my left eye and I'd see Graig Nettles move toward the line. So I knew I was getting a breaking ball in, so I didn't have to worry about the fastball, you eliminate certain pitches.

If you see the outfield play you straight up, maybe a step to the right, you're going to get something away, a fastball away. You see a shortstop playing in the hole, they were going to try to pound you in. So you try to eliminate certain pitches. I mean, you can't cover the entire seventeen inches of the plate, so my strong suit was the middle in. So if they threw me a changeup in, they threw me a slider in, a fastball in, I already had the zone taken care of so I didn't have to worry about looking for the wrong pitch and going out over the plate looking for something away.

I got hit at the plate 267 times. John Denny hit me in the head, and he was a headhunter, pretty much. And I always swore if I saw him at a church picnic, I was going to get him.

Dick Pole hit me in Boston. Out of all places, I charged the mound in Boston. I had more messages left for me in my hotel box—"I dare you." And Dennis Leonard threw at me deliberately. Sal Bando just hit a 3-0 pitch out of the ballpark. Leonard gets the ball back, never took a sign. He hit me right in the middle of the back. Buck Martinez was the catcher, who was my roommate in Puerto Rico. He kind of walked me down halfway, forty-five feet down, and then left. And Leonard was picking up the rosin bag and I charged the mound.

The only way that he knew I was coming was the crowd let him know. He looked up and he ran toward our dugout, where Billy North, I think, Claudell Washington met him. And George Brett comes out and, you know, we all get into a big fight. Oakland and Kansas City. So brushback pitches, that was part of the game. Today, they don't understand what brushback pitches are. Umpires stop the game, warn the teams. Players took care of themselves at that time. That was just a part of the way you played. You tried to intimidate the other team, and I was not going to be intimidated.

Reggie Jackson was a great star, great player. He comes to the Angels in 1982. Now we have four former MVPs on the same team. Freddie Lynn, Rod Carew, Reggie, and myself. What fun we had, you know. Because Reggie came in and we all knew he was "The Star," and Gene Mauch was the manager. Gene didn't have to manage. I mean, we have Bob Boone on the team, Tim Foli, Doug DeCinces, so we had enough managers on the team already. You know, Reggie, we would always talk about his home runs, always got on Rod Carew about being a Punch-and-Judy .300 hitter with seven batting titles.

We'd always talk about Freddie; you're always hurt, you know, when are you going to play? And DeCinces asked him one day, he said, hey, Reggie, how about you? How about that strikeout column of yours? Reggie could strike out with the best of them.

Speaking of my past temper and things, there's a long hallway in Anaheim Stadium that I walked up one night and I just fired the bat and it bounced off this wall and that wall and the door opens and here comes Nolan Ryan out. What a great competitor. He threw at people, there's no doubt. He was intimidating. He had the best fastball. I could hear Bert Blyleven's curveball. I mean, you could hear the seams as they went by you. But Nolan was intimidating because of his fastball. Then he would throw a curveball at your left shoulder—if you buckle, see you later. He had the best fastball and the best curveball. The best fastball I saw as a player. Seventh inning on, forget it. They threw the pitch count away with him. And the next day, he would be out playing catch with somebody after throwing two hundred pitches.

When I first came to the big leagues, where they had four 20-game winners at Baltimore, pitchers threw batting practice. The BP that they had to throw, it was their throw day, which was the second day after they pitched. It was great hitting off of those guys because they threw strikes, they knew how to throw strikes. It doesn't happen today at all. That's why Greg Maddux was so great, and Tom Glavine, John Smoltz, those guys in Atlanta when they pitched. But young pitchers today, they don't think about nine innings, they don't think about shutouts.

After the Angels, I joined the Yankees. I had avoided New York because I didn't think I could handle the city as a young player. The West Coast was the place that I thought I could handle—not as much media attention and things. I didn't realize what was going to happen after I left the Angels. I could have gone to Texas and played for the Rangers, but I chose New York. I played for Mr. Steinbrenner, knew what I was getting into, I thought, playing for Billy Martin. Tommy John had kind of warned me, because Tommy and I played together at Anaheim, and he says, you are going to the zoo, you know.

It was a very interesting place, a fun place. I played with Ken Griffey Sr. and Willie Randolph, Dave Winfield, Roy Smalley, Graig

Nettles. It's just a great place to be a baseball player, in New York. My managers were Yogi, Billy [Martin]. Lou Piniella traded me to Boston. It was the spring of '86.

I was traded for Mike Easler. It was a good trade for both, and I had to consent to the trade. I didn't hold Mr. Steinbrenner up for money in my no-trade. I had finally worked the contract where I had a no-trade, but I was ready to leave New York at that time and go play for my ex–third-base coach John McNamara, the manager there.

I came to New York about August or so, in 1986. One night, they walked someone else to get to me, brought in Brian Fisher, a right-hander, to pitch to me. I hit a bases-loaded double and I stood out there on second base and kind of looked toward George's box and kind of gave him one. I remember Marty Barrett and probably the entire Red Sox team, everybody was lined up, standing on the top step, and they knew we were going to win then. So I had a great series coming in. I think I had ten or eleven hits in three days.

It pulled something out of me, too, that inner strength that you really needed to get. Coming from the Yankees, now you're playing for the Red Sox. I remember, my first at-bat after that series, I got a standing ovation from the Fenway crowd and that was day and night, two different things.

The best game I was ever involved in was Game Five of the 1986 ALCS in Anaheim. We're down three games to one at the time. We're down 5–2 in the ninth inning, going into the last at-bat for us, the Red Sox. I could see they're getting ready for a great celebration. I see on the other bench, Reggie Jackson has his arms around Gene Mauch. I looked in the booth and there's Mr. Autry standing. Everyone's getting ready for a celebration. And Jimmy Reese is over there and I said, well, if we don't win, there's three people that I'm pulling for; Gene Autry, Gene Mauch, Jimmy Reese, if we don't win. So it comes down to our last at-bat. Mike Witt is doing a great job just getting everybody out except Rich Gedman. Rich has him with a home run, a couple of singles.

Marty Barrett gets on, with one out. I hit a two-run homer, that makes it 5–4. Angel fans are on the screen, the backstop there, it's deafening in that ballpark, and I never sensed that at all. Dwight Evans is hitting behind me, and he makes an out, so it's two outs. We're down to our last out, and Gedman is up and Gene decides to bring in Gary Lucas, a left-handed pitcher, to face Gedman. Hits him on the first pitch. Dave Henderson is the next hitter, and Gene goes out and brings in Donnie Moore to pitch to Hendu.

And he throws a split-finger fork, split-finger pitch, and Henderson hits it over the left-center-field fence. We go ahead in the ballgame. They tied the game in the ninth. They had a chance to win it. They had bases loaded, one out, and didn't. Well, we got a tie out of it and Donnie Moore is still in the game, hits me with a pitch. I'm sacrificed over to second, come over on another hit or so, and I score from third on a sac fly by Dave Henderson. Yeah, we won that ballgame. Now we have to win Game Six, but on that flight home, Clemens, who was going to pitch Game Seven, knew he was going to win. Everybody else knew, Oil Can Boyd had Game Six, and we already had it planned out. We were going to win it.

In the '86 World Series, we won the first two at Shea Stadium. We go to Fenway Park. We lose two out of three. Gary Carter has a big game, he hits two homers in a game. It gave them momentum, so we come back to Shea Stadium. That's 3–2, Red Sox. Everything is going great. Clemens is pitching a great game. He comes out of the ballgame. During the playoffs, World Series, you really forget that you play 162 games, that you should be tired. You don't have that feeling at all. You know, it's euphoria for two weeks. It was kind of whispered on the bench that Clemens had taken himself out of the game.

But somehow, they rallied. They had one out left and, we're in a similar situation to Anaheim a week before. Ray Knight had a key hit in that Series where he was down no balls, two strikes, so we needed one out. For a brief second, they flashed "Congratulations

Boston Red Sox, World Champions" on the board. It was a ground ball hit to Bill Buckner, just a routine grounder; he misses it, they score the winning run. It was silence in that clubhouse.

We had another game to play but the momentum just turned again. But we had Game Seven won also, you know. We were ahead in that game, but Game Six was just really tough to deal with. You know, in the clubhouse, they had the champagne there. They had to get the champagne out of the clubhouse in no time.

We all knew Billy Buckner had played with bad ankles all year. John McNamara was a player's manager, plus he was a veteran player's manager. He wanted the veterans on the field at that particular time. And I think he probably got caught up in that, because he had always brought in Dave Stapleton to play defense for him. He let Billy Buckner stay on the field that day, and the rest is history, they say.

My first thoughts of being a manager came while I was standing in left field in 1975. Billy Martin and Earl Weaver were making their moves. It's the first time I really kind of thought about managing a ball club. You know, just watching those two self-appointed geniuses go at it. So I kind of always thought in the back of my mind, especially the next year, when I believe Frank Robinson got his first chance to manage. So it was something I had thought about.

Frank Robinson was still playing when he managed in Puerto Rico. Reggie Jackson played on that team because he had a very difficult season, fighting over his contract, whatever, with Charlie Finley, so he came down to play in Puerto Rico, and he was the biggest star since Roberto Clemente playing in the winter ball. So Frank was the manager and still a player. And Reggie, one night, hit a fly ball and didn't run it out. I mean, he stood there and watched it. Frank says, the next time you do that, it's going to cost you five hundred bucks. A couple of weeks later, Reggie does it again. He doesn't run it out. Frank said, that's $500. Reggie says, no, I'm going home. Frank says, well, I'll be up to help you pack. And he never had problems with Reggie from that point on. And if you watched Reggie play, he ran out every ground ball like it was going to be his last, so Frank never had any problem with Reggie. That turned his career. Frank stood up to a superstar himself and Frank was a bona fide superstar, MVP in both leagues. No one else has ever done that. And Reggie was, you know, taken aback by that, but he also learned from that.

In August 1987 I was traded from the Red Sox to the Twins while we were in Minnesota. I went from one locker room to the next.

They were a game and a half in first, and so I've been to the World Series a year before and coming to that clubhouse, Kirby Puckett, Jeff Reardon, Blyleven, Frank Viola, Tom Brunansky, Roy Smalley is on that team. Kent Hrbek. Gary Gaetti. So it was a good bunch of young guys, you know. My first comment to [manager] Tom Kelly was, I'm here to help you stay right where you are, you know, not to be disruptive at all. So I got a chance to play some, DH some. It was a fun team to be a part of. There were no egos there at all. So we all had fun, just trying to win baseball games on the turf there. The first game of the playoffs, I'm called to pinch-hit and I drove in the winning run in that game. And I remember Gaetti said, now I understand why they got Don Baylor over here. You know, just the pressure situation.

Winning Game One, I think, it really helped a lot of guys on that club to get over the hurdle, because they hadn't been there before. So it was a fun series to be a part of.

In the World Series probably my biggest hit was off of John Tudor in Game Six. I faced him many times with Boston. I knew what he was going to try to do to me. The pitching coach had gone out and told him how to pitch me, and he went away from his plan, because he always tried to throw the ball in on me. He always thought he could get the ball in on me, but he threw me a changeup kind of down and away. I hit it over the left-field fence with Puckett on.

Running around the bases there, there's so many things that you think about. I don't know if I stepped on first or second. I don't remember stepping on home. You just kind of float around the bases. My mom was in the crowd and my dad; my wife-to-be, Becky, was there, my son, my brother, and my sister. So everybody had a chance to enjoy it. That's one trip I enjoyed running around the bases.

I was a free agent after 1987. I had an opportunity to go back to Oakland and play there. Tony LaRussa had already assembled a pretty good team, but some of the pieces were kind of missing somewhat. Tony and I had always had kind of run-ins before when he was with the White Sox. He needed somebody to protect his back, so I kind of think that's why I ended up over there. But Dave Parker, we split DH duties. Carney Lansford was another player I played with on the Angels; Dave Stewart, Bob Welch, let's see, who else? We had some guy named Mark McGwire, another young player named Jose Canseco. They were two great talents. Dave Henderson was on that team, again. So, well, Tony also had Walt Weiss playing shortstop. I mean, there were so many players that knew how to play. They assembled a great team. Eckersley was the closer.

We won in '88. We kind of breezed through the American League, really. No one could touch us. Bruce Hurst pitched in the playoffs against Dave Stewart. Stewart beat him both times. So we breezed through the playoffs in Boston, got to the World Series, and played the Dodgers. Orel Hershiser had a phenomenal year, but he was just the one pitcher that they had on that team. And we felt, offensively, that no one else compared to our club. You know, we're winning Game One, when Canseco hits a grand slam, they fight back, and that's when Mr. Kirk Gibson walked out of the dugout for his only appearance. There's nothing like the World Series.

He walks out, and Eckersley is throwing strike after strike. Gibson is fouling balls to left field, you know, can't catch up to his fastball. Then Eckersley throws the backdoor breaking ball. On one leg, Gibson reaches out and hits it into the seats. Now I've been stunned again, you know, you just can't believe that that happened. I asked Ron Hassey later, how can you call a breaking ball? The guy's late on everything, and all of a sudden, now you're going to speed his bat up?

You always want more. What if Buckner catches that ground ball? That's a World Championship; '87 was one, and '86, it should have been one also. It's nice to be a part of the World Series, but you like to win, you know. That's a regret I have, you know, not having three World Championships in a row.

Being a manager was something that I really wanted to do. When I lost out to Bill Plummer at Seattle, I was totally disappointed, there's no doubt about it. Then I was hired by Joe Torre to be his hitting coach in St. Louis.

I'd never been in the National League, I've always been an American League guy. To go to the National League and work with Ozzie Smith, just being around the Cardinals and just talking to Joe Torre about managing and watching his unique style, because he was never a hollerer, a screamer and yeller as a manager.

I run a charity golf tournament for cystic fibrosis and we were playing that particular day. I just finished a round and one of the secretaries came out and told me I needed to call Bob Gebhard with the Colorado Rockies. And he told me that you're going to be named the manager tomorrow, can you get here? I don't even know if I asked for a three-year contract, I don't know what money he was paying me. And I had to tell my wife, I was trying to keep it a secret, we were trying to keep it till the next day and make the announcement in Denver. I had to call her over and tell her that you are looking at the first manager of the Colorado Rockies. She starts to cry.

I played for so many managers. Gene Mauch is the strategist, you know, he was always thinking the game. Tony LaRussa, as far as organization, being organized every day. John McNamara, the coddling that you need to deal with players, he was good at that. Billy Martin, you learned some good things, you learned some bad things,

Joe Torre

you learned what not to do, but Billy's toughness, not tough love but just toughness, you know, he was not going to back down at all.

Joe Torre is a person I think about—when you're in a tough streak, you really need to kick guys a couple of times, and you say, well, I'll do it tomorrow. They're playing that way again the next day and you say, okay, I'll do it tomorrow. You know, you keep kind of putting it off, then finally I said, Joe, I'm sorry, I can't do it anymore and you know, I got to blast these guys right now. But Joe was a person that kept that inside and under control. He taught you how to really sit down and talk to players, see what was on their mind a lot of times, what was bothering them. He knew how to control a clubhouse. Respect everybody's privacy in a clubhouse. Not a lot of loud music and things, so I think that's where I got that from.

My world was just a little small neighborhood in Austin, Texas. To this day, I'm the most valuable player in that town. Being a part of the Texas Sports Hall of Fame is one of those things that my family is very proud of. And it could happen to just about any kid in America, really.

OZZIE SMITH

Known as "the Wizard of Oz," Ozzie Smith combined athletic ability with acrobatic skill to become one of the greatest defensive shortstops of all time. In his nearly two decades of jaw-dropping work at one of the game's most demanding positions, he thrilled fans from coast-to-coast with both his game and his sunny demeanor.

Always a base-stealing threat who would later turn himself into an above-average hitter, Smith used his glove, his magical tool of the trade, to make plays for the San Diego Padres and St. Louis Cardinals that often left those watching assured they were witnessing something that had never been seen before on a ball field.

Though Smith would finish second to Atlanta's Bob Horner in the 1978 National League Rookie of the Year voting, it was his defense that caught everyone's eye. His manager with the Padres, Roger Craig, said at the time, "Ozzie is the best young infielder I've ever seen. . . . Very soon he's going to be one of the best shortstops in baseball, if not the best."

After the 1981 season, Smith's national recognition blossomed when he was traded to the Cardinals for fellow shortstop Garry Templeton. Now possessing the kind of defensive shortstop needed for Busch Stadium's quick artificial turf, the Cardinals would go on to win the 1982 World Series over the Milwaukee Brewers. Cardinals manager Whitey Herzog said of Smith that offseason, "He took two hits or a run away from our opponents every game last year. That's just as important as a guy who drives in runs."

In the 1985 National League Championship Series against the Los Angeles Dodgers, with the teams tied at two wins apiece, the switch-hitting Smith, in one of his most memorable moments, faced Tom Nieden-fuer with one out in the bottom of the ninth and hit his first career homer batting left-handed after 3,009 at-bats to win the game.

"Ozzie, besides being a terrific ballplayer, was really the heart and soul of just about any club that he played on," said Mike Scioscia, current Angels manager and Niedenfuer's catcher when Smith homered. "He taught himself how to be an incredibly productive offensive player from a guy they thought was really only going to be a terrific defensive player."

As Smith's career continued through the 1980s and early 1990s, the accomplishments and milestones continued to pile up: In 1991 he set the NL record for fewest errors in a season by a shortstop with 8; in 1992 he collected his 2,000th hit, 500th stolen base, and his 13th consecutive Gold Glove Award to break the NL record held by Willie Mays and Roberto Clemente; and in 1994 he passed Luis Aparicio for the career assist record for a shortstop.

Retiring after 1996, Smith, in his nineteen big league seasons, finished with a .262 batting average, 2,460 hits, 580 stolen bases, and fifteen All-Star game nods. Elected to the National Baseball Hall of Fame in 2002, he set the following major league records for his position: most assists (8,375), most double plays (1,590), most total chances accepted (12,905), most years with 500 or more assists (8), and most years leading the league in assists and chances accepted (8).

"He's someone I idolized growing up, and every time I see him I'm always telling him to help me out and give me some pointers," said Yankees shortstop Derek Jeter. "He tells me to just keep doing what I'm doing, but I have to try and pick his brain a little bit more."

Ozzie Smith

Having been born in the baseball town of Mobile, Alabama, my earliest recollection was my uncle. We had a pecan tree in the backyard, and we used to take a plastic bat and throw it up and knock the pecans down. And we had this little plastic ball that came with it, you know? My mom tells a story that one day, we're out and he's playing catch with me and he says to her, boy, what an arm this kid has on him. So that was my earliest recollection of baseball. We moved to L.A. when I was six years old. So most of my growing up was done in Southern California, where we lived across the street from a recreation center. We used to go over and get the broken bats. And we would tape the bats. So we would put little tacks in there to put the bats back together, and then we would hit rocks, you know? That was really the start of it.

My formal introduction to sport was actually through the YMCA, where I played flag football. I played basketball, and of course, we played softball. And that was the real beginning of organizational sports. Growing up in Southern California there, in the early sixties when we moved to L.A., I was in the riots, and '65, the National Guard actually set up camp in the recreation center that we lived across the street from. So that was kind of a tumultuous time for us, not really understanding all that was going on, just watching the television, remembering having to sleep on the floor because of gunfire and fires and the like.

I was a young kid at that time. So it was kind of an awakening and a scary time for us, because we did not know exactly what was going on. And from there things got a little bit better. We were in the time of, kind of a social revolution. And of course, Dr. Martin Luther King was always the person out in front leading the way and trying to do it in a nonviolent way. And those are the things that resonate, that really kind of stand out, the marches. And then one day, things finally got to a point to where it got back to normal after the riots and all of that stuff.

And then my endeavor in baseball kind of started, because we used to go over and watch the semipro teams play. At that same recreation place was the first time that I joined a team, a baseball team. The team was called the Angels. We had the halo and the "A," just like the California Angels did at the time. When we first moved to L.A., we were close to the old Angels stadium, which was on Avalon. It had closed, but I used to go over there and stand and look at the gate and think about what a big gate that is, and the ballpark. And there is always something about a ballpark or a stadium and the lights that electrifies you, that brings something out from down deep.

I remember going over there and actually throwing rocks into the stadium over the big fence, which was, I guess, what kids did. But then we moved over off of Manchester Recreation Center. And I joined my first team, and it became the Angels. The one part of my

Roberto Clemente

uniform that I didn't have, my mom worked at the time. My mom and dad were separated, my mom worked, but she caught the bus and she had to walk through the park to get to our house. And I can remember her getting my stirrups. I didn't have the stirrups that go on the outside of the socks.

So when you're that young, the excitement of being able to play for the first time and just being a part of the team, my uniform was on probably eight, nine hours before game time. Back then, we ironed all of our stuff. You had a crease in your pants and the uniform is all ready, always hung upright. That was the one thing that we took care of. My mom came home from work, and I know she had stopped by the sporting goods store to get those socks.

So that was one of the happiest days of my life. When I saw her,

I went flying and she had my stirrups and stuff, and that was really it. That was one of those moments that you never ever forget, yeah.

My childhood hero was Roberto Clemente. We used to catch the bus out to Dodger Stadium. And living in South Central Los Angeles, we were good enough kids you would trust that we would do the right thing, so she would trust us to catch the bus out there and watch the games. In watching all of the teams that came in, we used to sit in the bleachers, get our tickets out in the bleachers. And you'd get there early enough to watch batting practice and watch what the pros did. There was just always something about the way Roberto Clemente went about his business every day.

From batting practice to the very first pitch to the time he went after a fly ball, there was such a grace and elegance in the way that he did that that it was very hard not to notice. Those arms and legs flailing when he hit a ball. It was hustle. It was excitement. And it was that that I think triggered me, because it was very hard to emulate his style of play. But the thing that really caught my eye was the aggressiveness with which he played and the excitement that he created.

In high school I played baseball on a team with Eddie Murray. It's very hard to garner a whole lot of attention when you have— I think he had four brothers that all had a chance of playing professionally, up to Triple-A, anyway. They played a lot of baseball and they were pretty good at it. He was pretty good at it. He was ambidextrous because he would throw with either hand. He could play first, second, short, third. You could put him anywhere, he was that type of athlete. But he hit with power from both sides of the plate, which, you know, when scouts would look at the young kids in high school, that's what they see. A lot of times when scouts would come around, that would be their focus. You know, watching this young kid who had all these skills but also had brothers before him and brothers that were right around his age that were still playing. They're also very talented players.

I wasn't one of those guys who at the time hit with any power or anything. I was just that little guy running around there in the middle of a diamond and people would probably say, as they said even when I got to the big leagues, I'll never hit. So, little guy with a good glove, so-so. But we got this guy here who can hit with power, hit for average. He can pitch. He can catch. He can do it all. So all of the attention was focused on Eddie when scouts came around. For a lot of the other guys that played on the team, it was just about getting an opportunity to play at some point in time, never really thinking that, well, you know, I have the ability to make it to the big leagues.

I think that was the real goal, to get a chance to play professionally at some point in time. And that never happened for me out of high school.

One of the only schools that showed interest in me was Cal Poly at San Luis Obispo, which is a small school in central California between Los Angeles and San Francisco that gave me the opportunity to both get a good education and also play the game I love. I walked on and got the opportunity.

Of course, being a walk-on, you know, you play on the B squad and all that stuff. And being the kid that I was, never getting drafted out of high school, and never having anyone show a whole lot of interest, I didn't think that I was ever going to get the opportunity. So I got it. I was away from home, got a little homesick, and I do remember calling back one day and saying to my mama, I'm not really sure that this is the place for me. Because I had not been moved up to the varsity baseball team. I was playing and I had made the JV squad, but there just didn't seem to be a whole lot of movement. And being a young kid, you know, we always deal with trying to be patient. My mom always told me, when it's your turn, it'll be your time. You'll know. Just be ready, when it's your time. Keep yourself in a position that when that window of opportunity does present itself that you're ready to step through it. And so just about the time that I was ready to give it all up, go home, I'm homesick and stuff, the varsity shortstop gets hurt.

And there was that window of opportunity. I stepped through that window and I never looked back. That was the little opening that I needed and then—let me back up a little bit and tell you that when I did call home, I said, I think I'm coming home. And she said, what home? You don't have a home. You *are* home. She had my high school coach call me and tell me very sternly, little so-and-so, you are not going anywhere. You are going to stay right there, and you're going to stick it out. And it was about that time that the varsity shortstop got hurt. I stepped in and never looked back. I think it might have been after my junior year. After you finish your baseball season, you're going to play semipro baseball.

And most of the big schools, the Arizona States, the UCLAs, the USCs, they send their players that they think have a chance to programs like in Alaska, Cape Cod, all of those leagues. Well, for players like myself, there are other places. Other places like Clarinda, Iowa, where you live in homes with families. You work during the day and you play baseball at night. And it's like old-town America, because these people in these towns, they don't lock their doors. I come from South Central Los Angeles. There are still communities around this country that people don't lock their doors. This is crazy, you know?

So here I was, a little black kid from South Central Los Angeles going to a predominantly white town in the Midwest, and getting an opportunity to do what I love to do, but at the same time being taught a lot of responsibility. When I first got there, I had to stay in the dorm a little bit, and you had to kind of cook for yourself, a little hot plate and all that stuff. And then they eventually move you in with a family. I got a chance to do that. You have to wash your own clothes. You become an adult very quickly. You learn the responsibility of being a man. You work a job during the day, which for me was construction.

This recreation center, those things have become very, very important parts of our lives. I think one of the things that has kind of been lost, from a societal standpoint, is that a lot of the programs that mold the young men, and I'm speaking about African-American men, a lot of those programs have been eliminated. I'm talking like trade schools, schools that would teach someone a trade so that he could go out and make an honest living. When you grow up poor and you don't have anything, and the few things that you do have are taken away, it leads you in a different direction of corruption. I'm hoping and praying that somewhere down the road here, we'll get back to understanding how important trade schools and things like that are for young men who have trouble finding their way.

My baseball field is now a soccer field. So the dynamics of the whole area have changed. That whole area now is more Latin than it was back then. Consequently, we've had the problem of being able to find young black athletes that want to play the game of baseball. I think what's happened is that you've had such success with guys coming out of high school and going into the pros from a basketball standpoint and, in some cases, from a football standpoint, probably more so from basketball. So kids that have athletic ability now, they look in a different direction to be able to make it. They're looking for instant gratification.

And this is where I think it hurts when they see a player that has the ability to come right out of high school and make it in the pros. They see the instant success. They see the money. They see the glamour, the glamour of it all, and I think that that really hurts because it's a very, very small percentage of guys that have the ability to do that. So it's kind of a false sense of reality for those kids, and we're having a hard time now getting young black kids to play baseball.

And it's been a challenge for all of us that are involved in baseball at getting it back together. I think Major League Baseball has done a good job. I think more emphasis has been put on building these programs in the Dominican Republic, Puerto Rico, because it's so much easier. One of the things is the red tape that you have to go through here. It's easier to set up a program in the Dominican Republic, a camp in the Dominican Republic, and audition those kids under those circumstances than it would be here.

I got drafted my junior year. I played my first year in Clarinda, Iowa. And the scouts see me. I finally get on the board, you know. Finally, my name is now on the board. So, they come to me and I talked to Mr. Eberly, who has been running this program there in Clarinda for forever. It's been one of those little neighborhood programs that just goes. They take these young kids that want to play and they play.

It's the Hawkeye League, whatever it is. And you go to the NBC Tournament down in Wichita, you know. So, it's one of these things that it's just been there forever. So, I get drafted at my junior year by the Detroit Tigers. I talked to Mr. Eberly, and I've talked to a guy who's played professionally. We're trying to get an idea of what I should sign for. And keep in mind, now, for me, this is an exciting time because finally I might get the opportunity to do what it is I love to do. I don't know where it's going. I don't know where it's going to take me. But just to get the opportunity to say I play professionally. This is 1976. And they draft me and at the same time they draft Alan Trammell. I didn't know this at the time.

You're going to go to Lakeland, Florida. We got this bus ticket and stuff for you, and you're going to start on this day. Okay, I need some change. I need a little something. So, they finally make their offer to me. And their offer to me was $8,500. So now, I'm sitting here and I'm thinking, well, in my infinite wisdom, I'm thinking that if I don't get at least ten grand, you know, ten grand being the cutoff point. If they give me ten grand, they got to take a real good look at me. Anything less than that, you know, because you can go out and get a job, you know, because I'm real close to my degree in social science now.

So, well, yeah, I can go out and get a job making ten grand. So, I asked them for ten grand. They promptly told me they didn't have that in the budget and so forth. So, I said to myself, well, now that I'm on the board, I'm going to go ahead and get as close to my degree as I possibly can in hopes of getting drafted again in my senior year. Many seniors don't get drafted. But once you're on the board, you know, at that point now, it's just the opportunity more than anything else. So I go back to school. And sure enough, my senior year I get drafted by the San Diego Padres. I got drafted in the eighth round by Detroit, and I got drafted in the fourth round by the Padres.

I'm ready for the big time now. We're high here, I'm ready now. So, sure enough, the Padres offered me $4,500. So, I end up signing for $5,000 and a bus ticket to Walla Walla, Washington, to start my big league career in 1977. I spent sixty-eight days in the minor leagues there. I'm doing what I love to do. I don't want to be here all the rest of my life but at least I'm getting the opportunity.

My approach to the game never changed. I was going to give it my all each and every day out there. If in fact I had to become a sanitation engineer, I was going to be the best sanitation engineer that I could possibly be. Whatever it was that I chose to do. But I finally got a chance to experience my dream, and it's the same thing that I ask from my kids now, that my kids find out what it is that they're passionate about. Whatever that is, just find out if it's what they're passionate about. I know they'll get the most out of it and that's all you can hope for, that you find that thing that you're passionate about in your life and go full bore.

People say you're blessed with great hand-eye coordination. Why do you have to go out there and take infield every day? As I mentioned earlier, I wanted to maintain that because I know that could be taken away like that. Yeah, I was good at what I did. But there's always room for improvement. There's no such thing as perfection. Consistency is as close as you're going to get to perfection. The more consistent you are, the more successful you are. And I didn't want to be surprised by anything that happened out there. When you play on Astroturf, and especially on a hot Sunday afternoon, the ball bounces higher. I'd have the guy hit high choppers, and I catch the ball and I throw it. I have people on my teams say, well, why do you do that? Well, it might happen during the game.

You never know. Or, why do you turn your back away from the in-field to catch the ball over your shoulder? Well, it might happen in the game, so I never wanted to be surprised by that. So, I always took a lot of ground balls. I always wanted to know where the bad spots on the field were, where you had to be cautious.

Your senses had to be a little bit sharper because it may be that bad spot. And just knowing that that bad spot is there sometimes gives you that edge, knowing that the senses have to be a little bit sharper in this area. So I took a lot of ground balls.

Think about it. Not all turf fields were laid the same way. You may play in Montreal, where the seam is right in front of you, whereas in Pittsburgh, the seam may be over there. There has to be a seam on the turf. You want to know where those seams are because at that point the ball may take a bad hop. One of the things that playing on AstroTurf did, too, is if you're not careful, you become very lazy because the ball gets to you so much quicker. And my thing was always to be as aggressive as I could on the turf, because the min-ute you laid back is when that ball hit a seam or something and bounced out.

I tell my son, tell young kids all the time that if you're playing a sport, you don't want to be outmanned in two or three areas. If you can't outplay somebody, you better be able to outthink them. If you can't outthink them, you better be able to outplay them. You cannot be unable to outthink them and outplay them. What's the purpose, why are you here? So you've got to decide. You know, this guy here, boy, he's so talented. How am I going to outthink him? How am I going to come up with a way to chop it down to make it more of an even playing field?

You have to have an idea of where you are on the field, getting back to taking those ground balls. It's all about knowing where you are at all times on the field so that it just becomes instinctual for you to be able to, if you get a ball over there, to have an idea where first base is. I used to have fun with my third basemen, especially Todd Zeile. We'd be talking, man, what did you do last night? I get a ground ball and I'm looking at him and throwing and I said, what did you do? I said, we went to a movie and stuff. And so, he starts cracking up, he's going, how did you do that?

In 1978, I get to big league camp. I'm there with players, notably Dave Winfield. Oscar Gamble had come over. George Hendrick was there at that time, Rollie Fingers, Gene Tenace, Gaylord Perry. These were all free agents that San Diego had signed, and I was this puny little kid, coming in talking about playing shortstop behind a guy who was the number one pick out of Brown University. So I just tried to fit in, you know, stay out of the way and just do my thing every day. If my name is in the lineup, go out and play and hopefully play well. Alvin Dark was the guy who had given me this opportunity. So I certainly did not want to let him down. And then what happens? He gets fired in spring training. When he gets fired, I'm sitting around thinking to myself, oh, what happens to me now? He calls me into his office on the day that he gets fired, and he says, young man, don't let things like this discourage you. This is the game. This happens in baseball all the time. He said, I want you to remember, all you do is pick that ball up and throw it across the diamond, just continue to do what you do because you're going to be a great one. And that was—I mean, how much better does it get than somebody showing confidence in you like that?

I was traded in the winter of 1981. Looking at the type of player that I was, I had always figured that I would probably be more of an American League type of player, a little guy who didn't hit much but had a good glove. I had never thought about San Diego being a place that I would have the opportunity to play. And I was still down in Southern California there. That was reassuring, because it gave my family and my friends an opportunity to get a chance to see me play on a regular basis.

I lived across the street from a wood factory where they had sawdust and they had stacks of wood. We used to go over and put a board in between the stacks of wood and use that as a springboard to flip into the sawdust. And then we used to go to a family-fun center where they had trampolines on Thursdays, you know, the in-ground trampolines. That's really where all my tumbling and stuff started, and it just becomes a young kid who would take a dare. We used to jump over these metal fences that had the little spikes on them. They had little twisted spikes on the top. If you don't make it, it's not a pretty scene. So you learn to jump very, very high.

So the last day of the season in San Deigo, the PR guy, Andy Strasberg, says to me, we've got fan appreciation day. We have fifty thousand people. He says, why don't you do your somersault in going out to your position? I go, oh, no, no, no, no, no. No, no, no, no. I'm not gonna do that.

He says, no, it will be great. And keep in mind now, at this time, the Chicken [the Padres mascot] was the bomb in San Diego. So I don't want to steal the Chicken's thunder. But I decided to do it. I did it reluctantly, thinking that I didn't want to be a hot dog. I don't want to be labeled a hot dog because I wasn't a hot dog. I just enjoyed what I did and just did it.

So they talked me into doing it. The fans went crazy. They got excited about it. And then I promptly go out and a ball goes between my legs. Now the Chicken comes out the next inning, goes down, and pretends. So that's how the flip got started. They liked it so much that they asked me to do it Opening Day the following year. So now, it's the thing that little ladies come up to me and say, we know who you are. You're that guy that does the flip. Which is great.

The name the Wizard, I think, came from the fact that my real name is Osborne but all my friends call me Oz. And when you make all of these great plays, they just called me the Wiz.

We were playing the Atlanta Braves. And I was about to say this earlier that, you know, when you talk about great plays, you make a great play and you let it go. You make a bad play, you let it go, because the next play may be the one that determines whether you win or lose. So you don't harp on those plays.

This particular play, on this Thursday afternoon, Randy Jones is pitching. Any time I go to my left or right, three or four steps, the first thing that comes to mind is dive. That's just an instinctual thing that has always been there. Don't ask me why, how, whatever. It's just an instinctive thing. This particular player hits a bullet up the middle. And I started running that way. And just as I dive, the ball hits and it goes back the other way. So now my body's going this way, the ball is going that way, my glove hand is gone. So now, while in the air, the only thing I can do is reach back like this.

Well, the ball stuck in my hand. I caught it and I scrambled to my feet and I threw him out at first base. Now, keep in mind, I'm just doing what I do. They call me a rugrat because I cover a lot of ground. You can't practice a play like that, but here, again, it's keeping your-self in a position to be able to make a play. In that particular play, for whatever reason, it all worked. Now, that ball could have hit my finger, whatever, but it hit the palm of my hand, stuck. I scrambled to my feet with all my hair, and I threw him out at first base.

So it's not until the next morning that I wake up and I'm listening to the radio, and the announcer says, I think I saw the greatest play I've ever seen in the game of baseball yesterday. And I go, well, I don't know if it was that great a play because I was just doing what I do, and it just happened. So it was all so surreal because I didn't look at it like that. I was in the place that I was supposed to be and it happened. That's the play right there that's always rated the number one defensive play that I've ever made.

Less than a week later, I think I made one that was as good but it wasn't caught on tape or anything and people didn't talk about it much. You know, in San Francisco, when that wind is swirling, you can hear a pop in the ball and it goes out of the ballpark, but then the wind shifts and it blows the ball back in. Well, there was a ball hit and I think it was, I want to say it was Gene Richards. I think he was playing left field. Well, he had gone back to the fence and I could see that—I had gone out—and I could see that the wind was now starting to change and the ball was starting to come back.

The ball was hit good, so he had gone back to the fence. So I started running out and I dive and I catch this ball. Now, personally, to me, because I had to dive—sometimes when you just go back and you don't have to dive or anything, it becomes an easier play. But when you've got a wind like that and it has shifted, to dive and be in the right place and catch the ball, that to me was a pretty good play. But nobody ever talked about that play. So you know, that's the way it happened, man. I just did what I did.

You want to be that guy that when the game is on the line, your teammates and everybody says, I want it to go to him because he's gonna give us the best chance of us making that play. You want to be that guy. If you're that guy standing out there saying to yourself, I hope it's not hit to me, that's not good. That's not good. You don't want to be in that frame of mind because you put yourself in a negative spot right from the start. And I think that when you talk to the guys who have plaques hanging in Cooperstown, guys who have made twenty, twenty-four All-Star teams, if you ask them, they will tell you that they wanted to be that guy when the game was on the line. And it's that thing right there that separates them from the rest of the pack.

We always wanted those guys the team could depend on when it needed them the most, and I certainly was one of those players. A lot of players, a lot of people look at momentum as being strictly offense. Momentum is not strictly offense. Momentum is defense as well, because it's defense that puts your offense in a position to win. So it's not heralded as much, but the importance is just as great. That is probably the greatest compliment that I could be paid if the stat was kept. What is the difference between driving in 100 and saving 100? If a stat is kept, you know, on that base hit there, this run would have scored; if that stat is kept, I'd like to think that I would be pretty high on that list.

When you put a team together from an offensive standpoint or vice versa, there's gonna be something lacking. If it's put together from a defensive standpoint, you're probably not gonna get as much offense. And if you put it together from an offensive standpoint, you're probably not gonna get as much defense. So there's a tradeoff there. Which would you do? Well, I think most people and most fans, anyway, they like the offense, they like to see the ball fly out of the ballpark.

But at the same time, from a defensive standpoint, we all know now, not only in baseball but in basketball and in football, it is defense that puts that offense in position to win, because if you can't stop the opposition, it just becomes a slugfest. People used to ask us in the eighties, what was the difference between the Mets and the Cardinals? Well, we knew that if we kept the ball in the ballpark, we were a better defensive club, especially late in the ballgame when that pressure is on, when you hear those people out there saying, I don't want it hit to me, as opposed to a team that was very sure-handed, which we were.

And I think that's why in years that we were able to win, it was because we were more defensive-oriented. We weren't as good offensively, but we knew that if you kept the pressure on, as we could with our overall team speed, that over the long haul, that defense was gonna win out for us. And defense starts with pitching.

That's why we were fortunate enough in the eighties to go to the World Series three times, because we were able to keep the nucleus of the team together to make that happen and we were fortunate enough to win it all in '82.

As a baseball player, when I was coming in, if you made $100,000, boy, that was good. And then all of a sudden, the salary structure took off under the tutelage of Marvin Miller, who, to me, was what the Players' Association is all about. The players wouldn't be where they are today without the courage of Marvin Miller or the courage of Curt Flood, coming up with the game plan to battle the game as they did. We knew that it was changing. But here, again, this was what we love doing. So we were able to kind of separate that—that's over there, I still got to do my thing on the field. So there becomes this balancing act of getting compensated for what you do but, at the same time, keeping things in perspective. I had no idea when I started, when I signed my contract in 1977, that the salary structure would go as it did. I think when we first started hearing about these million-dollar contracts, we were talking about what the ceiling is. We got to be close to the ceiling, can't get any higher than this. We sit here today, 2009, and there's still no ceiling. Contracts are still being signed like you wouldn't believe. It's mind-boggling that we can be talking here some thirty years later and we still haven't reached the ceiling.

We're not business guys, but we had to rely on the expertise of someone. And I don't think that we could've had a better leader than Marvin Miller. The whole time he talked about the team concept, which we were all a part of. If you do it as a team, it makes it very hard on the other side.

You want to be that person, that young guy that comes into the game and says, you know, man, I got to put out just like he's putting out. People ask me, you know, late in my career, when I'm taking all these ground balls, they said, why do you continue to work hard? I said, because it can be gone tomorrow. You never want to leave this game feeling that you didn't get everything that you can get out of it.

In the 1982 World Series Milwaukee beat us 10–0 in that first game. We took a scouting report and we looked at the scouting report. And they said, play Robin Yount here, play Paul Molitor here. Everywhere we play they hit it somewhere else. It was just terrible. Paul Molitor had five hits. Robin Yount had five hits. I'm going, man, this is crazy. I mean, they're hitting balls all over the place, and we're a pretty good defensive team.

We're going to find a way to beat them. We're going to beat them. First of all, we're going to get rid of the scouting report because it was just disastrous. We got away from doing what we had done all year. You know, when you play, there are certain instincts that you have, you've got to go with, because the person that's doing the scouting report is not out there every day. You can use it as a guide, but it can't be the bible. So we got rid of that scouting report and we started playing our game. And as I said earlier, defense starts with pitching.

Now, a lot of the weight went on the shoulders of our pitchers to be able to keep the ball in the ballpark because as I mentioned, if we can keep the ball in the ballpark, we've got a chance. They were a decent defensive ball club but they weren't like we were. So it started with our pitching. Our pitching started to keep the ball in the ballpark and we started doing what we had done all year. Scoring out there and catching it and throwing the baseball, getting timely hits. We realized we were not a power-laden team, but we knew we had the ability to string it all together, to keep innings going.

We had Ken Oberkfell at third base, myself at short, we had Tommy Herr at second, we had Keith Hernandez at first, we had George Hendrick in right field, we had Willie McGee in center field. He alternated with Tito Landrum, and David Green in left field. We had Darrell Porter as the catcher. And we had Jim Kaat as the pitcher; we had Bob Forsch. We had, of course, we had Bruce Sutter, the bearded closer who came in. And we had a lot of fill-in guys. We didn't have a bunch of 20-game winners.

We had Joaquin Andujar, nutty as a fruitcake. But, you know, Joaquin won 15 games for us and Forsch won 15 games. But we just had guys who knew how to throw the ball, keep the ball in the ballpark, and we made it work. We had a young kid by the name of John Stuper. I think he's the Yale baseball coach now. But he went out and threw the game of his life in the rain, and we were able to put it all together and win because we all believed in one another.

I don't know if there's been any infield any better. When you have a Keith Hernandez at first base—people have no idea how good he was over there. You probably had a chance to see him a little bit in New York, in the latter part of his career. But he was one of those guys that could throw to any base.

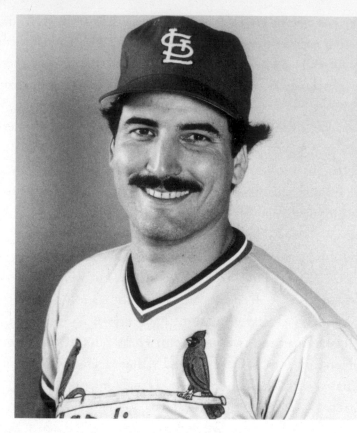

Keith Hernandez

He charged the plate, especially when we knew the bunt was on. He could charge it from first base all the way over to the third-base line. I've seen him charge the third-base line, get balls, and throw them to get the guy at second base, especially guys that didn't have the ability to run. Now, of course, he had to play a little closer with the guys who had speed. But with guys who couldn't run, if the sacrifice was on, he'd catch balls over by the third-base line and throw to second base.

Tommy Herr knew his craft, second base; I knew my craft, shortstop; Ken Oberkfell knew his craft at third. When you have people who can cover ground either way it makes it so much easier for that person playing on the other side of them, because now you can do things that you otherwise would not be able to do. And we had an infield that could do that. It was just amazing. It was fun going to the ballpark every day, playing with a group of professionals, guys who, at some point, all wanted to be managers.

With Jim Kaat, on many occasions, if you looked away, you'd get yourself in trouble, because Jim Kaat never ran into a really big windup. You know, if a guy put his foot in the batter's box, Jim, with that quick little head movement, was gone. A lot of times as an infielder you're kicking dirt or kicking rocks or smoothing out spots. A lot of times I was kicking spots and he was throwing the ball to the plate.

In 1982, we were able to rise to the occasion more than the Milwaukee Brewers. Not that we were a better team, because when you look at a team like that, they had 216 home runs as a team. And here we are, you know, a little 67. We just came in there, well, what are we going to do against these guys? But we proved that David and Goliath theory, you find a way to make it happen.

The year 1985 was a surprise, because I had gotten a lot stronger. I had learned how to pull the ball and hit the ball in the gap and back the defense up. The Dodgers had always been pounding me inside, pounding me inside. So, we're in the playoffs in the ninth inning. They bring Tom Niedenfuer in and the ballgame is tied. Niedenfuer as usual pounded that fastball in. Well, I take a couple of good swings on balls that if they're out a little bit more on the plate, I get it down in the corner. But he kept it in here. He kept pounding me in and I think the count goes to 2-2.

And he threw a pitch that I fouled straight back, and I said, oh, God, if he gives me another pitch like that right there, I can get the ball down in the corner. Sure enough, he throws another fastball but he didn't get it in far enough. And so, in Busch Stadium you got the foul line which is 330. Well, it starts out at an angle here and there's a little spot where the curve starts, if you get the ball airborne there, that's the only place that I'm going to have a chance to hit the ball out. I wasn't trying to hit the ball out, I was trying to hit the ball down in the corner.

Well, he gets that fastball in and I put the technique on him. And the ball starts going, and as I'm going to first base, that ball has got a shot of getting out of there. So I'm running as I always did because I don't hit home runs. So I hit first base and I see that the ball hit on top of the pillar, over the line. And Mike Marshall was playing right field, plays it like it's off the wall, which he should do. But the umpire out there is circling like this. And now I'm going around the bases and I'm going, what the heck just happened? Because the whole stadium is rocking now, you could feel it was shaking.

It was electrifying, and that was the moment where we got the great call from Jack Buck. He says, the ball hit down the line. Go crazy, folks, go crazy. And the place, it was just a madhouse. I get to home plate, and there's all my teammates there now, because 1985 for me was a breakout year. It was at that point that my teammates start looking to me for more than just defense. I became an important part of the offense of this ballclub now because Jack Clark had gotten hurt earlier in the year, and lo and behold, I got to hit third in the lineup.

I can remember seeing the guys when I got to home plate. They ripped my chain off and they made sure I stepped on home plate. And from there, we just rode the momentum into Game Six out there. Jack Clark hits the home run off of Niedenfuer late in the ballgame, where you see Pedro Guerrero, who, the following year, joined us, and we reminded him of throwing his glove down out there in left field when they decided to pitch to Clark. Niedenfuer struck Clark out the time before. And Clark hit the crushing home run that put us ahead and we were able to get those three outs and off to the World Series.

So we got to Game Six [of the 1985 World Series, against Kansas City]. I tell people that when you play Game Six on the road, you have a chance to win, and if you don't, Game Seven is almost academic. It's very tough. Game Seven is very tough to win on the road. I think up to that point we were 86–0 with a lead going into the eighth inning. Todd Worrell was our closer. We had not lost a game with the lead going into the eighth inning. And then that disastrous ninth inning, I think the score was 1–0 at the time and we're all, I mean, all of us were exhausted and it's been a long, hard season.

So we had put everything into this game. We had clawed and fought our way here again to get that one run, and our pitchers have vowed to protect it. The ball is stopped at first base. Jack goes over to get it. Todd Worrell runs over, stretches a little bit, keeps his feet on the bag, guy's very clearly out, they call him safe.

No appeal, and they didn't ask for any help at all. That's what hurts. So today, am I for instant replay? Yes, I'm for instant replay, especially in the playoffs and World Series, when technology can help you get it right. If the goal is to get it right and you have the technology, then by all means use it. I'm not saying take the personal element out of it because that's what, that's the first thing that comes up, you know, it takes the personal touch out. It's not about taking the personal touch out. It's about getting it right.

There was a lot of emotion because we were tired as a team and we wanted it over with, and this was our opportunity to get it over with and we're right there and we hadn't lost a game with the lead and this comes up and we don't get any help from anybody. And we very clearly saw that he was out on the play. It's called "The Call," and there are pictures all around. I see pictures all the time of The Call that remind me of that but, you know, they got it wrong. The umpire finally admitted that he got it wrong. My only problem with it is that there were some other umpires out there that probably could have helped him to get it right and they didn't. And so we lost the game, 2–1.

Game Seven was anticlimactic. All of the energy that you have as a team we put into Game Six. And when Game Seven rolled around, we were drained, we had nothing. They beat us 11–0.

* * *

In the 1987 World Series we won every game at home. Minnesota won every game at home. My good friend Kirby Puckett is playing and any time you play against a player like that, he's one of those guys that has a plaque hanging in Cooperstown, because the story has been told many times now.

He walked through the door, the clubhouse door; he says, guys, get on board. I'm gonna take care of it this evening. Those type of players, they can be very, very dangerous. And he certainly was against us, as he was against everybody he played. When you get a player like that and you surround him with guys who believe in what he's capable of doing, you're going to end up winning more than you

Kirby Puckett

lose. And he certainly was a big part of that Minnesota thing, and you couple that with having to play in a place like Minnesota and the memories aren't too pleasant, so they were able to beat us.

In 1985, when I hit the home run in the playoffs, people said, wow, you know, he's more than just a defensive player. So that evolution just continued. I'd met Mackie Shilstone, my trainer, who I continue to work with, who I credit with probably adding eight, nine more years to my career. I'd learned nutrition. I'd learned, well, I don't always work with weights, but nutrition being an important part of that, learning how to take better care of myself and keep myself in better shape.

And so the progress, as far as offense was concerned, continued to grow—my understanding of what it was that I was trying to do as an offensive player. And it all came into play. I got bigger and stronger but I didn't hit more home runs because that was not the goal. The goal was to be able to drive the ball a little bit more, hit the gaps more, which I was able to do. When I came in in 1978, I wanted to win a Gold Glove and I wanted to win a Silver Slugger. As you know, the Silver Slugger is given to the position where the guy has the highest slugging percentage and other factors in a year. And I did that in 1987. So there is one lone Silver Slugger sitting there in my case with 13 Gold Gloves.

Each generation was different. Red Schoendienst and Stan Musial had a chance to play together. Red managed Bob Gibson and Lou Brock. Being a part of an organization that is rich in tradition, as the Cardinals are, I knew that coming over, that one day, hopefully, I'd be mentioned in the same admiring terms as those guys were. All of that came to fruition for me just by going out and doing my job every day, doing what I love to do. It's great to be a part of an organization that has five living Hall of Famers. I think there's very few clubs that can say that.

Bob Gibson has become a very good friend, Mr. Tough Guy. I

said, if I hit against you, I ought to hit you in your knee. And he said, let me tell you something. If I had played shortstop, people wouldn't even know who you are.

Originally the shortstop position was one where the guy was the defensive guy, he and the center fielder. Not much was expected from them on offense. Whatever you got from them offensively was going to be extra because through the years you've always had to be strong up the middle with your second baseman, your shortstop, your center fielder, and your catcher. That's the lifeline there.

If you're strong in those positions, especially from a defensive standpoint, and then you throw the pitcher in there from a defensive standpoint, then your club automatically has a better chance of winning because you've got somebody who can go and catch the ball. You've got a guy who is smart enough behind the plate to call a game. You've got those position guys out there that are gonna be consistent at turning the double play when you need it, getting that pitcher out of trouble.

The position of shortstop, as we've gone, larger guys were given the opportunity. You know, Mark Belanger basically was a defensive player. He was tall and rangy but he was basically looked upon as a defensive player who got a little bit better as the years went on. Through that same Orioles organization, because of that, when Cal Ripken came in and Cal proved that, I don't think that it was always fair to expect a guy who is going to give you all that offense to be able to cover as much ground and be as great a defensive player, but they found a balance there.

So he was the impetus, I think, for what we see today in shortstops. And there's always a trade-off. For those guys who are going to give you that great offense, we don't look for the same range. If you get that range, it's wonderful. But it is very hard to find guys who have outstanding range and can be a great offensive player as well. You have a Cal Ripken who—he's a great position player, very smart, and a great offensive player. Defensively, he's not going to hurt you.

You know, he's going to make the routine play every day and that's basically what you want at that position.

When you look at so many shortstops today, there're certainly great offensive players that possess the ability to be much greater defensive players, your Hanley Ramirezes and people like that that have been given the opportunity because Cal Ripken proved that a big guy can play the position, probably not as effectively as a prototypical shortstop, an Ozzie Smith or an Omar Vizquel, but good enough to be able to hold your team in and give your team a chance to win.

I think Omar Vizquel is the last of the Ozzie Smith shortstops. He was one of those players that came in notably as a defensive player, who continued to work hard to become a better offensive player. Jimmy Rollins, on the other hand, comes in as a pretty good offensive player to start with, who also was a good defensive player. So there's been a transition in the position. I think that when you play the position today, you're looked upon to be more rounded.

A-Rod [Alex Rodriguez] realized that if he was going to have a chance to win a Championship, if he was going to play in New York, he had to play third base. He certainly had third-base numbers. You'd get the production that you would get from a third baseman from him.

God forbid, if anything happens to Derek Jeter, then he certainly could fill in over there. But Jeter has been one of the best things that's ever happened to New York. You know, he's one of those guys that just kept his nose clean. He's played every day, has been successful. He's handled the pressure. New York is never an easy place to play, but he's one of those players that comes along every now and then that the city falls in love with and can do no wrong. So he's just been a steady rock for the city of New York.

It's a very unfortunate thing that happened with baseball and steroids. Especially for some of the people who have been suspected of using. In the Hall of Fame, we get all the questions about this era and whether there should be asterisks and all of that stuff. The thing that hurts the most is that numbers are tainted. You know, baseball has always been a game where we knew what was real and what wasn't. And what's happened now is we don't know what's real and what's not. And I think some people are feeling the effects of their use of steroids.

I don't think that fans are apathetic about whether a guy used because they've all been entertained by him. I think the thing that they're most interested in is whether or not a guy is going to be a stand-up guy and admit that he did, be a man and say, yes, I did. Now, was it right? No, it may not have been right, but I did. I did it. And, you know, forgive me for whatever wrong I have done. Two perfect examples are Andy Pettitte and Jason Giambi. I think people look at them much differently than some of the other guys.

You're always going to have someone who's going to be willing to test the system, because they know that you can have one of those magical years, and behind one of those magical years come big dollars. So there's always going to be somebody willing to test the waters.

When I came in in 1978 there were outfielders like Ellis Valentine, Andre Dawson, Warren Cromartie. They dared you to run. It was just a beautiful thing to watch the way that they played out there in the outfield. And I played against Michael Jack Schmidt, who was a great third baseman. He was never given credit for how good a defensive player he was over there. Great arm, he could charge that ball, barehand that ball with the best of them.

Of course, playing against the Big Red Machine, Johnny Bench, Joe Morgan, Tony Perez, who always tried to knock me over, you know? Having the opportunity to play against the people that you grew up watching play, never thinking that one day I'm going to be able to do that. I'm not going to say it wasn't a dream. The dream wasn't just to be able to play professional baseball but to be able to rub shoulders with these guys in the same fraternity.

It's just been beyond anything that you could ever imagine. And, you know, Sandy Koufax walks into the room and Hank Aaron, Willie Mays, I can go up and say, you know, sign this for me. It's surreal because I never looked at myself as a Hall of Famer growing up. I was just a little kid who had this idea that one day I'd get a chance to play professional baseball. I'd make a decent living and be able to tell my grandkids, look at these clippings here, this is what I did.

I always leave this with young kids. You're only gonna get out of something what you put in. If you don't put anything in, you shouldn't expect anything in return. That's life.

CAL RIPKEN JR.

At six-foot-four and powerfully built, Cal Ripken Jr. redefined what a modern shortstop looked like. Not only could he field his position with the best of them but he added a slugger's bat to the equation.

"Cal's one of the players I looked up to when I was growing up," said longtime Yankees shortstop Derek Jeter. "He really set the stage for taller shortstops, more offensive shortstops. When I was coming up, people would say I was too tall to play shortstop. My first line of defense was, 'Look at Cal Ripken.' It's been fun getting to know him over the years. When I was younger I was afraid to say anything, but Cal would go out of his way to be nice. He's fun to watch play, but he's even a better person than he is a player."

For all his accolades, honors, and accomplishments, Ripken will always be remembered for "the streak." The ultimate gamer captured a nation's imagination by playing 2,632 consecutive games from May 30, 1982, through September 19, 1998, shattering what was thought of as an unbreakable mark of 2,130 set by Lou Gehrig.

A pair of former teammates, Brady Anderson and B. J. Surhoff, considered Ripken an inspiration both on and off the field.

"He's the best," Anderson said. "As a player he was someone you could look up to to see how he went about preparing for the game and how he played the game. As a person, every good thing you see or read about Cal is legitimate. He's pretty much one of the most consistently honorable guys you'll ever meet."

"He's one of the guys people always looked to talk to," Surhoff said. "And what he did on the field, his commitment to the game, was unparalleled."

Baseball was the family business for Ripken, whose father was in professional baseball for more than thirty years and whose brother played in the majors for twelve seasons. "When they were little, I showed all four kids how to catch a ground ball and how to catch a fly ball. Other than that, I just let them play, like kids are supposed to do," Cal Ripken Sr. said. "I didn't talk hitting with Cal until his junior year in high school. When I saw him play that year, he showed me the tools that made me know I wanted to come back to see him again as a senior."

While Ripken's consecutive games streak is certainly impressive, it's possible it overshadowed what a remarkable all-around career he had. In a twenty-one-season big league career, all spent with the Baltimore Orioles, Ripken methodically accumulated 3,184 hits, 431 home runs, 19 straight All-Star game nods, 2 Gold Gloves, 2 Most Valuable Player Awards, and a Rookie of the Year Award. The ultimate honor came when he was elected to the National Baseball Hall of Fame in 2007.

It seems like my whole life is a memory of baseball, because from the earliest days, Dad was in minor league baseball. We talked baseball almost every chance we had. And if I remember correctly, my toys as a boy weren't your normal rattle, it was a ball or something that came home with Dad, a plastic bat. So I remember a yellow, thin plastic bat I used to drag around and a variety of balls. You know, I can't tell you if it was a major league ball, I can't tell you if it was a Wiffle ball. I just remember walking around dragging a yellow bat

Cal Ripken Jr.

and having a ball in my hand. And that's just how I made it through the day.

It seemed like we lived in a new place every summer. And when we got old enough to be in school, Dad would go out, go to spring training, then go to a minor league town: Kennewick, Washington; Aberdeen, South Dakota; Dallas, Texas. And then we would load up into a blue station wagon with a red trailer attached to the back, and my mom would drive to wherever it was, including cross-country, with all the little kids in tow. I had a sister that was older than me, a brother that was a year younger than me, and then a brother that was three years younger than me. And I remember the car broke down a lot. I remember the little six-ounce bottles of Coke, real thick bottles that we had, while we were sitting in a gas station trying to get right. And I just remember being with my mother's family a lot. I mean, when you leave your home structure and go to a new one, you really rely on the closeness of your family as your friends.

So we did everything together. We played cards together, we sang and did games, we did license plate games, sign games on the highway. We really looked to our own little family unit as our friends as well as our family. Now that made us laugh a lot; that also made us cry a lot and fight a lot and all the things that families do. But it seems like we had to rely on our little unit a little bit more than other families because we would constantly sort of move our home base to where Dad managed.

Baseball really took Dad away for the majority of the time. And even when he was home, since you're not getting paid a whole lot in the minor leagues, he had to work temporary jobs that were available.

He had probably three part-time jobs, driving a beverage truck, working in a drugstore, or just picking up odd jobs that he could get in the off-season. So it seemed like we saw him even less when he came home. And Mom played the role of Dad and Mom in most cases. And sometimes, that made for some traumatic moments. If you have a bully picking on you, you really want your dad to give you some sort of advice. Mom can't necessarily solve that as well. But in all other respects, Mom was there in that role and as Mom. And again, she was the doer.

I always had an aptitude for baseball and I always had a love for it. In some ways, it made Dad so happy. And I think at the start, you wanted to find that happiness that Dad had. Baseball was a joy. It was wonderful. You know, it almost seemed like he transformed when he would take me to the ballpark or we'd be around the ball-park. As soon as he put on his uniform, he transformed into a happier person, I think. I always associated baseball with that sort of happiness.

And I guess being around the game, watching the game, trying to emulate what you see, trying to make your dad proud is what I tried to do in many ways, early on, being a kid. And a by-product of that was that I liked it. I liked playing it.

It came really easy to me. I was always more advanced pitching with the other kids because normally, nowadays, you have Tee ball and many other things in which to start out your baseball a little bit earlier, more organized activities that start sometimes as early as four. But organized athletics or baseball for me was eight years old, because that's the age when kids could start to pitch to each other. They couldn't pitch that well to each other, because the control is not really where it needs to be, but it's the first stage.

And I knew that I was a little bit more advanced at that age because I could control the ball. I could throw the ball where I wanted to. I could hit the ball. I could track the ball. I could perform all the skills that were there. And sometimes I couldn't understand why other kids couldn't. You know, if I was throwing pitches and maybe my wildness would turn out to be hitting a couple of batters. You know, the coach one time came out to the mound, I think when I was eight years old, thinking I would be all upset because I just hit two batters in a row and he wanted to ask me about that and kind of calm me down. And he comes out and says, you know, okay, what's the problem? And I said, those kids don't know how to get out of the way of the ball very good. And so, he comes back laughing and he tells my mom that story. So I was unaffected by that. But I knew that at that point I had some skills that were better. I wasn't physically the biggest kid. At shortstop, I was thought of as a bigger shortstop. At almost six-five and I played at 225, you know, I'm getting credit for somehow changing the mind-set and redefining a position just because of my size.

But when I was younger, I grew very late and I went through other kids who were stronger, they threw the ball harder, they could hit the ball farther, whatever else, but my overall skills were finer. I knew that I was a little bit better than they were. I knew that I was good when I was eight and nine and ten. I was always among the All-Stars in the top of the level. Did I know that I could play professional ball at that age? No. Did I know that I was gonna be a better player in high school? No, at that point. But I would say probably at the age of sixteen that I start to measure myself around other kids and the success that I started to have, then I felt that I had a chance to play at another level.

The really ironic part about my childhood development is most people think that Dad played a significant role in teaching me the game of baseball hand to hand, arm to arm, working with me in the backyard. But I can't remember, you know, times when that occurred. Normally, you could remember as a kid playing catch with your dad. But that wasn't my existence at all. Dad had his responsibilities at the ballpark. Periodically, he could do something with me at the ballpark in between his responsibilities.

And in many ways, I was left to the other members of the team to actually play catch with or play pepper with or kind of demonstrate how to play. Early on, and I can't remember exactly what age it was but I'm saying it was before eight, Dad came to me on Saturday mornings and he tapped me on the leg and asked me if I wanted to go to a clinic with him. And, you know, I knew that my brothers at that time and my sister weren't gonna go. And so I wanted to go just to be with my dad. Those clinics, they'd just put you in these stands and you sit and wait and you listen, and it's the most boring thing in the world because all you hear is words about how to play, and kids want to play.

And I was miserable sitting in the stands, but I was listening to the words that my dad was saying. This is how you field the ground ball, this is how you hit, this is all the fundamental things. And I guess that I soaked them in really well, but Dad never went out and hit me ground balls or worked with me in those sorts of cases. I would do those sorts of things with other people. And every once in a while, Dad would say, how did you learn how to do that?

I made the varsity baseball team as a freshman, I think, only by default. They didn't have a really good team and they needed a second baseman. I mean, I could catch the ball and throw the ball, but was pretty overmatched physically in some other aspects of the game. But I remember I was five-seven, 128, because we had to actually stand on the scale in our underwear in front of the team and then somebody would announce, okay, five-seven, 128.

And when they did that to me, everybody laughed and made me feel about this big. And I was a boy among men because other people had developed and they were shaving and stuff like that. I truly was a boy at that point. And I remember that distinctly. So, as my season went along, I remember the coach that was coaching the varsity when I went out for tryouts that particular year, he heard that I was there because of my last name, had a little bit of local pickup to it. Never met me, never saw me, and I came up to him and asked him where I was supposed to be in a high, squeaky voice.

And he says, sure, you know, tell me what your name is. And I told him my name was Ripken. And then he said this was supposed to be the savior of his program, you know, all that kind of stuff, and he laughs about it and he tells that sort of joke around. And I was overwhelmed. I hit about 5-39 at that time. As the season progressed, I got better and better. In the playoffs we had, nobody could hit this guy that we ended up losing to, and I hit ninth and I ended up getting two hits off the guy, the only two hits that we got.

And progressively, you know, I started to get a little size. By my tenth-grade year, I grew a little bit more and then I started contributing. And then in my eleventh-grade year, probably I was six-one at that time but I could throw the ball pretty hard. I could control. I started pitching and I started hitting really well, and I started to become a major part of that team. And by my junior year, I had scouts looking at me. And in the senior year, all the scouts were looking at me at that point. So we won the state, I think, in the playoffs on the benefit of my arm, I think, because I pitched nearly every game.

We were very active kids. We loved the game of baseball. We were around a ballpark all the time. We used to roll up programs into little bats and create other balls or whatever else. We played a lot of games with hand-eye coordination. A broomstick was very popular, and then old tape people would discard for taping their ankles or something, we'd roll it up into a ball. So we were very innovative playing ball, Ping-Pong balls and those little wood bats, souvenir bats, giveaway bats that would be at ballparks.

All those were the tools of our trade. And we didn't really think about it, but we played those games nonstop over and over again. And I think hitting moving balls with different sizes and different shapes really did help my hand-eye coordination, because I think when you end up going to the real bats and the real balls, it seemed a whole lot easier to play that game than it did the games that we were playing.

In the state playoffs, I pitched virtually every game. I split time with another kid on the staff, and we played roughly two times a week in tough weather. You know, I think we played a total of twenty-some games in my senior year. So it wasn't like what it is now, where kids are actually logging a lot of time. And usually I had ample time to actually rest in between. So, in the state playoffs, it just happened to me that I was pitching over and over again every game because the games were against better talent.

There was one little funny story that in the state finals, I had pitched all the way through. We played every other day. And by the last game, my arm was pretty tired. And I made a mistake with a pitch early on and gave up a double, and I was down in the game, 1–0 or 2–0. And this big rain cloud came over the field. And I remember having somebody on first base that I walked on the 3-2 pitch. I struggled a little bit. I must have made ten throws to first base in a stalling sort of effort.

And the rain came down. It rained for a long time, washed the whole game out, and they rescheduled the game for a week later. By that time, I was rested. I'd gotten drafted in between. You know, that game, I came back stronger than I ever was and ended up striking seventeen batters out. We won, and we won the state championship. I don't know what would have happened in the rest of that game, but I had at least the wherewithal to know that I was limping to the finish line. I threw ten pickoff throws over there just to stall.

At first, I thought I was different because the other kids had their dad around. You know, for all our games, Dad and Mom would come to the games, and it was just Mom for me. But then I really started to think about it and thought how lucky I was during the summers that I went and I was there every single day at his place of work, which was minor league baseball. Now, granted, as a minor league manager, in those days especially, you didn't have any support from pitching coaches or hitting coaches. Dad was all of those.

So he had to deal with twenty-five guys or twenty-two guys, whatever the roster size was, and he had to be all those things, so his responsibility was pretty constant. But I felt really lucky to be around

Cal Ripken Sr.

that ballpark and see what I had a chance to see. And I look at it now, I had the baseball encyclopedia of Dad, so I could ask him any question I wanted and he would have the answer for it. But I also had all these books, these other smaller books of how to play short-stop and second base and first base, in the form of players in the minor leagues. I asked them questions all the time. And the real in-teresting thing that happened was everybody had some instruction for me. At the end of the day I would tell my dad what I learned and I asked, is that right?

And most of the time he would say, yes, that's very good. And then I would know that I could go back and play catch with that guy. But if an outfielder was messing around with me and told me, okay, the way he catches fly balls is one-handed off to the side like this, it really gives you the chance to do X, Y, and Z. And I would go back and tell him that this is what I learned today. My dad would say, no, that's wrong. And then I would x that guy off my list. I wouldn't talk to him.

Locally, my dad was considered with professional baseball. But nobody really knew what that was. We didn't have minor league baseball as a model around where we were. So people knew that he went away. They knew that he played a role for the Orioles in the developmental system somehow, but they really didn't know what it was. So, in some ways, it carried a little bit of celebrity that you are a son of someone that is attached to baseball.

So at times the expectations from my coach in freshman year, that was kind of normal. I'm the son of a professional baseball guy, so therefore I should be able to play. But when I compare it to my son right now, my son is under more scrutiny, you know, than I ever would have been under, and I can't protect him from that. It is what it is. He has to figure out how to deal with it the same way that I had to figure out how to deal with my little bit of scrutiny and expecta-tions. But I never felt the pressure, and I think mostly because my dad didn't help exert the pressure.

My parents didn't put any pressure on me whatsoever, and maybe they were the wisest and the smartest to recognize that there already was some and that they were gonna try to defuse that, similar to how I think now.

As a batboy, I was watching the Double-A team out there and I thought, you know, this is the greatest job you could ever have. And at that time, I aspired to be a Double-A player, not a big league player. I had this sort of dream and this goal, and was working toward it, and then it kind of slowed down a little bit when I became a freshman and sophomore. The challenges became great. But then it picked back up again as a junior. And then all of a sudden, I was getting attention and scouts were actually looking at me. I was being invited into some invitation-only sort of tryout camps to be observed and looked at.

Everybody knew the scouts were there when they came to a small town like Aberdeen, Maryland. We didn't draw the crowd. We didn't have fans per se. So when there were people sitting behind there with their little notebooks and those sorts of things, after a while you could start to tell who were the scouts and who weren't. And the buzz would continue to go around. And ultimately, when I started to perform and the small pocket of scouts grew to this many and then this many, it became a bigger deal, and I started to think, maybe I do have a chance to do that.

So when I did get past my state championship, I was drafted on the second round by the Orioles. The Orioles had four second-round picks that year. I think I was the third one in the second round. I think roughly fortieth, forty-fourth in the country, I think. A lot of the cross-checkers and the scouts were only interested in me as a pitcher. Most all of them in the Orioles were split in that regard, but the Orioles had some interest in me as a regular player because I had the chance to try out and hit in front of Earl Weaver. He'd be down at the stadium at that point, and I'd kind of show off some physical skills during batting practice. And so they had a kind of read on me from there.

And many of them said they're gonna get a cross-checker in to draft me number one, you know, as a pitcher. So I really didn't know what was gonna happen. And I was drafted number two by the Orioles. Part of me wanted to actually not be drafted by the Orioles, to kind of step out of Dad's shadow a little bit, and part of me, the majority of me wanted to be drafted by the Orioles because it was my team, it was close, and it was part of the dream. And I remember then entering into some sort of negotiations, and my dad was sort of an adviser and sort of an agent at the same time.

I got drafted in 1978 and the issue at that point was I was a high school kid, seventeen years old turning eighteen in August, so I was young. And I didn't really have much interest in going to college. But the thought process around that time was, Dad said, look, you know, I want to get the real talent into the minor league system and if you want to have college as a backup plan, you want to find out if you can play, let's ask for that in the contract negotiations. So in 1978, I think the bonus, the total was twenty grand cash.

I think I had an incentive of $7,500. As you progressed to the minor leagues, I think it was $1,000 right away, maybe $2,500 Double-A. And then when you got to the big leagues, it was another 5,000 bucks. So I had that working for me. And I think my first contract was worth $500 a month. I remember that in Bluefield, West Virginia, because after taxes, we had $406 to spend for our rent and everything else. And the good part about it was we found an old house. Mrs. Short had a house that was there. She took in four ballplayers. She only charged a hundred bucks a month apiece, which included two meals a day and your laundry.

You couldn't beat that sort of deal. So at the end of the day, I think we made a little money on $500. The next year was in Miami. I made $700 a month at that time, and the rent exceeded that right from the start, so I lost money in the Florida State League. But it was a good start. It wasn't about the money. It was about trying to develop and prove yourself as a baseball player.

As soon as I got to the minor leagues, I started to gaze at the talent around, and there was a lot of older guys there that came out of college, some were twenty-two, twenty-three years old. And all of a sudden they were in different levels of development, and then that confidence turned into being scared, thinking, okay, I was a pretty big fish in a small pond, but I'm a really small fish right now. And I remember there was a guy by the name of Bob Bonner, who was a shortstop from Texas A&M, that got drafted in the fourth round, I think.

That was two rounds behind me and I was taking ground balls with him. I thought he was the greatest thing I've ever seen. He had a great, strong arm. He could catch the ball. He was more fluid. He turned double plays as quick as lightning. And I kept thinking to myself, I'm never gonna make it, I'm never gonna play. As a matter of fact, I called home and told my dad, you know, this guy, I can't beat this guy out. He's way better than I am. And he said, always remember, wherever you are, you belong in that level, okay?

And two days later, they sent Bob Bonner to Double-A. He was far advanced for that level, so they sent him up the ladder, which then brought the shortstop position back to me and allowed me to develop at that point. And in a few short years, I had caught Bob Bonner and essentially passed him on the way to the big leagues.

When I got drafted, in the negotiations, there was a difference of opinion inside the Orioles organization about what to do with me. The scout assigned to me, Dick Bowie, said, I want him to play shortstop. And I think the director of scouting at that point said, no, he's pitching. He's a can't-miss pitching prospect. And that conversation internally in the organization took on another level. And Dad and Earl Weaver got into that conversation. I believe Hank Peters also got into that conversation.

Hank Peters was the general manager at that time, Tom Giordano was the director of scouting, and Dick Bowie was the scout assigned to me. They said, look, you know, if we're unsure about him and we're split apart, in my experience in development in our organization, you can take a guy and start him out as a regular player, and if he doesn't work out or if he doesn't develop like we think he is, you can always then go to pitching.

But it's very difficult to put him in at pitching first to determine if he could make it pitching, and then put him back, because he's missed some of his development in hitting and it's too big a window to really close. Now, that could've been a really cool way of getting me what I wanted, and ultimately I was asked, okay, Cal, we don't know what we're gonna do: What do you want to do? I was called into a meeting with Mr. Peters and I said, well, and it's ironic looking back on it, but I said, pitchers only get to play one in every five days in professional baseball. I want to play every day.

And they allowed me to do that. And the funny part about it was, talk about scrutiny and pressure. When I went in there, having made the decision and then seeing Bob Bonner at shortstop then having moved up, I think I made 32 errors in that short season, that sixty-game season, and I think I made 9 or 10 of them in the first week.

When I first came in after Bob Bonner got sent up, we had an exhibition game and I hit a home run that went through the light tower in left-center field. So, again, I was feeling pretty good. I didn't have a lot of power to my credit and my stats in high school. But all of a sudden, I said, okay, yeah, I could hit the ball over the fence and now I proved I can hit it over the fence in a game. Then I went to the next sixty-some games, where I didn't have a homer at all. I had a big goose egg on my homer column, and I didn't hit a homer all the way through, but I showed some signs. I think I hit .260, .264, drove in some runs, got some hits, hit some doubles where there was enough there that they thought that I was developing.

I got invited to instructional league. I went down to instructional league to work on hitting and also fielding, and that development process really started.

I graduated high school at six-two, about 180, maybe 185. So I was like Mark Belanger. Mark Belanger was a shortstop that played for the Orioles for many years. His nickname was Blade. So I was more tall and lean. And then I went on to grow almost three more inches after that and put on the feedlot consequently. But when I went in there at shortstop, throwing was the most difficult part, consistently getting the ball across the diamond. I was throwing every possible way I could. I was told to catch it, get up there, and then don't try to just lollipop it over there, put something on it. So I threw mostly overhand. And, you know, once the mental part of throwing the ball away starts to build, then you have less confidence about being able to do it. And I was having trouble with the timing on the speed of the game, because when you go from high school to pro ball, with guys getting down the line much faster, you have to execute your plays a little faster. And I was having difficulty knowing when to rush and when not to rush, and those sorts of things, which affected my throwing.

So when I went to instructional league, I started to solve that a little bit, started to become a little bit more accurate. They took a couple of shortstops down there. And to my great advantage, one of the shortstops became ill or hurt or injured and they sent him home, and they didn't replace him with another one, so I played all forty-five games at shortstop down there and made really great strides. The next year, I played shortstop the early part of the season in Miami, Florida, and the same sort of thing came back where I made a lot of errors in the beginning. I was out there working hard to try to control my throws. That was 1979 in the Florida State League A ball.

So I went from rookie ball, which is the Appalachian League in Bluefield, to Miami, which was our A ball affiliate, Florida State League. And then we had an injury. Our number one pick, by the name of Bob Boyce, got hit with a pitch and broke his wrist, so we didn't have a third baseman. So we had two shortstops on the team when I was there, and my size had started to take over and they said, well, let's move you over to third base. When I went to third base, my throwing problems got solved really quickly because the timing was different.

I started à la Graig Nettles. I saw Graig Nettles perform in the World Series, have a wonderful Series with the Yankees, and I started to look at him and I started to emulate his style over there. And I found out that I could be really accurate with that particular style of throw. So I did so well at third base as a defensive player, and my offense really started to pick up at that point, that they said, he's built for third base. Let's leave him at third base. And basically, I stayed at third base, you know, from that point all the way until I got to the big leagues, when Earl Weaver had the idea to put me back in my rookie year.

There was certainly an Orioles way and it was very, very evident when I was young and growing up in it. Did I have the capacity to fully understand what that meant? No. But there was a great pride in the Orioles' success and there was a great pride in how they taught and their philosophy, and it was made up by people that paid attention to the game. And they essentially took what worked and kept developing it and then discarded the things that didn't work. And they developed systems, whether it's bunt plays, whether it's cutoff and relays, whether it's just normal strategies of the game, or normal secrets of development.

They were there to develop the player, not necessarily develop winning, at the lower levels. They wanted to win at the big league level, but they were developing the tools and the talent to get to that point. They had such a good system. And I'll tell you, at the same time, the Dodgers were considered a very good fundamental organization at new baseball. And many of the game's managers came out of both those organizations or models. They looked to those organizations for the expertise to have success in other organizations.

And Dad, I remember, would address the minor league guys as a group when they were in spring training. And one of his opening lines was, welcome to the greatest organization in baseball. You know, it's great to be young and an Oriole. And he said, if you make it through our system, you will play in the big leagues. Might not be with us, but you'll play in the big leagues if you make it through our system. So that's how that whole thing started, and they all believed that. And the Orioles had people sprinkled around all over the big leagues because you could only develop one third baseman. You couldn't play two third basemen at a time, two shortstops. They made timely decisions. They traded players at the right time, and they were sprinkled all over the place. So there was a great sense of pride.

I can remember my dad's style of teaching. I think he really understood that you couldn't teach in the moment of the game. You know, that was for the experience of understanding how to play the game, and Dad would keep track on the pitcher's chart. The pitcher who's gonna pitch tomorrow would keep the chart in the dugout, and when something happened in the game, whether it was situational, whether it was something else, he would ask the guy to make a note or put a little red dot on the game chart.

And then after the game was over, he would replay the whole game in his mind from the game chart and then take his little three-by-five index cards and write out the individual lesson that he wanted to talk to the player about the next day. So then he would have maybe six or eight or ten cards sitting on his desk, and he would lay them out and then he'd put them away, get dressed, and go home. The next day he'd come there early at one in the afternoon for a seven o'clock game, and he put his uniform on really quickly and then he'd get his cards out.

He'd spread them out on his desk and he would wait for someone to come through the door that was on one of his cards. And when they came through the door, he would say, can I have a minute with you? And he would say, I want to re-create something that happened in the game last night, and he would talk about it openly. And, you know, the emotions would die down. He knew what he wanted to say. The player didn't feel like he had done something wrong. There was a value to that sort of moment. And thirty seconds, sometimes to two and a half minutes, it would take to actually do this, and the guy would get the situation. And then before he sent him out the door, he said, by the way, I love how you're playing, I love how aggressive you are. And they'd walk out with a bounce in their step. Philosophy helps you learn the game. Now, another thing is, bunt plays or things were taught in the same way in Bluefield A ball, Double-A, Triple-A, all the way up. So when you got to do the bunt plays, when you're in big leagues spring training, it was a refresher. Bunt plays or rundowns, when you had to go over those things, it was just a refresher to you. It wasn't teaching.

You know, you've done all those things and you already learned the principles of those rundowns, and the cumulative effect allowed you to execute them better and better and better. When I came to the minor leagues, quite frankly, it wasn't that way. You know, there was some teaching. I knew how to do that, but each of the different managers or different people at different organizations had backgrounds from other places and not all of them did it the Orioles' Way or the same way. They had their own opinions. And the hard part was to remember and be respectful of the ways that the manager at the time wanted you to do it but also remember what the Orioles' way was.

And I remember Dad used to always tell me, no, son, that's not the right way, that's not the Oriole way, but you've got to do it that way because that's your manager. But remember what the right way is. And he said, no matter what, you're gonna run into many different managers, many different coaches along the way, and some you're gonna think know a whole lot, some you're gonna think don't, but there's always at least one thing you can add to your game from every manager. Sometimes you've got to look a little harder for that one thing.

The year 1980 was my breakout year. I hit 25 home runs, 80 RBIs, whatever the numbers turned out to be. And all of this at the age of nineteen. I hit in the middle of the order and I was the third base-man, I was the all-star in that league, Double-A, in Miami. So that was a breakout year, and they kept me there the whole year of 1980.

And then after the '80 season I was asked to go to winter ball, which was in Puerto Rico at the time. I had been to two instructional leagues in the off-season in my first two years, the '78 instructional league and the '79 instructional league. And then my breakout year in '80, first time I played every game, by the way. I played 144 games. My manager in 1980 was Jimmy Williams. He was in the Dodgers organization, then they brought him over, a great baseball guy. My dad had a lot of respect for Jimmy, and Jimmy was very instrumental in shaping me as a player. And I remember at the halfway point, he was gonna rest his regulars. And he went around and asked everybody, I'm gonna give you three days off, and he asked me, and I said I didn't want them. And he said, okay, and he allowed me to play. If there was any foreshadowing that might take place—I played 144 games and I never was so tired in the last week of August.

My numbers were really good, and going down the stretch I couldn't get a hit. So my numbers kind of stayed where they were, and then I got reenergized for the playoffs. We won the Southern League pennant that particular year. And then I took a week off and went to winter ball. When I was down there, Ray Miller was the manager in Caguas, Puerto Rico. I'm one of the youngest guys on the team. They didn't have guys coming out of Double-A at that time. There was mostly Triple-A, a lot of big league guys.

And I came in there and turned out to be the team MVP. Played well, did well, and then that went all the way up until February. So I came home for a week and then I had to report to spring training. That was my first big league spring training.

I was a typical kid going away, as you'd go away to college. People ask me all the time, you didn't go to college, you missed that sort of fun or that exploration or independence that every kid goes through. And I said, well, I went to the minor leagues. I played the game during the night and could sleep until two or three in the afternoon if I wanted to every day. And all those things, the staying up late, going out with your friends, going to different places, they were all temptations that I succumbed to in many ways, but it's all part of growing up. It's about being part of a team. We all had a lot of things in common. In the big leagues, you get there, a lot of people are married, you already get into different stages in your life, but in the minor leagues, you are like a college team in many ways, so you act like college kids. And I certainly did, but at the same time, you knew the importance of food for your body, rest for your body, because you had to perform and this was your chance.

And I think, growing up around the minor league model and listening to my dad advise other people and witnessing other people throwing it away by either staying out too late at night or running around all the time and not taking what they did seriously, it fully affected their ability to make it. In some cases, they were released and let go for other reasons besides baseball. And that always resonated with me. Clearly, I knew why I was there and what I really loved to do, and I hated not being successful.

So I really placed a big emphasis on sleep because I needed it. Eating regularly, you know? It brings me back to one of the bits of advice that my dad said: When you're going to the minor leagues and not making any money, don't be afraid to dip into your savings. Go spend your own money to actually eat right because you need to fuel your body.

So I think, logically, it was an advantage to be around professional ball. It was an advantage to understand other people's mistakes. But I didn't look at it as baseball taking away my fun off the field. No. I could have fun on the field. I could have some fun off the field, but let's keep a balance in place so you can perform, because that's what you're there to do.

Brooks Robinson was my childhood hero growing up. I think he did a lot of things right as a baseball player. But he was a good person.

Brooks Robinson

And I think in some ways, a lot of the people growing up around Baltimore might have been conveniently brainwashed by their parents, pointing Brooks Robinson out because of his character, who he was as a person, as well as the talent that he displayed on the field.

And I emulated him, at third, when I got to third base, I tried to be Brooksie. And I tried to do all the things that Brooksie did. Nobody said a bad word about Brooksie. He was always the most popular guy everybody aspired to be. And maybe you don't understand at first why he was that popular, why he was a nice guy, why nobody said anything bad about him. He was a great player. But my parents knew that if you want to be like somebody, you should be like Brooksie.

Now, in the minor leagues, my dad managed many guys that

turned out to be big league players. One of the guys who took a special interest in me was Doug DeCinces. Doug DeCinces always had time for me, always had a kind word to say about me, always would show me how to do things as an infielder and as a player. Doug replaced Brooksie at the big league level. But at the time, I think he was toggling back and forth between second and third, middle infielder. And he was really helpful to me.

And the irony is, when I broke through the big leagues, in order to make room for me on the big league roster, they traded Doug DeCinces. But Doug always was very helpful to me. And I remember coming back to Dad many times and saying, Doug told me that I should spread my legs out, put my butt down, and get my hands out front for a ground ball. Is that right? And he'd say, yes, that's right. So I knew that Doug was the person I was gonna continue to go to. And he really was nice to me and really made me feel really comfortable. So, he was really probably my minor league model. And there was Al Bumbry. Al Bumbry was on my dad's team in Double-A and there wasn't a faster guy in the whole league. There wasn't one that smiled and laughed as much as Al Bumbry.

Ron Shapiro was my agent. And it's always funny when I tell a story about Ron. Many agents are coming out to recruit you, especially when you establish yourself at Double-A, and now you have a chance to make it to the big leagues. There's a value there. So I played the agent game in the next spring training and everybody came to me to solicit my services, and they wanted to take me out to dinner. Some would send a limo and put me in a car and take me out to dinner and wine and dine me and tell me why they want to come on.

And many of them were very showy. They dressed in really nice suits, had a whole group of people with them, you know, festive party situation. It was like that with some of the coolest ones. But the thing that resonated the most from Ron Shapiro was he did none of those things. He had me over to his office. He ordered in tuna fish sandwiches and we talked about the substance of what was going on, not the fluff. And to me, that whole agent game was more about the fluff and it was sort of artificial.

And in the end, I talked to my mom and my dad about it or whatever else. And the fact that Ron wasn't any of those things gave him the advantage. And I signed with Ron Shapiro as an agent. He was a wonderful agent for me, but he was a wonderful adviser, for the different life changes and the decisions. I played in the same place for twenty-one years and most people would think that I didn't go through change, but I went through a lot of change. I think I had nine different managers, maybe ten different general managers, and many different rebuilding processes. And there were three owner-ship changes, too.

So, in order to stay there, you had to actually make a decision not necessarily based on where the value of your money is, but where do you want to play? Can you withstand the rebuilding process? Where do you want to live?

But I moved from Double-A to Triple-A. I had maybe one or two guys that went from the championship team up to Triple-A with me as we started off. And then Triple-A started out so wonderfully, got off to a great start and I really never looked back to continue the same sort of hitting and those things that I had done in Double-A.

I was the league leader in home runs. I hit three home runs in a game for the first time in my career in Rochester, and I felt that I had a chance to be on my way at that point.

In 1981, I'm knocking on the door of coming to the big leagues. And I could have gotten called up earlier but there was a rumor of a work stoppage, a strike that was gonna happen as a form of leverage from the players to get negotiations started. None of that stuff mattered as much to me at that point. It was just developing and playing baseball.

And that strike stopped me from coming to the big leagues a little earlier than I would have, as Doug DeCinces got hurt and I was on the doorstep of being called up, but they didn't want to have me frozen in the big leagues and not playing so they locked me down.

Now, in a great, wonderful, positive way, I always believed when things happen, and sometimes in a negative way, there's always a silver lining. There was no baseball in the big leagues as the strike went on for the majority of that summer—I think baseball started again in early August. But when the strike was on, television started popping down to cover the Triple-A games, and therefore, I started to come on the radar and get some coverage down there. And I started to be looked upon as one of the better prospects in the International League. Once the strike was over, they expanded the rosters by two, which was my entry to the big leagues.

So in some ways, the strike was a good thing even though it was a bad thing for baseball and it's, you know, it's a shame that the business side and the collective-bargaining agreement get in the way of the season for fans and for all of the players. But in this particular case, I came to the big leagues after the strike was over and spent from August 1981 to the end of September on a big league roster. I think I only got 39 at-bats.

When I first got called to the big leagues, it seemed to me like the biggest stage. You know, again, you go through a little bit of fear, and adrenaline starts to come through you, and Earl Weaver liked to get you in there as soon as possible. And I think in the first opportunity I had, my debut was as a pinch-runner for Ken Singleton. Ken Singleton hit a double and I came running on the field to run for him. I never was known for my wheels, but I could run okay and score on doubles. And he looked at me and said, you're going to run for me?

And he started laughing and shook my hand and went off the field. John Lowenstein hit a ball down the right-field line and I scored the winning run in the game so I didn't do anything but actually touch home plate on the play, and I got mobbed a little bit for having success. That was my first chance to be on that big stage. But when I ran out of the dugout to second base, now I was in the middle of the stage and the lights were all shining on me and I was kind of looking around and there was a sort of a moment that I thought,

God, this is really terrifying. But yes, it's really exciting at the same time.

Frank White, it was against the Kansas City Royals, Frank White was the second baseman. And immediately, he put a pickoff play on on the very first play. And he caught the ball, I got back safely, and he says, just checking, kid, and went back to his position. Was I so nervous that I'd actually be a deer in the headlights and wouldn't be able to get back? He checked on that and then that started the whole process.

Shortly thereafter, I started the game at third base, and Paul Splittorff was the pitcher, a big left-handed pitcher. And my first at-bat, a little bit conservative, I get behind. I think there were two strikes. He throws me a fastball. I hit a chopper over the mound that's heading into center field, my very first at-bat. And from my vantage point, as I'm running down, nobody is even close to it. It looks like it's gonna be a clean hit to center field, my first big league hit.

And then out of nowhere, Frank White comes into the picture, catches it on the backhand, jumps up in the air, and throws. And I jump at first base and he throws me out by just a smidgen. And so my hit that was gonna be a hit turns into an out. And I run back into the dugout and someone in the dugout, I think it was Ken Singleton, said, welcome to the big leagues. In case you don't know, that's Mr. Frank White. And then the whole process started.

It took me, I think, seven or eight at-bats to get my first hit. And I remember George Brett asked me, you get your first hit yet? George Brett was the third baseman for the Kansas City Royals, Hall of Fame player. And I go, no. And he goes, how many at-bats you got? And I go, about seven. And he started laughing, really uncontrollably out loud, you know, and kind of went away and, you know. And I remember those sorts of feelings. But those same guys, they are the characters of the game. And in a way, they were trying to make me feel comfortable in the big leagues, I believe.

The Orioles were a classy organization and they had good-quality people. Not only did they have good players, but they had good-quality people, and they prided themselves on that. So everybody was pretty similar in welcoming me there and making me feel comfortable, those sorts of things. Jim Palmer certainly was. He was reminding me that he knew me when I was four and those sorts of things. But everybody else genuinely came over and shook your hand and brought you in.

Eddie Murray probably was one of the most influential people because I think Eddie could feel a similarity between his situation, coming to the big leagues, you know, being a young guy, and my situation, coming to the big leagues and how I would feel. And I think he knew that inside. So he went out of his way to kind of include me in going with him, going to events, doing things, offering advice. So Eddie probably went out of his way more than anybody else to make me feel welcome.

My first full year in the big leagues was 1982. And we went into spring training with a pretty good nucleus of a team and good pitching. The Orioles always prided themselves on pitching and that's the reason they were successful to that point. We had some pretty decent hitters as well.

And in the '82 season, I'm thinking, as an Orioles fan and somebody that watched the recent history, you know, we're struggling along, we're under .500. I'm thinking, how in the world did a team like this win a hundred games, you know, because that's almost 20 games over .500. When are we gonna get 20 games over .500? And as we're going along, the Milwaukee Brewers were in first place. We were chasing them as we went down the stretch. And as the year went on, Earl Weaver got his team. He got the engine running and we started knocking off games and we started winning and we started catching up. That was the year we went down to the last four games of the season against Milwaukee. We were three back with four to play. We won the first three games, including a doubleheader in Baltimore. So the whole season came down to one game, game number 162 of the season. And Jim Palmer was pitching, hadn't been beaten, I think, in 15 games. Don Sutton came in and pitched for the Brewers. He came over in a trade. Robin Yount decided to spoil every-thing for the Orioles, hit a couple of home runs, he was the MVP that year, and Milwaukee went on to play in the World Series.

Now, that particular team, all of a sudden, you realize you were a good team, you know? We all watched the celebration for Milwau-kee. And the very next year, 1983, we almost went wire to wire and won the whole thing. We won the World Series. But it was the expe-rience of '82 and us internalizing that and the slow start we got off on that there was an attitude coming into spring training that we could have made up that one game anywhere along the year before. Let's not set ourselves up for that.

So in 1983 we got off to a much better start and we played really well. Now, having said that, I thought my career was gonna be all about being in the playoffs and having a chance to win the World Series all the time. The most satisfying feeling by far came on the 1983 World Series team. I caught a little humpback liner from Garry Maddox, closed my glove around that ball, and the sense of accom-plishment, sense of fulfillment is off the charts. I've had laps around the ballpark, the game-winning home runs. I've been celebrated at the All-Star games. I've done a lot of individual things that are pretty cool. But for the feeling that I'm talking about, nothing at all is even close to that one. My regret is that I didn't feel it again. I didn't feel it enough, and you long for that.

By the '87 season, my dad finally got a chance to manage the club. We were clearly in a rebuilding process or whatever else, but wouldn't admit to it publicly. We didn't win a whole lot of games in '88, my dad's second year as a manager. And then after the first six games of the season, he was fired and Frank Robinson replaced him and then we went on to lose fifteen more so we were part of the team that was 0–21.

And then rebuilding was recognized as where the organization was heading; we're on ground zero and we're gonna start over. And so then from that point on, it was, you know, a series of rebuilding processes. And I think, looking back on it, the most challenging part of my career was wanting to play for a winner but enduring and dealing with the transition and the change of the Orioles' way into something else and then trying to hold on to some of the principles and the values that I was taught under Dad from the Orioles' way and trying to keep that alive. You're able to make some contributions to a point, but you weren't really able to affect the whole thing.

So the challenging part of that was after Dad was manager. I could have left as a free agent at the end of that year, but I made a conscious decision that I was young enough to withstand a rebuilding process. The Orioles were the team that I really wanted and I was willing to endure that to get to the other side. And that was really looking inside yourself and saying, okay, I'm from here. This is where I want to live. This is where I want to raise my kids. This is a decision that's a life decision as well as a baseball decision.

I think I was shaped and molded by my dad, that it's a sense of responsibility to be a player and come to the ballpark and play every day. And you couldn't play 100 percent healthy all the time. If you're a professional baseball player, you're playing every day, you've got to figure out how to make contributions when you're less than 100 percent. And I would argue that you're probably less than 100 percent for 99 percent of the time. There were stories that my dad as a catcher would have, where he'd get a foul ball hit off his finger and his finger would split open, you know? And even Earl Weaver, who managed my dad in the minor leagues, would come out and say, come on, Rip, we've got to take you out of here.

He'd say, no, you manage the game over there. Put a little tape on this and I'll keep playing. That was sort of the stories that I grew up with. Having a dad that's on the team when I got called up, there's sort of an expectation that you come out and play. Now, there's an honor being that sort of player and being considered a gamer that you come to the big leagues ready to play, but it's still a responsibility of the manager to choose the lineup, to choose who plays, and that's really when the streak happened.

I had Earl Weaver as a manager, and it was a fact that he wanted to put me in the lineup. Now, in my first full year, I was 3-5 Opening Day, and then I went 4 for my next 63. And there were times when he could have taken me out of the lineup, and he did take me out once early on, but he kept playing me through those periods or whatever else because he knew what he had on the other side. And I often look back and think that when I first came in, there might have been pressure for him to send me back, to sit me down, whatever else.

But Earl had the bigger picture in place and then I eventually caught fire, became the Rookie of the Year in the first year, and he kept playing me. Now Earl retired. Joe Altobelli came in and I was an everyday player at that point. I was hitting third in the lineup and Joe just put the lineup out there. And for 162 games, I didn't come out, not for an inning, not for a game. Nothing, I just played all the way through those games and responded and played well and I was voted the MVP and had a great season and a great month of September.

So, as the subsequent years happened, as the manager sat in his office, he made that lineup out and my name was in that lineup every single day. Nobody talked about the streak, nobody talked about playing all the games. It was your responsibility to play. And all of a sudden the accumulation of, you know, five, six, seven years all of a sudden gets to be a thousand games or so. It approaches the National League record and then there started to be some sort of understanding of that. But I still had the exact same approach as I did for Earl Weaver when I was 4-for-63, that my job was to come, be ready to play. And if the manager chose you, you played. It was as simple as that. And those middle years got to be a little foggy because rebuilding had taken place and all of a sudden there was blame to go around and people were pointing their fingers all over the place about why we weren't winning, what happened to the Oriole organization. I got a finger pointed at me. Eddie Murray got a finger pointed at him. All those things happened and there were some negative periods where I felt that I had to defend the fact that a ballplayer would come to the big leagues and come to the game that day and want to play.

And that's all it was all those years. And after you endured those middle-of-the-road things and then you started to turn that around, then it ultimately became a positive and a lot of the critics then turned out to be supporters. And some even say that it was really good for the game of baseball. There were two close calls about the streak. One was an ankle, and it was really early on, before it was a streak. So I think it was about 1985. I had a pickoff play at second base in a day game, Opening Day. Caught my cleats on the top of the bag and my ankle turned all the way under, sprained my ankle really bad. I taped it up really tight, finished the game, everything turned out fine. As soon I took the tape off, it blew up, got it X-rayed, and it wasn't broken. We had Thursday off. It was an exhibition game against the Naval Academy.

So I spent all of Thursday in rehab, trying to get the swelling out and I missed the game at the Naval Academy and somebody actually wrote that my streak was over because I missed the game at the Naval Academy. And then Friday night was a game against the Blue Jays. I believe it was an eight o'clock game. So I really had almost two full days to get the swelling out. I taped it up really tight. And in this game, baseball, you can't hide any sort of injury. I had to actually beat out an infield hit with a really bad ankle to score a guy from third base. I hit a ball back to the mound and it deflected off the pitcher's glove. I had to hurry to get to first base, jump at the bag. It hurt like crazy jumping on the bag. But the run scored and it proved to me that, hey, I'm gonna be okay with that. So I played through that. It took a little while for the ankle to get better.

The streak didn't matter. It wasn't the motivating force. It was the fact that you should play if you can. And I did everything I could to play, and they put you in the lineup and you play. I had another knee injury. The knee injury I had that was really a close call was in a brawl. It was against the Seattle Mariners. Mike Mussina had hit

Bill Haselman after he had hit a home run. There had been some issues early in the game about them throwing at us. That resulted in Bill charging the mound.

And I went in to help Mussina on the ground or whatever else. And I realized he was okay because our first baseman, Paul Carey, was already there. And I turned my attention to the whole Seattle Mariners dugout. And for a brief moment, I thought I could stop a whole dugout from jumping onto the pile. And as I turned toward them, my cleats caught in the grass and I heard a big pop in my right knee. So then I end up on the bottom of the pile on my back, not a good place to be in a brawl, and worked my way out of that and then everything was kind of pushed to the side, all the action was over.

And then I had to hit the next inning. So I came to the on-deck circle and I felt this pain start to develop in my right knee. It really hurt to push off of it to swing, so I took my at-bat. I don't really remember what I did, the game was really out of hand at that point, and then I went in and told the doctors. And the next day, I woke up and tried to put my foot on the ground to get out of bed and I couldn't put any weight on it. And I was really scared and worried about it, so it got to a point where I couldn't walk, I couldn't play.

So I called up, I told my wife I wanted to play, but I called up my mom and my dad and I said, I just want to give you a heads-up. I haven't got it checked out yet, but I mean, I hurt my knee in the brawl yesterday. It looks like I can't walk, so I probably can't play. And my mom and dad lived forty-five minutes from my house. And in exactly forty-five minutes, they were at my door. And so I iced it and I talked to the trainer. I did some different treatments or whatever else. I exercised it toward the end of the day. And I started to get a little feeling in my leg and I started to have some movement, went to the ballpark, continued that sort of treatment, and then the moment came and I said, okay, can I play or can I play?

And I said, well, I have to go test it. So I tested it privately in the cages of Camden Yards to see if it was okay. And I could hold on to it a little bit and I went out and played in the game. Now, again, baseball will find any sort of weakness you have right away. As soon as I got to the field in the first inning, I was playing shortstop, there was a two-hopper hit in the hole, I think the very first play of the game. I had to go backhand the two-hopper and then plant, with all my momentum stopped on my right leg. And I'm thinking in the middle of doing this, it's either gonna hold or it's not.

And I put my knee down there, it held okay. It hurt, and I made a good throw to first base and I thought, I'm gonna be okay. So I got through that. Those were the two really difficult injuries. There were many times when you had injuries, you hyperextend your elbow sliding into a base, and you don't know if you'll be able to do it or not. This really probably proves the point a little bit better, that you play for the purpose of playing. Maybe the only time in my whole life that I thought I was selfish for trying to play with an injury was when I herniated a disc in my back in 1997. I went in and got the X-rays and they said it's a herniation. They said, okay, you're done. You're out for six weeks. And I started to question the doctor a little further. I said, okay, look. Can I do any permanent damage to my knee? And he goes, I don't think you can right now but, you know, you can't play with this. The pain is so bad, you're not getting the signal to your leg and all that stuff. And I said, okay, if I can endure the pain, will I be doing any serious damage? So I tried it and it was the worst sort of pain in the world.

But we were in 1997 and this was two years after the streak was broken. The record was broken. The celebration was all, was all there. But we were good. We were good for the first time in a long time. We made the playoffs in '96. We're beating the Yankees from the first day of the season to the last, and it was July. And we're in the pennant race and we have a lead. And Robbie Alomar, I think, went down. I think that was the year that Eric Davis was diagnosed with cancer. So we were starting to break down a little bit and I'm sitting there thinking, I'm not sitting on the sidelines of this.

If I can, I want to play. So I went out there and tested it, and I didn't have the same sort of mobility or movement and I had to do a lot of things or whatever else. But from that point until September 1, I was able to contribute and push them back and score some runs, had a big series in Yankee Stadium. One of the most gratifying things I've done, one of the hardest things I've ever done, is play through a herniated disc in my back, and it had nothing to do with the record. It had nothing to do with the streak. It had everything to do with being part of a team that won.

Frank Robinson was really, really instrumental in sharing his experiences as a player with me and taking me on as a personal hitting coach and actually pulling me back from that time when I had a lot of doubts about the longevity of my skills.

So, the '91 season, I had one of my best years and became the

Frank Robinson

MVP at that time, but there was the period before that, I think it was 1990, the year before, that Frank actually brought me back as a hitter and got me fundamentally back strong again or whatever else and the second half of the '90 season was really good. I dedicated myself to working out harder and continuing what I had done with Frank. And then once the '91 season started, you know, I hit .450 or close to .500 in spring training and that seemed to carry on all the way through the season. It didn't seem like I had a problem or a slump.

But it was really Frank who was instrumental in taking a special interest in me and giving of himself. And he really kind of guided me on the right path. The '91 season was directly related to Frank Robinson taking a special interest in me.

In 1996, B. J. Surhoff and Bobby Bonilla were the choices to play third base out of spring training. Davey Johnson chose B.J. and put Bobby Bo in a DH role and then ultimately in right field. When B.J. got hurt, Davey came to me and said, you know, I'm thinking about playing you at third. This was out of the blue. I said, well, B.J. is only gonna be on the disabled list for fifteen days. Is this something that you really want to do?

We decided that I would come to the ballpark early and we went down to a private area and started discussing that. We went through the whole thing about the move over to third base and whether it's permanent and all that kind of stuff. And it turned out to be temporary. He wasn't that passionate about it. He was just thinking about ways in which he could improve the team. I think he wanted to get a look at Manny Alexander. He wanted to play him.

I don't know the full story, but it ended up not happening at that particular time. And then later on, it did happen. And then I went over to third base and then played there and played pretty well, and then he asked me to come back to that. Now, the only thing that I would say is Earl Weaver didn't ask me to go play short. He just said, I want you to play short. It would be better for the team. And if that had been told to me, I want you to play third, I think it would be better for the team, then I'd do that normally and naturally.

So sometimes, it just felt like things weren't always done the way that I would like them to be done—not that I would like them to be done as a baseball guy but just as a normal way of doing things. The only controversy there was maybe in the way it was handled or the way it was thought of or the way that I was thought of. I moved the next year to third, to make way for Mike Bordick. In the process of that whole move, I went to Japan and had a wonderful year. In '96, we ended up in the playoffs.

I hit 26 home runs, drove in 102 runs, went over and represented the All-Star team in Japan as a shortstop over there. And while I'm in Japan, I'm getting stories written about me that I've lost three steps or those sorts of things. And I don't understand why you need to do that sort of stuff, and I suspect that it came from inside our organization. So, when I came back, I wanted to kind of bring everybody together and say, are we not all on the same team, because if you say you want to improve the left side of the infield because you want to put Bordick at short and me at third, that's your right, that's what you want to do, and I would agree with you.

So what's the big problem? What's the big deal? So I don't know what the whole issue was. There was never any real controversy about whether I was willing to do anything. I would have gone over there in a heartbeat just like I did in my first year. Earl Weaver never consulted with me. He just put me over there.

So that was the controversy and I don't know how it was played out. The only other thing I can say was that Davey, when we had a discussion and we decided that we were gonna keep it between us, he told the media. And then I confronted him on that. I didn't harbor any sort of resentment about it. Matter of fact, Davey was a breath of fresh air. As a manager, he came back and he guided us to '96 and '97, and I couldn't be more happy that he was the manager that did that. I was a little bit unhappy that he didn't manage in '98.

In '96 and '97 we came back to respectability and you just stick your chest out that we made the playoffs. They were great, fun years for us. And in '98, there were high expectations. We had virtually the same team, but we didn't accomplish that. In thinking about the streak and thinking about going through it, there were a lot of things going on at that time and I thought that the timing was right.

And the way that I rationalized it in my own mind was saying, look, I have an obligation to continue to come out. It would be the same exact approach all the way through until it doesn't matter anymore. And it wouldn't matter anymore if we fell out of the playoff run. Then I was gonna end the streak and put it back to where it was from the very beginning where the manager, with all the freedom in the world, could decide who was gonna play without feeling that he was restricted. And in some ways, I said, okay, I'll turn the clock back and I'll guarantee you, you'll still pick me. I thought that I'd take the last day of the season off, and it turned out to be in Boston that particular year. I discussed it with only one person, my wife. She started talking about it and she said, I understand what you're saying, and in some ways you kind of want to make a little statement. You could have played 162 if you wanted. But you know, you end up on the road. If this thing is gonna end, it should be a celebration. It should be a celebration with all the people that have gone there with you and you should do it at home. And it just so happened that the last home game that year was against the New York Yankees. I waited until ten minutes before the game started. I was in the lineup, everything was normal, all that kind of stuff, then I went to Ray Miller, our manager, and I said tonight is the night that the streak is gonna end.

He kind of looked at me really baffled and puzzled and said, okay. And he called up to John Maroon, who was a public relations guy, to bring him down. And I told him, I said, look, guys, I don't want to make a big deal out of it before the game. I waited until ten minutes before, not to put you in a bad situation, but I wanted to deal with this after it's all over. I want it to unfold, however it's gonna unfold, and then I'll talk to the media. I'll talk to everybody. But now let's just make it unfold.

And my thinking was, you know, it's too late to change the line-ups. All of a sudden, you just run out on the field and then it'll gradually start to be noticed that I'm not there, and then we'll see what happens. And the real cool part about it was that the Yankees recognized it very early, very fast. I don't know if it was Boomer Wells or Derek Jeter or Joe Torre or who it was. All of a sudden, they all kind of got up and looked at me in the dugout. And when Ryan Minor took the field they started clapping.

They knew what it meant, what it represented, and it really turned into a wonderful tribute and a wonderful celebration. And then the whole crowd started to understand what it was and then the buzz started to unfold and went all across the country and the world. And I treated it as a celebration. I felt like I was on the outside. I never had not played the game and I thought I'd sit in the dugout, see what it felt like to sit in the dugout, thought I'd feel what it felt like to be in the bullpen, watch the inning on TV inside.

I mean, when you're out of the game, what do you do? I just felt like I was lost, you know? But, in the end, the fans reacted really great to it, the Yankees reacted really well. It turned out to be the right advice from my wife to treat it as a celebration. I still played every game after that, I still played 161, and I still was approaching the game in the same exact fashion, but the thing called "the streak" was done.

The streak, first of all, happened as a by-product of something else. It didn't happen because I wanted it to happen and it was my life goal to do that. It was a by-product of doing what I thought was the right thing. And what I thought was the right thing came from my dad, who said, you as a baseball player have a responsibility, you know, to the team and you have an individual responsibility as a player to come to the ballpark ready to play, and it's the manager who chooses you to play.

And that's a simple game-by-game sort of analysis that I used every single day. Sure, there were days I didn't feel like playing. There were days where I was tired. There was days where it was hard and it would've been easy not to do it. If I really wanted to look out for myself and really be selfish, I could have picked many days where I wasn't gonna do well. Fifteen-inning game against the Red Sox, you know, the night before, then you got to wake up and face Roger Clemens the next day and you're 0-20, by the way, and you haven't got a hit in four or five games.

Those would have been easy days to say, you know, let me have somebody else deal with that problem. But I thought there was an honor to being part of the team and a sense of obligation and responsibility you had to the other team. When the going got tough, it was more important for you to actually be there to try to meet those challenges. So to me, the wonderful part about the streak is that many people related to the values of the streak, not the number, not the record, but that's how they approached their own lives, that they have the control, they have the power to show up and try to make a difference.

Guys I've played against? I'm tickled to death that a lot of people now don't realize I played against Carl Yastrzemski. And Carl Yastrzemski, at the end, he was so fascinating to me because he was a great player but he made adjustments. He made adjustments all the time. He wasn't satisfied. And in many ways, some of my crazy sort of stances came from witnessing some of the adjustments that Carl Yastrzemski made as he got older to still be good. And, you know, Yaz played a long, long time and I guess our careers crossed over for a couple of years.

During that time frame, it was pretty cool to kind of go back and see that. Some of the guys I played against I absolutely loved playing against and competing with. Probably my number one favorite would be Don Mattingly. Don Mattingly, Donnie Baseball, was, in many ways to many people, an overachiever. He wasn't thought of as having the most talent, although I would argue with that. You know, gritty, understood the game, very intellectual in how he understood the game of baseball.

And talking to him at the All-Star games and competing against him, we spoke the same language. And I really loved his overall attitude of playing the game, the way that he went about it, the honor with which he handled himself. And it was sad to me that—he had a fulfilling career, but I wish that he would've had a chance to play twenty years and be recognized for being the great player that he was in the Hall of Fame. I don't know if he'll have a chance. I certainly hope that he would be in the Hall of Fame.

A couple of talents that I wish that I had of people I played against: one was Ken Griffey Jr. When Ken Griffey Jr. came on the scene, there was nothing that he couldn't do on the baseball field defensively, offensively, power, running the bases, making the right play at the right time. He could do it all. And he did it so easy and he had such a smile about it and he really had happiness toward the sport that I liked.

Alex Rodriguez. Alex Rodriguez came along with the same sort of talent and zest and I just looked at him in awe. And the things that he's been able to accomplish as a baseball player and the way that he goes about playing the game is wonderful.

Eddie Murray really showed me the sense of responsibility, playing every single day, and even though we don't think of Eddie Murray as the streak, if we look up his numbers and look at the amount of games that he played, there was an honor and obligation or responsibility that he felt, far greater than people know. He was the number four hitter in our lineup, he was the stability at first base, and it made a difference if he was in the lineup or not.

And very few people have that sort of perspective. I would say that Eddie Murray probably is the greatest leader by example. You know, maybe Eddie didn't have all the right words to say and he struggled with communicating a message or two from time to time, but he understood the importance of going out there and doing it

Eddie Murray

and he just did it. He was a great example for me, and he did show me the importance of being in the lineup every single day.

There are the number one guys, the starters that are up there on a level by themselves, and you hope to try to make up ground against the two and three and four guys, but this is the big leagues. One of the more terrifying pitchers I faced was Goose Gossage. You know, Goose Gossage just went into the Hall of Fame this past year. A really intimidating sort of presence on the mound.

When I faced him in my very first spring training, I think Doug DeCinces didn't want to face him at that point. But I think he came into the spring training game in Fort Lauderdale, and it was the year, I believe, after the World Series or closely thereabout. I remember seeing the image of him accidentally hitting Ron Cey in the head.

And it looked like it didn't faze him one bit, it looked like he didn't care. That hundred-mile-an-hour fastball, when I faced him, it seemed like my left leg wanted to bleed. I stepped in the bucket when I faced him. He was quite intimidating and you had to figure out a way to get past that.

Nolan Ryan: growing up watching Nolan Ryan, I mean, totally amazing. He pitched until forty-six? Was he forty-six years old when he pitched? Kept himself in marvelous shape, lifted his legs up. I faced him I think for the first time in the All-Star game in '85 in Minnesota. And I thought he was the hardest guy I've ever faced, the hardest velocity guy. And then, he was already about forty years old. Here's a guy with a resilient arm. To me, it was just totally amazing. Great control, great breaking ball, just an explosive guy, I mean,

Nolan Ryan

it was an honor to compete and face him. And the way he handled himself was very professional and marvelous.

The guys that bothered me were the guys that had natural sinkers that ran in, sinker-slider types. Duane Ward comes to mind really quickly. His ball was so heavy. Scott Erickson, those kinds of guys that would run the ball in on you. Yeah, I have trouble getting those sinkers out of there. The guys I absolutely liked to face were the guys that tried to set you up with breaking balls and changeups and those sorts of things, because that was a strategic-thinking way to get you out. And I was all about thinking about what they were doing to me patternwise, and what I could look for. For example, Bert Blyleven was a wonderful pitcher and had a great curveball. And I prided myself on being a good curveball hitter. Every time I faced Bert Blyleven, it was his strength against my strength in many ways. And it always seemed like even if you hit a home run off his breaking ball, he was gonna say, that must not have been my best breaking ball. Here it comes again. And I love that about him. He competed and did those things. Young Roger Clemens coming on the scene. He reminded me a lot of Nolan Ryan. And I'm sure he prided himself on being that way, a power-type pitcher with excellent control. That's a very odd combination to be able to have someone with explosive stuff, but pinpoint control as well.

Dennis Eckersley is a closer. I faced him as a starter with Boston when he came over and then he went away to the National League for a while. Spirited, energetic, really helped define the role of closer. Goose or Eck, they really start to show you the value of specialized roles in the bullpen.

John Smoltz, thank goodness he was in the National League most of the time. We got to face him a few times. But certainly, those types of pitchers helped redefine pitching in general because they have the ability to go out and be a starter and be a Cy Young–type pitcher as a starter and then go to the bullpen and save fifty games and show you their importance there as well.

* * *

It's interesting, growing up around baseball, many times, you think the world revolves around baseball, and intellectually you know it doesn't. You know, it's just a phase of your life. It's part of what's going on. But while you're in it, you're very narrow in your approach and everything outside is just a distraction and you kind of go that way. Now, when you first come into it, you want to make it. You don't really think about the future, you don't think about the rest of your life. Even if you had the longest of careers, you might play twenty-one years, you might play twenty-seven if you're Nolan Ryan, but at some point, you're gonna get out.

And if you really start to look relative to your life, most of your life might still be ahead of you. And for some reason, I had an interesting sort of view on that. It's that when I came to the big leagues in '82, we're good. In '83, we won the World Series, then we started to go through a little bit of an aging process and many players retired around '84, '85—Ken Singleton, Al Bumbry, Jim Palmer. And I would look at their situations and I would wonder what they're thinking at the time. What are you gonna do now? What's gonna happen now and do you have any regrets about your playing career? And we talked about that.

For some reason, I was fascinated by what happens now to these great guys that, you know, you're not old, you're not retired, you're not ready for this, and what are you gonna do now? And I started internalizing that sort of thinking and saying, okay, even for a long career, you've still got to prepare for what's gonna happen afterward. If you have a thought in your mind that there's gonna be life after baseball, then you could start to do certain things in the off-season, start to set up some of your interests, start to get in touch with what you might like to do after that.

When I started looking at kids' complexes and building fields and creating programming, and all that kind of stuff, I felt that I was much more motivated by that sort of thing and wanting to help grow the game of baseball.

I don't say that I became an ambassador for the game of baseball, but my success and my attention for my success and some of the things maybe you stood for, you know, really represented some good things and you could use that sort of platform to guide kids. They're not all gonna be big league players, but they can benefit and they will learn a lot from the benefits of sport. And that's really what I was trying to accomplish, and trying to give them the sense of what it feels like to be a big league player and still play the game.

We have twenty thousand kids that come through in tournament sorts of destinations. And I guess if you did a quick sampling, you'd probably think that there would be fewer black players coming through than before. But I don't know. I don't tend to think about it and look at it that way. I know through our foundation work and through the spirit of the Cal Sr. Foundation, we go through the inner cities a lot to show them the game of baseball.

And it's amazing to me, in some of the inner-city environments or some of the boys' and girls' clubs, this is the first time they've seen and swung a bat, which really kind of blows me away. You live in a country that we think that baseball is around all the time, but it's not necessarily around all the time. But we try to go around and spread the good word of sport in general. We're partial to baseball.

We want to actually show you the values of sport through baseball, and that's what we do in many ways. And we use sport and baseball in a foundation sense to get in front of them so we can talk about other things that would affect their life.

I move around and speak to many different audiences about many different subjects—mostly the secret of perseverance. And part of the speech kind of deals with controlling things you can't control. And one of the examples in your personal life is bringing some control over some of the areas you don't think you can control. And I used the example of the streak and the birth of my kids. My first six years of my career, I wasn't married. You're working off your own schedule. You can stay up until two or three in the morning in the parking lot and sign autographs if you want. You could sleep in the day, it doesn't impact anybody else. Your life is your life.

Then I met my wife and got married. And things didn't change too much after that because she had the flexibility in her life where she can get on the plane and see me in Chicago or New York or anywhere else. So we could actually move our life. And then when you have kids, your life changes, all for the better, but it certainly changes. So then I go on and tell the story that my daughter was born in 1989, November 22. And for those of you thinking in the baseball sense, that is the off-season.

So when my wife had to go in the hospital, she had to have a C-section at the end. I threw a mattress down. I got to bond with my daughter first. I got to feed her first. I got to stay in the hospital, support my wife in ways we as a team and a parent could figure out. We could support each other. And by early February, when I had to go to spring training, we had a pretty good handle on it, we felt pretty good about it, and that's wonderful.

My second child was born July 26, 1993. And as most of you know, it's right in the middle of the baseball season, and it was two years prior then to the record-breaking year. Now, the streak had gotten to the point where all my critics who said that I need to miss a day off, da, da, da, da, da, they turned out to be the most positive supporters of it, and they started to say things like, this is good for the game of baseball. Cal has to continue this streak. He has to break this record for the good of baseball even if it means missing the birth of his own child. And my wife actually read those things.

So then I had to deal with this at home and try to figure out what the answer is. So I support my wife and I said, honey, I'm gonna be here. I know my place. This is the most important thing in my life. And then I walk out of the room going, oh, crap, what am I gonna do now? And then, the more you think about it and you start to think about, what can I do, what can I do, how can this thing work out, the moral is, sometimes it's dumb luck. But I would say, you know, honey, even if I were to miss a game as a result of the birth of my own son, I would have no regrets. It'd be the absolute right thing to do. Do not bother about it. Do not worry about it. You should not feel bad but, you know, this will be the date forever stamped in the history of baseball that the streak ended and that would be our son's birthday. Is that fair to him?

Then I go on to say, you appeal to a mother's protective instinct, nature, whatever else, and it worked out. It worked out in sort of a dumb-luck way. My boy was really big. He was nine pounds and he was still a couple of weeks early. The doctor wanted to get him out. And it just so happened that there was an off-day right in between Minnesota and Toronto. I flew in for the birth of my son, then flew on, and hit a home run off one of the hardest guys I hit a home run off, Duane Ward. I hit a home run to celebrate his birthday. So, I don't know what I've done, but I can only tell you that it was important for me to be there for the birth of my son.

First and foremost, I was someone who loved the game of baseball, was absolutely crazy and passionate about the game of baseball. I don't care about being remembered as a hitter. I don't care about being remembered as a shortstop; that might have changed the mind-set. I love to be thought of, and I think it's the most highly complimentary thing another player could say to me, is that I was a gamer. A gamer just means that you're willing to meet whatever challenges have faced your team today and you're willing to do it with your group of guys. So when you're called a gamer, that's the highest compliment.

BRUCE FROEMMING

Bruce Froemming umpired more seasons in the major leagues, thirty-seven, than anyone else, and his 5,162 regular-season games is second only to Hall of Fame arbiter Bill Klem. For that longevity and solid service, Froemming has earned the respect of everyone connected with the game. MLB president Bob DuPuy said, "He has been the consummate professional throughout his career."

After serving a thirteen-year apprenticeship in the minors, Froemming reached the big leagues in 1971, serving on the crew headed by Hall of Famer Al Barlick. Froemming maintained that he "learned more from Barlick" in that first year than he had learned in the minors. By the mid-1980s he was a crew chief himself and has mentored dozens of other young umpires.

Froemming never doubted his destiny to umpire, calling his first game as a high school freshman. "I love being on the field" was a credo he carried to the end of his career, acknowledging the vital role umpires play in the game. "Every decision is important," he said. "This is bread and butter for the players and for the managers. Your job is to get everything right."

Those players and managers recognized his enthusiasm for his job.

Ken Griffey Jr. said, "He's still real good. He nips arguments in the bud. And you know, he looks like he enjoys the game." Indeed, he believed that "the easiest part of the job is being on the field. The toughest is the traveling, being away from home."

Froemming's career included assignments in five World Series (1976, 1984, 1988, 1990, 1995), three All-Star games, nine Division Series, and ten League Championship Series. He also called four no-hitters, including the September 26, 1981, gem by Nolan Ryan, the fifth of his career. Despite those achievements, Froemming maintained that "when the pitch is thrown, I'm not thinking about who's at bat [or on the mound]." That was his dedication to his job and the concentration it demanded.

"You've got to have guts," said Froemming about what it takes to make a good umpire. "Good partners are important. It makes the job easier. But when the roof caves in, you've got to be able to face the situation and not hide and run for help. You've got to stand on your merits and your hustle." Froemming maintained those qualities for a longer career than any other umpire. When asked about what he thought his best call was, he replied, "getting into umpiring."

"He's like a four-star general out there," said Alex Rodriguez. "He's got great passion and great respect for the game." As Froemming put it, "I just love walking to home plate every night. We're all competitors. The player wants to get a hit. The manager wants to win. I want to get it right. I just love that competition."

I grew up in a small farm town—it's like a city now—Hales Corners, Wisconsin. Around the fourth grade, during recess, we started playing ball, and that was a big deal. And recess, you only had fifteen or twenty minutes and you run outside and you play ball. Going into the fifth grade, I had rheumatic fever. And between fourth and fifth grades, I was bedridden almost all summer. And at that time, we had the Milwaukee Brewers, which was a Triple-A club in the American

Bruce Froemming

Association, and you had the Chicago Cubs that played all day games, and you had the Chicago White Sox that also played at night. And being bedridden, the radio was my best friend. There wasn't anything like TV, especially in our family; we didn't have the resources to have a TV, but I listened to baseball morning, noon, and night. And as a matter of fact, when the Brewers were on the road in the American Association, they had an announcer, his name was Heath—I think it was Mickey Heath—they re-created the games.

And a guy would hit a ball and they'd dub in the crowd and everything. But I became a big, big fan of the game that summer because that's all I had to do. I couldn't get out of bed. And when I did get out of bed, I was cheating, because my mom and dad would go somewhere and I'd jump out of bed. A couple of times, they'd catch me next door by the neighbors' throwing, playing, catching this and that, because that's a terrible age to be bedridden. That was 1948.

In 1951 I went down to Borchert Field, where the Milwaukee Brewers played. And I'm sitting outside the ballpark at Borchert Field one afternoon about three-thirty, just sitting against the boards, and this gentleman came by and I knew it was Charlie Grimm, the manager. I just watched him and he said, what are you doing?

I said, just waiting to get in and shag balls. When they hit batting practice, you'd stand outside. At Borchert Field, they'd hit them over the fence a lot and you'd get a lot of balls outside. He said, why don't you come in with me? You can shag balls for me in the outfield. So I went in with him and went to the clubhouse and Charlie said, you just wait here and when the players are ready to go, you can go in the outfield. He said, I don't want you in the infield because of a ball possibly getting you hurt.

So I went to the outfield. And I was out there about fifteen, twenty minutes and the groundskeeper came over to me and he was a grumpy guy. He said, you have to get off the field. And I said, Mr. Grimm said I could be on the field. And he said, I'm telling you you got to get off. So I started hemming and hawing and Grimm came over and said, leave him on here. So the groundskeeper made me get a letter, a note from my mom saying that I could be on the field and the club wouldn't be responsible, this and that.

I got the letter from my mom and I went back the next day, and the guy was on me right away. He said, you got your note? He read it and he said, you never go in the infield. He was a tough guy but, you know, he was in charge. That was his ballpark. And as a kid, you don't understand it, but I understand it now. The rest of the year, I was with the Brewers, and they were in the playoffs that year. They played Kansas City, and I think in '51 they went to the Junior World Series, but I'm not sure.

In '52, I went back to Borchert Field and I'm a veteran. I'd get to the ballpark after school was over and everything. And they'd have errands for me to run. Unlike the players who have twenty, thirty pair of shoes now, they had one pair of shoes. Johnny Logan's spikes were loose one day. Logan was playing with the Brewers in '52. They gave me the spikes: Get on the bus, go up to Twenty-fourth and Burleigh, there's a shoemaker there, he's waiting for them. He's gonna fix them, bring them back to the ballpark.

I mean, that's unbelievable when you think of it. I ran errands. Across the street, there was a tavern that had these roast beef sandwiches. I did everything, and everybody was nice to me. Think of the players on that team. They had Gene Conley, Dick Donovan, Billy Bruton, Johnny Logan, George Crowe, Billy Klaus, Buzz Clarkson, all these guys playing. And some days I'd get to the ballpark and everybody had different things. And the guys started to take to me a little bit because I was hanging around.

Some guys, you were a pain in the neck to. But most of the guys were good to you, and you'd get a quarter tip or something. Somebody gave me a quarter tip or fifty cents. Man, I mean, that was a big thing. And you always went home with five or six batting-practice balls.

Del Unser was Al Unser's child, and during the game, they had a little pigeonhole down the left-field line in this ballpark that I would sit up there during the game and babysit Unser's kid, who was maybe four or five years old.

And I'd sit there until the game was over. Then we'd walk on the field down to the clubhouse on the left-field line. So I babysat Del Unser. Now, when I get to the big leagues in the seventies and eighties, Del Unser is playing with the Phillies. And I put it together and I said, you know what, and he said, yeah, Al Unser was his dad.

I did make the varsity and played three years of varsity ball at Custer High School. I was a second baseman and pitcher to spell the guys that would pitch too many innings.

So now, I'm gonna graduate from high school in '57, and what am I gonna do? There wasn't any money in the family. School to me was like a sports academy. I went to school to play sports. I didn't really buckle down in school until I was a senior. At that time, the girl I married was a very good student. So, when I started dating my wife, Rosemarie, I started taking books home because it looked good. I never looked at them when I took them home because I was also in the gym at night somewhere.

But I graduated from high school and I saw an ad in the paper and I call a guy that's still in the game today, Roland Hemond. He's with the White Sox, I believe. And I called Roland Hemond with the Braves and he put me on to an umpire that was in Milwaukee at that time, Stan Landis, and I saw an ad for an umpiring school. Landis recommended that I go to the umpiring school in Florida. You won't get a job because you're so young. But you can go down there and maybe in the second year, you'll get a job. Well, I went down to the school in 1958 in January. The Al Somers umpiring school. In a six- or eight-week course, I got a job. They gave me a job.

Al Somers never made it to the big leagues. Al Somers was a Triple-A umpire out of the Pacific Coast League. And he was like a lifelong Triple-A umpire. There were players that wanted to play in the old Pacific Coast League rather than the big leagues because they got more perks and they made almost as much money as you could make in the big leagues.

When I graduated from umpiring school in 1958, I was assigned to a rookie league in June which was called the Nebraska State League. The league started in June. But before I went out there, somebody quit in the Midwest League and they optioned me. So for the first two months, April and May, I worked in the Midwest League. My league didn't start till June because it was a rookie league. And I worked with a guy with an airplane. We traveled in the Midwest League. He had money. He was from Columbus, Ohio, and he was a friend of George Trautman, who was then the president of the minor leagues.

And he was gonna get to the big leagues because the guy had connections and he had money and this and that. Well, I ended up as his partner because his partner had quit. And we flew into cities like Paris, Illinois, that didn't have an airport. I didn't like flying. At first I got sick and I was scared to death. He had a beautiful airplane, a twin-engine Piper Apache with all the commercial radio equipment and everything. But we flew and we had some experiences. We had an off-day, we went into St. Louis, stayed at the Chase Hotel.

Can you imagine, you're eighteen years old? And at that time, the Chase Hotel was *the* hotel in St. Louis. I mean, that's where all the ball clubs stayed. And we had a day off and we were in Clinton, Iowa. We flew to St. Louis to see the Cardinals play in the old stadium where they were.

My grandfather gave me money out of his pocket for umpiring school. He said, if this is what you want to do, go try it. There weren't any guarantees that you're even gonna be into the game. So, I go to the school. And the process of the school early on was, first of all, everybody knows the game, and they tell you, you all know the game, right? And they give you a test, twenty-five questions. You might get five right. And there were rules questions, this and that. So right away, they break you down, you don't know the game. And from there, they take you from the morning sessions of learning the rules. You will then go out early in the first couple of weeks.

Maybe about eleven in the morning you go out to the field. At that time, it was a two-man system. Working the bases, how to take plays into second base and where to go in the outfield and the plate umpire had to cover you. And it's all mechanics, mechanics that you had to learn about the two-man system. And about four to five weeks into the school, you knew on the field where you ought to be because you did it every day.

A two-man system would be, you walk out to home plate, you have two umpires, the plate umpire and an umpire that stands at first base. And you've got all four bases with two umpires. So when the ball is hit, the first-base umpire has to come into the infield. He has to take a pivot. They showed you how to do the pivot. If you didn't do the pivot right, they hollered at you. And guys would fumble with the pivot for a week or two. But when you had it down, the system worked. And of course, you're young and everybody could run like deer then.

Before the pitch, you're stationary at first base, and you're always about four, five feet behind the first baseman, wherever he's playing. There's a reason for that. If you're in front of him and there's a ball hit, you could be in the way of the ball. So, you play off the first baseman, you're four, five, six feet behind him.

Now, when the ball is hit in the minor leagues, you run in toward just in front of first base to the cut of the grass, and you take what they call—and it was a big word in the umpiring school—the pivot. You would come in and you would pivot left to take the runner, watch the runner tag first base, the batter runner. And if he went to second, that same umpire would take him into second base.

You would follow him. Now, if he stops, you stop. And if he went back to first, you had to be ready because maybe they had the cutoff throw and there might be a play at first base. So far, the first-base umpire has got everything. So, now, on a base hit or on an extra-base hit, you would take the pivot—the big word, the pivot again—and you would follow that runner to second base.

And if he's going to third, you got him all the way to third, and you would take him. And in a two-man system, the plate umpire could not leave the plate because you had to protect the plate. So, the base umpire had the three bases on a triple. If there's an overthrow, you've got the plate umpire there. And you learn all that.

I think it was in the thirties they went to three umpires in the major leagues. But when Bill Klem started in the big leagues in 1905, there were two men. And I think in the thirties, they went to three. And then, when Klem was retiring, he retired in '40. In '41, he came back as a supervisor. They started to work the fourth man into the three-man crew. As a matter of fact, Klem himself worked ten games in 1941 to work the four-man system to see where they were going.

And by the end of the decade, in the forties, they had gone to the four-man system.

The first summer in the Midwest League, in 1958, we got $250 a month. And that was everything. That was the expenses and everything. So, I had a guy that had money that flew that airplane. And he checked in hotels that, there was no way I could check in the same hotel, but because he had money, he fronted for my room and helped pick me up.

We got $106 clear every two weeks. The Midwest League was a place to start in. It was a D league. It was a good league and good cities, but the money wasn't there. The money in the minor leagues has always been pathetic. It's better now.

I then went to the Nebraska State League and I finished the summer. You then were a free agent. Because it was a rookie league, they didn't bring you back for the second year. The Nebraska State League was a rookie D league. It was only a seventy-game schedule. So, when the season was over, there was a guy with the White Sox. His name was George Noga. He was the manager in Holdrege, Nebraska. He wanted me to come to spring training in Hollywood, Florida. The White Sox had their training down there. I was all excited to go there. The year before, I was in Daytona Beach with the Cleveland Indians. And that was fun, too. I mean, spring training; as a kid, I'm single and everything is fun. You're on a field where you love the game and everything.

I went home, and I was home about two weeks, and the Northern League president, Herman White, who was there forever, his secretary, Barney Neary, called me and said, we'd like you to come to the Northern League. That was a C league. So I went from a D league down to a rookie league. And now, I'm in a C league. So, I spent a couple of years in the Northern League, and it was terrific. I then became a free agent again. And I went to the Northwest League, which was a B league. And from the B league Northwest League, I went to the Texas League, which was a Double-A league, and spent a couple of years there. And then I spent five years in the Pacific Coast League. And all the time, your contract was sold from league to league. They would purchase your contract. And at one time, the big leagues bought your contract from Triple-A.

When I went to the Texas League in 1965, I worked for a guy by the name of Hugh Finnerty out of Tulsa, Oklahoma. And I had a play that year at the end of the season in Tulsa with the Albuquerque club there. Buzzie Bavasi was there sitting with Finnerty. A guy by the name of Bobby Pfeil missed third base, which would have been the tying run, and the winning run was coming around. There were two outs. There was a ball hit down the left-field line. We had four umpires in the playoffs. The third-base umpire went down the line, Don Denkinger. When Pfeil came around through the base, he missed the base.

I came up to cover third base and make sure he touched the base. So the Tulsa runner misses the bag. I've had trouble with Tulsa all year. And it was a big turn in my career there. The boss, Finnerty, he lived in Tulsa.

Roy Hartsfield, the manager for Albuquerque, was coming out to change pitchers after the base hit. And the third baseman, Braxton Bailey I think his name was, said, "Stay there. We've got a guy who missed the bag." They don't know if I'm gonna call him out or what. So, I'm just saying, man, don't appeal this because I've had trouble with this club all year. So, they appealed it. And of course, you had to call him out. And the place went nuts. There were four ejections, including the manager, Vern Rapp. It wasn't pretty; the field was littered with beer cups. It was an ugly scene.

We got it all settled. We finished the game. Tulsa lost the game. And Don Denkinger, another umpire, and I were going home after that game. We had my car. They gave us police protection on the highway out to Highway 44 until they felt like everything was cleared, and that's how we left Tulsa. Now, when I got home for the winter, the first thing you start thinking of is, you know, is Finnerty going to have me back? He was a good guy. He was tough on umpires as a GM with Tulsa, but when he became the president, he was the umpire's best friend and he supported you.

So I don't know what period of time it was, but it couldn't have been too long when I got home that season in 1965. I called Mr. Finnerty and I said, that was a hell of a way for the year to end. He said, I was sitting with Buzzie Bavasi. We all saw he missed the bag. He said, you're coming back with me next year. So, I went back to the Texas League.

Hugh Finnerty sold my contract to Triple-A to Dewey Soriano. This was in June of 1966. Well, now, this is where everything starts to blow up in your mind because now you're in Triple-A.

I had to report to Seattle. This was on a Tuesday or Wednesday. He gave me until Saturday to get to Seattle. I went home. I'm all excited, going to Triple-A. Now you fly. These leagues, until then, you drove, and you drove your own car. And in the Texas League, for instance, the first summer in 1965, Don Denkinger and I, with my car, we put on over thirty-five thousand miles with trips like El Paso to Tulsa, eight hundred miles; Albuquerque to Oklahoma City, six hundred miles; and like that. You traveled after the game. In many cases, no day off.

We had a game one night in Dallas, we went twenty-five innings. We had a game the next night in El Paso, Texas. It's two in the morning when the game ended. You don't take a break and get to bed! You've got to get on the highway and make those six hundred miles and then work the next day. That's the life in the minor leagues. But now, when you go to Triple-A, you now start fantasizing. I'm in Triple-A. The next stop, if I can show what I'm doing and if I can do good, it's the big leagues. And that's when I would say that I started to think about the big leagues. It's when I flew to Seattle and I'm in Triple-A. And I know a lot of guys have gone from the Coast League to the big leagues. You start thinking, you know, maybe there's a chance.

The year that I went from Triple-A to the big leagues, I worked for a guy, Bill McKechnie. The Coast League used to give you half the sale price. The big leagues would buy you from Triple-A, and Dewey Soriano, who was the previous president, would sell you for $4,000, and Dewey would give the minor league guy $2,000 of the $4,000. When I was sold, I asked McKechnie for the money, and he said, oh, we did away with that system. So, I didn't get in on the deal.

You had to have a job in the off-season, including when I went to the big leagues, because the big league salary for an umpire after I came out at Triple-A, and my highest pay in Triple-A, was the $3,200 salary in 1970. And I was the umpire-in-chief.

I had good jobs in the winter. My brother-in-law helped me get different jobs. One of my first big-time jobs was at the Coca-Cola

Al Barlick

Company, sales and driving the truck, sales and delivery. Those jobs in the winter sustained me for the summer because we had to save. I got married in 1959.

I was with Coke three or four years, and then went to a dry-cleaning job. And then from there, I went to furniture and parcel delivery. And all those jobs were all union jobs that I got myself into. And that's what sustained you because even when I went to the big leagues, in 1971, I had to work in the winter because the pay was only $10,000.

In 1970 I met Al Barlick. And I worked a game at Dodgertown. Ted Williams came in with his ballclub, the Washington Senators. Barlick had the plate. I asked him if I could work the plate for him.

I had been assigned ten big league games, but they were all in Vero Beach. I didn't travel anywhere because I was in the minor league camp also. So, as a minor league umpire, I was working big league games. Barlick comes in, the senior umpire, and was watching us there. And Barlick came in the dressing room and I asked him, would you mind if I work the plate for you today? I was assigned second base. The reason I wanted to work the plate was, the only way you could get noticed to go to the big leagues, really, is work the plate.

You could stand at second base or third base, never have a call. And you have to show your trade and what you can do. I felt it had to be at the plate. So, everybody that came in, I asked if I could work the plate. And all the umpires gave me the plate. They couldn't wait to get rid of it. But Barlick said, nobody works the plate for me. He was real rough about it. He said, where are we, let's get lunch. So, we went over to lunch at Dodgertown and walked into the lunchroom, and he knew O'Malley—Walter O'Malley, owner of the Dodgers—and O'Malley came over and there was small talk in a snap.

He was in the lunchroom, and they're talking. And Barlick said, you got this kid over in the dressing room. He asked me to work the plate. And O'Malley said, well, you certainly don't need to work the plate with all these years you got. Why don't you let him? And Walter was—I'd gotten to know Walter in several parties. We had this thing, parties, and all the umpires were always invited. And I got to know Mr. O'Malley because I was in that camp seven or eight years, in the minor league camp.

And they treated minor leaguers just like big leaguers. It was a great, great camp at Vero Beach. O'Malley said to him, why don't you let him work? So, when Barlick came back to the dressing room, I don't know if I was in the Dumpster or what, but I wasn't thinking much of it. He came up two steps in that ugly dressing room we had. And he said, put it on. You're working the plate. Not real friendly, either. Man, I was excited. I'm going to work the plate for Barlick.

That was his thirtieth year in the big leagues. He went one more year. He went thirty-one years. So, I put the gear on and we went out to the field. And not very much talk. Barlick, you know, he hasn't talked to me much or, you know, ra-ra stuff or anything. And I worked the game. And I had a great, great pitching game. Both sides pitched really well. It was, I don't know, 3–1, 2–0, whatever. And when the game was over, and I was pouring it on, I mean, I gave it all I got, you know, because you got one shot. I got the senior umpire at second base.

And, you know, maybe you get lucky. So the game is over and Ted Williams came out of the dugout. And I got to know Ted later, which I'll talk about later. But Ted came out of the dugout and he went right to Barlick. And he said, tell Joe Cronin to get this guy in the American League. And Barlick said, the hell with you, we're going to get him in the National League. Now, man, why, my heart was fluttering, you know, they're talking like this. So, we go to the dressing room and Barlick had a guy with him that came up from West Palm. He was living in West Palm for spring training.

And Barlick said, where can we get a beer? I told him, if we went down to Vero, we've got a place downtown where we always go to have a beer. And he said, I want to sit down and talk to you. So, we get there at five o'clock. Game ends at four; by that time you showered and everything. We're down at the bar at five.

Both leagues, American and National League, actually competed for umpires. They would see an umpire and the American League would take him to spring training because they were interested in him, the National League would do the same thing. And every spring they would take four, five umpires there, to spring training to look at them. They had guys in the wings that they would bring up to the big leagues.

The National League had the best of it for many, many years. I mean, you wanted to go to the National League. You go to the American League, but the National League, there was something there because of the names, the credibility: Barlick, Augie Donatelli, Shag Crawford, you know, Tom Gorman, Jocko Conlan, and on and on and on. Of course, it didn't matter to me. To go to the big leagues, you were gonna get a raise, but if you have a choice you want to go to the National League.

We went downtown, Barlick picked my brain, and all of a sudden it's nine at night. And he had said to the guy he was with, about eight, he said, call Jenny, Al's wife. Tell her we're not gonna make dinner tonight. Just tell her to have something. He picked my brain for almost three hours, where I was, who I worked for, and why didn't I get a chance? He couldn't understand why I didn't get a chance to umpire in the big leagues with what he had seen that day. He liked my work. So that was that, and I go back to the Coast League and during the winter in '70 or early '71 I got a letter from Fred Flagg saying that the National League was bringing me to spring training, a full spring training, and that they were gonna look at me.

And Barlick took to me, and it was like a father-son relationship. And all the games I was working, he was almost at every game. In the beginning, Paul Pryor, another National League umpire, had told me, don't expect to get a job. But they got you in spring training and you know, next year, a couple of years, maybe something will happen. Well, spring went along and everything was going good, and I had a guy that was in my corner big-time. When you talk about politics, he was well-respected.

I worked a lot of games in St. Pete with the Mets, and Gil Hodges was the manager. Hodges raved about my work to Barlick. This just kept going on, and toward the end of the spring training, I had a game in Tampa, Florida. And one of the umpires I was working with, he said, you know, you've had a good spring. He said, they'll probably give you some insurance and stuff, you know, they'll probably do something with you. And that day when I walked off the field in Tampa, Pryor was there. He had an off-day. And he said, whatever you do, go right back to the hotel, hang around the bar. There's basketball at night. Barlick is gonna ask again, he set this all up. He said, Barlick's gonna ask again to watch basketball, the NCAA tournament.

And he says, he's got some incredible news for you. Pryor was the one that said I wouldn't get a job, now he was all fired up. So I go back to the hotel and I did what he said. I went into the bar, and Barlick came in six, six-thirty. And he said, you're gonna watch basketball with me tonight, in a grumpy way, and, you know, but now I'm getting to know Al, and I know he likes to tease. And I said, I don't know if I want to. Come over, he said. All the guys are coming over. So he had about ten, twelve people in his room. He had a nice big suite at that Holiday Inn.

And we're watching the game, and he gets to the small talk and he said, well, what do you think of your spring? I said—well, I know that Pryor had told me there was good news, so I had to play this thing out to the end—and I said, well, you know, they probably won't do anything. I've been in the minor leagues forever. And it just hit a nerve with him, and he said, go call home and Rosemarie. You're going to the National League. So, I mean, I get chills now when I say that because Barlick became my friend in 1970. He could've forgotten about me. He never did. And he stayed in my trailer in '71. I went to dinner with him and his wife at least half a dozen times during spring training, which was unheard of.

So I was working with Barlick. That was gonna be Barlick's last year. And the crew we had going into the '71 season was Barlick, Eddie Vargo, and Harry Wendelstedt. Three really solid umpires.

Vargo was Barlick's partner for most of his big league career, and they were close. I mean, everything Barlick said, Vargo would say, you're right, boss. They were close. Wendelstedt was a star pupil out of the midsixties. They came into the big leagues in '66 or '67. And Harry was a great personality and everything else.

Wendelstedt and I went back to the Northwest League. We worked the Northwest League together. So Wendelstedt was in the big leagues three or four years when I got there. That June, Flagg came into the dressing room in Cincinnati and Barlick said something that I'm sure Wendelstedt and Vargo will never forget. I never forgot it. He said to Flagg, this is the best crew that I've ever worked with on and off the field.

I've had five or six no-hitters. And when you think of the no-hitters, there was only one that I can remember was a little clumsy. It was Nolan Ryan's fifth no-hitter in Houston, Texas. We started slow, but by the fifth or sixth inning, he was there and they couldn't touch him the rest of the way. He started out slowly. He walked some guys. When the pitchers throw strikes, most of the time, most umpires, because all the umpires are looking for the same thing, you're gonna have a good game because they're throwing strikes.

When you have games where they complain about the umpiring, it's probably a 10–7 game, 14–9, a lot of plays, a lot of balls and strikes, a lot of relief pitchers. Those are tough games to umpire.

How you develop credibility is you give them all you got. And you'd be fair, and when I say fair, guy's got an argument, let him have his argument. When I say, that's enough, he has to respect that. If he doesn't, then we got a problem. And where you get the credibility is the consistency in how you handle situations. If a guy gets profane with me, he's gone and we don't even talk about the play.

Profane is anything with "you" in front of it. What follows usually gets you in trouble. Now, when you talk about trouble, I've got one ejection in the last two years, so when you talk about working 280 ballgames—we work about 140 a year now. With the time off, what you see there is I've been there a long time. Guys know which button to push and they know when to shut it off because that's my personality. I try to handle players with respect, and that's how you get respect. You give respect, you get respect. I'm not looking for trouble, I don't want any trouble. If he thinks you call a bad pitch or a bad play, he has the right to beef. But he has to do it in the right way.

And later on I worked with different guys, like John Kibler, and I worked with Eddie Vargo. You saw how they handled situations. And instead of trying to torture or throw more gasoline on it, they had ways to defuse it. A guy will make a statement, oh, that guy is a tough umpire, or say, Froemming is a tough umpire. I'm not tough. I'm not tough at all. I'm fair till you're not fair. Then we've got a different game. And if a guy has got an argument, if it goes too long, sometimes you have to say, that's enough. I heard it. Let's go.

Sometimes you won't even have to say that. A guy will say, oh, you missed that play, and he'll move on, because it isn't gonna do any good to go any further. He's only gonna get himself in trouble. An umpire's job is not to run ballplayers out of the game. Our job is to keep them in the game. The people are there to see the players. You don't want to throw the starting pitcher or a home run hitter out of the game.

I ran four guys on a play in Houston that I had right. Barlick was there and he was on the field with me. That was my rookie year, 1971. I'm learning how to handle situations. I didn't have a chance on this play. I had the play right. Tim McCarver caused interference at second base with a football block that knocked Roger Metzger out into center field. The ball is loose and two runs scored. I call a double play. The play was absolutely called right. Now, you talk about credibility, I didn't have any credibility because I was a brand-new umpire, and the Philadelphia Phillies came at me like a troop surge. Frank Lucchesi was the manager. I had Frank in the minor leagues, and Frank was a walking time bomb. He came out and he's pulling everybody back and the bullpen came in. It was a big play. The Phillies win the game with those two runs. I call it out. McCarver, you know, everybody is screaming and booing.

I had twenty-five guys at second base, and Barlick was on the field with me. And I'll never forget it because they clocked the argument at fourteen minutes. Fourteen minutes is a lifetime for an argument. But there were arguments, you got to tell them, you got to do this. But when it was all over, four guys were chased, all by me. One was a coach, the third-base coach for the Phillies. And what had happened was, during the early part of the argument, I said to Frank, look, I can't talk to all these guys. He's the manager. And I started to explain the play and the coach said, he's a so-and-so liar.

So that was the first ejection, then all hell broke loose. And when it was all over, Barlick said, is this guy gone? I can't think of his name. He says, is this guy gone? I said, he's gone. He said, for what? I said, for calling me an SOB or whatever. I got called so many names, I couldn't remember who called me what. And he said, that's a lie, I never called him that. Now, I looked at him and I said, no, that's right. He called me a so-and-so liar. Barlick said, get out of here.

We got back to the Shamrock Hilton Hotel in Houston and we got into the lounge area and Barlick said, we've got to get a phone and we've got to call Feeney. Chub Feeney was the president [of the National League]. And I said, you're not supposed to call Feeney on a weekend. He said, we're calling him on this. He said, I've never seen anything like this. So we did call Chub.

Once in a while, you even had to chase a guy that was a good guy because the players were going on and a good manager or a good guy will get run to protect his player. Now, people say, what do you mean by protecting his player? If he thinks a good player is gonna get run out of the game, the manager sometimes will take the brunt of the argument to get you off his case, keep him in the game. The manager's gonna go and he's gonna manage at the back of the dugout, anyway. They hide back there and you can't see them.

When you think of their careers, Paul Runge was an excellent umpire, as was Dutch Rennert. The three of us were in the Coast League together. We thought we weren't going to the big leagues. When I was working with Barlick in '71, when I went to the big leagues, Barlick asked me on the field one night, are there any other guys like you in the Coast League? And I gave him Rennert's and Runge's names, because they were both excellent umpires. They both were hired in '74. And that all had to do with Barlick. Barlick, to his credit, he was a Hall of Fame umpire, but he was a Hall of Fame supervisor, too.

In the minor leagues, from when I started in 1958 through 1970, you could not get home. When the season started in April, you were gone all year. The kids were small, my wife couldn't visit, you couldn't afford to travel. So when I got to the Coast League, there were a couple of Midwest cities in the Coast League, Indianapolis, for example. One year, they folded the association and Indianapolis became part of the Pacific Coast League. And I had a couple of trips here and both those trips, I got my family to Indianapolis. I went home to Milwaukee, I drove them down. And that was a big treat for the year. That was 1968. But you couldn't get home and you couldn't afford to go home and make $3,200 a year. You couldn't fly everybody around. For the minor leagues, the key date was right around the first week or second week of April when the season started. And the date you were looking at was Labor Day because that's when the minor leagues always ended. And then if you worked the playoffs, you might have to work another week or so. But everybody loved Labor Day because now you got a chance to go home and see your kids.

* * *

Why aren't there women umpires? Well, first of all, I don't think it's got anything to do with judgment. They have eyes just like we do, like men do. And they could see the plays. But the physical capabilities of a sport, like baseball versus basketball with a whistle and a ball, one ball and they don't throw it at you, it's a big difference. Women are not built to take a hundred-mile-an-hour fastball in the shoulder, the chest, or whatever. And I think that part of it—down the road, when somebody reads this book, somebody will say, well, this lady is doing it now. I don't know what he's talking about. Physically, it's tough for a man. I got hit in the forearm and it swelled up like a grapefruit. It was a Randy Johnson fastball, foul ball. You get hits like that. I remember Pam Postema—I was at Cooperstown; they brought her in that weekend and she worked the game, 1989. Physically, I don't think they can do it. But judgmentwise, balls and strikes, safes and outs, everybody's got judgment. But physically, I don't think it's a physical impossibility, but I think it's something where somebody can really get hurt bad.

Steve Dalkowski was reputed to be the hardest-throwing pitcher in the history of baseball. Any number of people said nobody threw the ball harder. He was a 170-pound left-hander, a young kid who could throw like nobody's ever thrown. I'll never forget it. It was in Aberdeen, South Dakota. Earl Weaver was his manager. And Chuck Hinton, who played later in the big leagues, was the catcher. Dalkowski was just incredible, an incredible arm. But he was totally wild. He didn't know where it was going. And the batters tiptoed into the box. Hinton was a good catcher. And I must have gotten hit one night, I don't know, two or three times, with balls in the dirt that got in front of Chuck and he couldn't get it or whatever, and then it hits you. And I told Weaver one night that if I got hit again, I was gonna go behind the pitcher's mound and call balls and strikes. I mean, it was scary back there, absolutely scary. And when you bring up the hardest thrower, I guess he probably was in the top three or four that I ever saw. Nolan Ryan, Nolan's pitches were hard, and there's a couple of guys now I can't think of.

We know when pitchers are throwing at guys deliberately in most cases. But the players get smarter every year. And maybe they'll even be smarter yet. They used to get you right away. In other words, Jones hits a home run, Smith's the next hitter, and Smith goes down. Now what they'll do is they won't knock Smith down. They wait an inning or two and then knock somebody down. Sometimes, they stay away from the guy that hit the home run. But they find ways. We even know that as umpires. So it's an alert situation. We have a rule, but it does not prevent you from throwing the guy out right away. And that's the good thing. If you got something that's flagrant, you used to have to give a warning.

You can throw the pitcher right out, no warning at all. And that becomes a touchy issue because the reason is you're saying intent was there, and the pitcher will say, how do you know what I'm thinking? But having said that, I still handle it that way, as do a lot of my colleagues. If you think it's flagrant, you have to call me tomorrow or have the boss call me. You're done today. And it works.

The only time you ever see that it's coming is if there's a group of guys, like there's gonna be a fight, and somebody will say, we're gonna get you. You better be ready this time. So, what it does is it throws up a warning sign, and preventive officiating becomes a very big factor in this. Because if you want to sit back and wait, it's gonna happen. If you want to take charge, which is the way I was taught by the greatest, which was Barlick, hey, you guys mess around, I know what's going on. You're gonna go, you're gonna go.

I remember one situation we had in Boston. Alex Rodriguez is the hitter. And the Boston pitcher threw an inside pitch. It was not a blazing fastball, by any means. But the ball was inside and it hit Rodriguez. Now, there's bad blood. These guys play, Yankees and Red Sox, there's bad blood between those clubs all the time. So, he gets hit. And it started innocently enough. He's gonna drop the bat and he, Rodriguez, said something to Jason Varitek, and I'm walking with him, and I walk about ten feet down the line with him. And now the words are going back and forth and one guy said you so-and-so. And the other guy said, you, too, and now they clash, and now they fight. And we have fifty guys on the field. And it's a TV game, it's a big series. I'm working the plate.

And it's a huge, huge game. And what made it worse even was we had like a three-hour rain delay in this game. We didn't start till like three-thirty in the afternoon. It was supposed to go off at noon or one-fifteen or whatever. So, when you talk about preventive officiating and handling situations, you've got to be lucky and the people you're dealing with have to believe in you or believe about you. I had Joe Torre on one side, I had Terry Francona on the other.

So, when we cleared the mess of the fifty guys, as the players started to spread out a little bit toward their side, I asked Francona to take his players off the field, all of them. And I asked Torre to do the same. You watch poker on TV. You've got to have a good hand when you're playing. You've got to get somebody to believe in you. They both cooperated. I got four umpires now on the field and I talk to my crew. One of the things that maybe we'll talk about later is how important the crew concept is. You don't do anything alone.

To me, umpiring, the most important people in my life are the three guys I work with because I work with them every day. And whether I like them or dislike them personally, they're my partners and we're there to do a job for the three hours on that field. So I got the crew together. Mike Winters was my partner, and I said, this is what I'm gonna do. We all agreed, this guy's got to go, this guy's got to go. And we took two or three from each team. They were done.

Varitek and Rodriguez, they're gone. And then there were, I think, two others from each team. The fight was good. There aren't very many good baseball fights, but this was a good baseball fight. This was all over the place and everybody wanted to get their punches in, and we finally got order and both teams were off the field. This is the game of the week. I then went to Torre and I got him out of the dugout. My partners all stood at home plate. I may have taken Winters with me because I like to talk with a witness. So, I think I took Winters with me and I said, Joe, here's what we're gonna do. You're not gonna agree, but this guy is done, this guy is done, this guy is done.

And Torre said, well, I can tell you right now, I don't agree. I said, having said that, that's what's gonna happen. Well, I don't agree, and I don't know if he smiled, but he may, you know, because the war was over now. And I said, that's the way it is, and I said, I'm going over to Francona and I'm gonna give him the same message. So I then went over to Francona. And the funny part about this is, they both said the same thing. I said, you're not gonna agree with this, Terry, but here's what's happening. And he said, well, I don't agree with that. So they both said the same thing. But they both co-operated and this was early in the game. We never had another problem.

I did say, if anybody moves or breathes like there's gonna be a problem, I said, I want everybody out of here and I'll put everybody in the clubhouse and we'll play with the nine guys on the bench. Neither manager indicated that there were gonna be any more problems. They didn't like who got thrown out. We got a couple of non-players that weren't playing in the game. They were part of the ejection thing. That's an umpire way of controlling something. You didn't hurt either team. A guy that's gonna pitch tomorrow, he's out of the game and somebody else.

But we got two of their big guys, which were Varitek and Rodriguez. We finished the game Saturday, nightmare situation, that inning, didn't have another problem. Sunday, when I went to home plate, the boys I was with, the crew, I said, there's gonna be a message at home plate. I don't want anybody talking. I just want you to listen to my message. And I asked both Torre and Francona to come out; they both came out. I said, the warning's in, everything is the same as it was yesterday. We're gonna play baseball. Nothing else. Sunday, nobody got dusted, nobody said boo, and that was the end of the series.

Now, for an umpire, that's a big deal. Why do I say it's a big deal? Because there's four guys, you're four guys against the world. You've got two teams that are feuding. You've got two good managers that both have good sense, and they both use their sense, and they control their athletes. Nobody challenged the situation, but they also knew that if anybody did, they were gone. And the reason I repeat that is because you asked about credibility and we talk about consistency. What I've hung on to my whole life is sometimes I'm not right, but I'm consistent.

And if you abuse something that I told you not to abuse or you abuse my partners, you're gonna pay the price that day. I do not carry it over to the next day. Umpires, to be worth your salt, you have to move on. I can't look back.

The thing that I like the most is the umpiring. And to go between the white lines at seven o'clock, I want to give the game respect, I want to give the teams respect, I ask for that in return, and everything is gonna go good. When we have a bump in the road, you have to handle it. And a good official worth his salt will handle the bumps in the road. Don't try to pretend they're not there because the bump will get bigger. Handle it and it'll be smoother than you ever think.

You can take me from the Texas League to the Coast League to the first year in the big leagues to where I am today, I still give what I think is the same effort. I learned it from Barlick, and go back to Barlick; I worked with Barlick his last year and I always thought, and I discussed it with Wendelstedt and Vargo, the guy could have coasted. He never coasted. We sent him home the last week of the season because he was worn out from the travel and he had had problems with his heart ten years before, and we knew it was his last year.

So we sent him home from Chicago for the last four days and he went home. But he gave 100 percent. And it's not a cliché. When you read this, I'll be retired, but I will work until I can't give 100 percent. When I have to compromise a position just to keep a job, I don't want the job.

We talked about Klem working in '41 as a supervisor; they were trying out the four-man system. We got the same amount of years now. This year, 2007, I will break the record. He had eleven games in his thirty-seventh year. This is my thirty-seventh year, so with the season, end of the season after the eleventh game, I will have broken his mark. Now, I would have broken his mark for total games also, but for the people who are reading this book, Klem never had vacation when he umpired. He worked 154 games every year. I've had twenty-eight days' vacation each year since 1979; twenty-eight years times twenty-eight days, and I've got another six hundred, seven hundred games in the record book.

The National League had the union first. The National League unionized in 1962 or '63, led by Barlick, Augie Donatelli, Stan Landis, and a few other guys. They got the guys together and they went to [National League president] Warren Giles's office and they said that they were gonna form a union. And he was devastated by it. The boys went to Giles and he was taken aback. And Barlick told me the story that, you know, he almost cried in his office. You can't do this. Well, they did it. And the reason they did it was because of low pay and the per diem wasn't sufficient, and they were carrying their gear bags for years, and on and on and on.

So to make conditions better, they unionized. Well, by the end of the years in the sixties, the American League still had not unionized. And then two umpires, Bill Valentine and Alex Salerno, tried to start the union to join with the National League. [American League president] Joe Cronin was all upset. He dismissed them. Somebody else picked up the ball, and they did finally unionize in the 1970s, either late '69 or '70. So, now, both the American League and National League—which were separate at that time, unlike what you're looking at today—Major League Baseball is all under one roof.

The salaries in 1970—Barlick was senior umpire, thirty-one years in the big leagues, he made $32,000 a year. That was in 1970.

The highest-paid umpires in the American League at that time, and remember, they were not unionized, were the crew chiefs at $16,500. So the National League pay at that time had doubled.

Now almost all the clubs are corporate. There's a lot of people in baseball that were never in baseball. I don't think a lot of people know umpires. And really, why would you? The only time they know an umpire is if he's not at home plate at seven or if he misses a game or whatever, then it comes up. But I think one of the things that I would like to see in future years, and I'd like to be a part of it, is umpires are part of the baseball family and they should be treated like part of the family.

A new umpire now comes in at $90,000-plus. His bonus—that's the playoff money that is pooled—is around $25,000. So, you're looking at about $110,000 to $115,000 for a new umpire.

We do travel first class and that's a big thing. As much flying as we do, we fly—nobody would even believe this—but we fly three or four times a week. To give you an example, on a Sunday night, using Sunday night as the end of a series, Monday's off, so you fly home if you're in the area. So that's the flight. Tuesday morning, you go to your next city, say, St. Louis, and you're there Tuesday, Wednesday, and Thursday. Thursday is an afternoon game, you fly to your next city, which now becomes your third flight of the week, and you're there for the weekend. And they could be long flights. And then you could go from St. Louis to Los Angeles or St. Louis to Seattle.

Bart Giamatti was a guy that could talk to the clubhouse guy and he could talk to the president of the United States and anybody in between, and he could communicate with them. He was incredible with his vocabulary and delivery, and he could put you in your place with a couple of words that I never even heard before and make you laugh. And when, in 1989, he became commissioner, he made me a crew chief that year. And he brought me into the room and he said, I'd like you to teach. I'm gonna give you a couple of people I want you to work with.

At that time, Eddie Vargo was his lieutenant and they gave me a crew and went off. And during that summer, whenever we were in New York, Bart would come into the room. And his personality was terrific. Now, in 1989, he became the commissioner. And Barlick was voted into the Hall of Fame. And about a month before the Hall of Fame induction at Cooperstown, I got a letter from the commissioner's office inviting my wife and me to Cooperstown on the weekend, which started on Friday night, for Barlick's induction.

And I had to call Vargo. I'm umpiring. How do I get off? Vargo said, well, the commissioner wants you off because you grew up with Barlick and he's going into the Hall of Fame. So, when we checked in Friday afternoon, my wife and I, at the Otesaga Hotel in Cooperstown, I put my credit card out there and the desk clerk said, everything is taken care of by the commissioner and you're just to have a good time. I couldn't believe it.

He was just a down-to-earth person. For a guy that had never dealt with umpires until two years before, he took such a liking to all the umpires. And the umpires loved him because he was just a real guy. You could tease him, and he teased back, he'd fire back. And with his death, I was in Atlanta that Friday afternoon, and one of my partners came downstairs.

I was sitting in the lobby reading the paper. I couldn't lie down and rest, I'd just flown that day, and he told me Giamatti had passed away. And it was like you lost an arm because he meant so much to us. You just felt like he was gonna build blocks for you in that umpire stuff all the way down to the end of your career. And just like that, he was gone.

Len Coleman was president of the National League. I had an incident. The pitcher's name that comes to mind is Jeff Fassero. My partner was Charlie Williams. We're in Montreal and Fassero, his record was 2–5 at that time, or 3–5, and he had just gotten a ton of money that year. And Charlie Williams had the play at first base, where Fassero covered from the pitcher's mound, and Charlie called it safe.

And Fassero went goofy in the paper, made some bad remarks about Charlie.

I don't do everything always right. The next day in Montreal, I called a press conference. I called upstairs and I said to the press, whoever I had talked to, I said, tell the press, whoever is interested, there'll be a press conference in the umpires' room at six-thirty. The room was full, cameras all over the place, this and that. And I took off after Fassero. I said, for a guy that's 3–5, he should worry more about pitching than chopping up my partner, and I don't appreciate it. Joe Kerrigan was his pitching coach. They came into the dressing room, they apologized.

They did everything right. Kerrigan and Fassero came in and they said they were sorry and it was the wrong thing to do to take Charlie on in a paper. And that's the way it ended. So, I thought it was all over. The next day Len Coleman called me, and he said, what the hell's wrong with you? You can't have a press conference. I said, well, I did. And I said, anybody who goes after my partner, I'm going to deal with.

So, a couple of months later, we're in New York, and Len invited me and Steve Rippley to play golf. And so we go, had a nice day, and it's hot as hell. And when it was all over, we go have a nice lunch and a big lemonade, and the day is terrific. We walk outside and Len is gonna say good-bye, and Rippley and I are gonna go back to New York. And Len said, Bruce, can I see you a second? And he took me to the practice green. He said, I'm gonna fine you 450 bucks. I said, you've got to be kidding. I played golf with him all day.

We laughed and joked. He said, no, that's for that incident in that press conference you called. So I appealed it. I got it down to $300, and he let me write a check to BAT, Baseball Assistance Team, the assistance program for the players. That's all it was. But Len was an excellent boss, and the fine didn't change my opinion of Len.

*   *   *

I can remember working a plate game with Eddie Vargo in spring training my first or second year. When the game was over, Vargo said, your stance, if you could just do this and drop back a little bit and suck the pitch in, you'll see that outside pitch better. He didn't even know how much he helped me. It was a big help. And when I explained to Ted Williams, when he opened that museum in the Ocala area, I took Barlick's ticket. Barlick got snowed in.

And I was with Al Kaline, Enos Slaughter, Bobby Doerr, that was our limo. Every day for three days, I was in that limo, and we go back and forth. On the last day, we had breakfast. Well, I was invited to Ted Williams's VIP breakfast. And his son came over to me, John-Henry came over, and said, Dad would like to see you. So, I went over and—how are you doing, like John Wayne, you know? As a student of a game, like Ted Williams, there weren't very many.

He asked me about working the slot versus working the shoulder, toward the catcher's right shoulder, and this and that, and I just was stunned. Here's the guy talking about working the slot. So, he said, tell me how you work. And I said, well, I don't work in the slot. I said, I drop back because it gives me full vision of the plate. That's what I want to hear, he said. Those guys up in that slot are looking across the plate. How would a guy, a hitter like that, even know what an umpire's looking at? But he explained it.

In 1999 the head of the umpires' union, Richie Phillips, decided, as his strategic move, he would have the umpires resign en masse on the theory that Major League Baseball couldn't get along without the umpires, and this would force Major League Baseball to make concessions to the umpires. One of the problems that developed early was, we were all together all the time. Whether it was good or bad, the union was all one body. We now had two bodies. We had a group of guys that wanted to be certified and start a new union, and you had the old guard. And meanwhile, guys lost their jobs as they came in and baseball took charge.

Major League Baseball sent letters out after we resigned en masse. They sent letters to us to rescind. You had two or three days to get those letters back, and if you rescinded, you were still part of the staff. Some letters came in late, some guys didn't rescind at all, never thinking it was such a serious thing. Well, when it all shook out, the ones that didn't rescind right away were dismissed. And then there was litigation.

I'd rescinded right away because my supervisor called me and said, you've got to get the letter in today or tomorrow or you're gonna be unemployed. That part of our life was not pretty. We all made mistakes. I think the lawyers made mistakes, we made mistakes. I think MLB made mistakes. Communication was the problem. But the guys that rescinded kept their jobs. We finished that year, '99, and we came in to new management in 2000 at the Marriott Hotel in Tampa, Florida, where we were introduced to our new bosses, which at that time were Sandy Alderson and Ralph Nelson. They brought in twenty-two guys from the minor leagues to replace the guys that hadn't rescinded.

We had a lot of new umpires come in all at once. And they were actually force-fed into the game. We had labor problems in the late 1990s, early 2000s. You had an input of twenty-two or twenty-five new umpires coming to the big leagues. The turnover to that point was you might have a guy or two come into the big leagues every year. But there was a big war and they put twenty-two on the field. And the challenges for twenty-two guys to come out of the minor leagues—some of whom were not ready to work in the big leagues—includes handling situations, knowing how to handle them. When I came into the big leagues, I was with Barlick, Vargo, and Wendelstedt. They didn't take any guff, any of the three of them. But you could see the smoothness in it.

MARVIN MILLER

To the owners, Marvin Miller was a labor agitator out to ruin baseball by challenging the long-sacred reserve clause. To the players, he was Moses leading them out of servitude and taking them to the promised land. No matter how you viewed him, he changed the way the business of baseball was conducted, swinging the balance of power from the owners to the players.

Carrying a degree in economics, Marvin Miller made his mark with the United Steelworkers of America before signing on with the Major League Baseball Players Association in 1966 as its first full-time director. The key issue for the players was the pension fund, but Miller soon discovered other problems, including the lack of an impartial arbiter for labor disputes. "My job was to right some wrongs, improve conditions of players," said Miller, "and that was done."

Miller had to overcome not only an ownership group that wanted to break the union but also the players' lack of experience with unions. "While players started with a tremendous deficit in knowledge of how to operate," Miller said, "they were among the most rapid learners I ever met." By educating them that baseball was indeed a business and that they were its primary commodity, he empowered them to fight for their rights.

"Through his work," said Hall of Fame pitcher Robin Roberts, one of the players instrumental in hiring him, "ballplayers for the first time attained dignity from owners. He changed a monopoly into a more realistic setup."

In addition to negotiating for the union through a series of conflicts with the owners over Basic Agreements, Miller's chief campaign was to rid baseball of the reserve clause, which in effect bound a player forever to the team that originally signed him. Through eloquence, patience, and the strength of conviction that he was doing the right thing, Miller outlasted the owners' negotiators, who were hampered by less unified support. Miller used a system of impartial arbitration set up in 1972 to push test cases, which eventually led to the demise of the reserve clause in 1976. That ushered in the age of free agency that brought greater competitive balance to the sport and ever-increasing salaries to the players.

Miller had a bigger impact on baseball than any commissioner, owner, or player in the past forty years. Hall of Fame pitcher Tom Seaver said, "He was one individual who had as large a ramification as anybody on the history of the game."

Two other judgments of Miller perhaps carry as much weight as any others. Hank Aaron said, "Marvin Miller is as important to the history of baseball as Jackie Robinson." In recognition of that importance, Miller was named by ESPN's SportsCentury as the fourth most influential person in twentieth century American sports.

I was born in the Bronx, New York. I don't remember it, obviously, but my parents bought a house in Brooklyn when I was less than a year old and I grew up in Brooklyn. Not surprisingly, I grew up as a Dodger fan. We lived not that far from Ebbets Field. And I got interested in baseball and sports in general, I would guess, through my father, who was a great sports enthusiast, a kind of championship bowler in his own right. And he was an anachronism in Brooklyn.

Marvin Miller

He had grown up in Manhattan and he was a Giants fan living in
Brooklyn

I'm not sure I remember the very first professional game I saw; I
think I remember it. And it would have been somewhere around
when I was five years old because it had to be before I started school.
My father was a salesman who worked on Saturdays, Sundays, and
holidays, so this would have had to have been on a weekday and
that's why I think it was before I started school. My mother was a
teacher in the New York City school system, so I doubt if she would
have let me play hooky to go to a ballgame. But more than the first
game I saw at Ebbets Field, I somehow remember what was called
semipro baseball games that my dad used to take me to.

Somewhere along Ocean Avenue, where there was a great big field, I can remember going to games where there was no admission price but they passed the hat for contributions. And I also remember seeing a professional team called the Bushwicks play, and I remember the House of David team. As I got a little older, somewhere around the time I was about ten, after much coaxing, my parents let me go to ballgames alone. And I remember taking a subway just a few stops to Ebbets Field and going on a Saturday or a Sunday when there was a doubleheader and standing in line outside the bleachers. The tickets cost fifty cents then. And later when the amusement tax was put on, it was fifty-five cents.

My father worked in what was basically a retail store selling women's expensive coats in lower Manhattan, where on one street there must have been thirty-five, forty competing stores all selling the same thing. He was really exploited as an employee. He worked, as I mentioned, Saturdays, Sundays, holidays.

When I was growing up, I would see him on his day off, which was a weekday, and I would see him on Friday night for dinner because he came home early from work on Fridays and not at any other time. And at some point, I've forgotten exactly which year, but I think it was in the early to mid-thirties, I used to visit my father down on Division Street on Saturdays and have lunch with him. I'd take the subway down there, and I vividly remember one day going down there and finding him out on a picket line.

I had not known that the retail and the wholesale department store employees had been organizing in that street, and there was my dad marching with a picket sign. And I got interested. And I got interested in the issues and the outcome, if it was a successful outcome and so on. I have a feeling that at least part of my interest began there. And my mother was an early member of the teachers' union here in New York City.

My father was a very unusual man. His formal education was not great. He had started working when he was really a young lad. But he was a small-d democrat. I would visit him at work on Division

Street and we'd go out for lunch. Division Street is really at the edge of what was called, and is called, Chinatown in lower Manhattan. And I remember my father would always have a pocket full of coins. We would pass the Bowery on the way to lunch, and the homeless in those days were down there. And there wasn't anybody that approached him who he didn't have coins for.

And he had, as I say, without the formal education, he nevertheless spoke Yiddish to the older people who we had gotten to know there. He'd learned rudimentary Chinese. And it fascinated me to hear him talk Chinese with the natives there. But it was more than just having coins in his pocket to give to the people who asked. In Brooklyn, I remember, well before we had oil burners, we had coal furnaces heating the house. And one of the tasks was that the ashes used to be shoveled out of the furnace into large cans that were probably waist high or more.

And those cans had to be wrestled up several steps and then out the alley from the back to the front where they would be picked up. My mother went off to school as a teacher early in the morning. My father usually did not leave for work until about 10:00, 10:30 A.M. This was a regular routine. When the ashman came, it would be wintertime, and they would heave the ashcan's contents into the truck, and my father, every week, would invite the driver and his helper, all of them full of soot and so on, into the house to warm up.

This was before the repeal of Prohibition, but my father usually had a bottle of Canadian Club squirreled away and he would serve drinks. When he didn't have this bootlegged liquor, he would make a pot of hot coffee for the driver and his helper. The driver was usually a white employee, the helper usually a black employee. And I learned that it made no difference, absolutely made no difference.

I was a member of the State, County, and Municipal Workers of America, CIO. And it's really there that I got my first training as an activist, as it were. I became a member of the grievance committee and I was involved in an actual sit-down strike. And I got to know the workings of unions through unorthodox unions. The Unemployed and Project Workers Union was the union of WPA workers. The Workers' Alliance was an organization of the unemployed and those on welfare. And so that really was my background experience.

It's important to understand the Depression, which started somewhere late '29, '30, '31. And in parts of the country it went on for ten, eleven, twelve years. It was probably the longest-lasting and worst depression that this country has ever seen. At its height, there were officially more than ten million people unemployed—ten million unemployed, it's hard to describe. The population of this country in the thirties was less than half of what it is now. But there were ten million people unemployed by official government figures, which meant the figures probably were higher, because nobody counted partial unemployment, people who only worked a few hours a week. They were considered working.

There was no such thing as unemployment compensation in the beginning of the Great Depression. Social Security was still a dream of Roosevelt. It didn't exist. There were such things as Workman's Compensation if you were injured on the job, but when you were just an economic casualty, when you were just laid off, there was nothing. Well, there was what was known as the poorhouse. There were church-run kinds of assistance—food, some clothing, and so on. But until the first Roosevelt administration with the construction of the WPA, the Works Progress Administration, and the NYA, the National Youth Administration, and the CCC, the Civilian Conservation Corps, and a whole raft of alphabet agencies, [the church-run organizations were] trying to pick up the slack in the most constructive way possible and not always successfully.

My father's work as the Depression went on became less and less; the fifty-two-week year became forty weeks and thirty weeks and twenty weeks and so on. But my mother was a full-time teacher in the New York City school system, and I can't say that we had personal hardship. But when I started to work in the Welfare Department in the spring of 1940, I saw what really existed.

And just to give people a flavor of what it was like in those days, if you were absolutely without means, you had no job, you had no resources, and you had no legally responsible relatives, meaning you didn't have parents or grandparents or adult children, then and only then were you eligible for some kind of welfare assistance. And I worked out in East New York, Brooklyn, and I remember the first time I saw an eviction. And evictions still occurred, welfare or not, because you applied for welfare and then it might take five, six weeks, even when you were accepted, before you got the first sort of rent check and so on.

People were being evicted all the time. The first one I saw occurred in the rain. I was making the rounds visiting the welfare clients on my list. And I saw a crowd around and men came out of this small apartment house carrying terrible sticks of furniture, not worth anything, and putting the family's belongings out on the sidewalk in the rain. And then the family would come out, sometimes with small children and so on. And the first time I saw it, I wondered about the people watching. They were silent, just absolutely silent, they said nothing to each other and nothing to the family moving out. And the sheriff and his deputies would deposit everything out on the sidewalk and then they would disappear.

After the sheriff and his deputy had moved all their possessions on the sidewalk and then disappeared, I saw for the first time the most remarkable sight. All of these neighbors and people who had been standing so silently began to pick up everything there was and put it back into the house. And I would ask somebody, what are they doing? And they said, we do this all the time. It's like a ritual. They said the sheriff knows this happens, but he's done his duty, he's put it all out on the street and then disappeared.

The neighbors know their role and back it goes. You learn what solidarity in times of crisis means, and they had it. And what I've described is something that used to happen a couple of times a week on my route. At any rate, yeah, I think the whole welfare department experience was a learning one in very many ways.

The War Production Board enticed me to Washington. My wife and I were married at the end of 1939. And the period I'm talking about is close to the end of 1942, three years later. I was hired as an economist. And at any rate, to make a long story short, I moved to the National War Labor Board the following year. And that was absolutely the most valuable experience in dealing with labor relations and labor management affairs. The War Labor Board had an unprecedented task. It had a dual task. One was to attempt to stabilize wages so that nobody could get a wage increase without an application to the board and the board approved it. But it also had a Disputes Division. And the purpose of the Disputes Division was to provide a mechanism for resolving disputes other than through strikes or lockouts. We were now in a war. War production was exceedingly important not just for this country but for those we were supplying. And Roosevelt had approached the brand-new CIO and the older AFL and he suggested that he would like to see a no-strike pledge for the duration. And of course, they wanted to know about industry.

And I think this was a learning period for Franklin Roosevelt, too. And he kind of learned that there were two sides to this coin, and he belatedly approached the National Association of Manufacturers and the U.S. Chamber of Commerce, asked for a no-lockout pledge from them, got it, and now we still had a problem. The labor movement, in effect, said, how are we gonna resolve disputes? The brand-new CIO, having organized millions of industrial workers; they were still getting Depression wages. Disputes were inevitable.

And Roosevelt, by executive order, created the Disputes Division of the War Labor Board. And believe it or not, they were to handle every dispute in the United States, every labor-management dispute. Nobody had ever done this before. The War Labor Board was created and it did an absolutely marvelous job. Again, I was most fortunate to become a hearing officer there in the Disputes Division and really learned what labor-management disputes were all about. Because in that role, you handled not just wages and salaries, but union security and seniority and shift differentials and insurance plans and everything; every issue that you can imagine would come up in these disputes.

In the War Labor Board in Washington and in the twelve regions throughout the country, each board consisted of public members, who were the neutrals, labor members, and industry members, and each board was tripartite in structure. And in any dispute, the disputing parties had to win a majority of those votes to have their way. The War Labor Board, as you might expect, ended when the war ended.

I began with the Steelworkers Union in the spring of 1950 as the associate director of research and took on more and more responsibilities as time went on. I was on all of the top negotiating committees. Philip Murray, who I had met when I was hired in 1950, died at the end of 1952, and David McDonald, who had been his secretary-treasurer, became president. And sometime after that, I was promoted to assistant to the president of the union and chief economist of the Steelworkers Union. In that role, I was involved with all of the top-level negotiations.

It really didn't matter who you were and it didn't matter that you were now working for the most prestigious of the unions and one of the largest and wealthiest. When you got down to negotiations, what mattered is, did you have the support and the understanding of the rank-and-file worker. All the rest of it was really secondary or tertiary. And that was true whether it was necessary to mobilize for a strike or whether the negotiations were relatively peaceful and constructive. It still always came down to what kind of support and understanding and solidarity did you have with the membership you were representing.

When the players first approached me about becoming the first executive director, sure, I had been a baseball fan ever since I was a small boy, but I just thought that there was much I did not know. So I began to read everything I could. And I remember my feelings at that time, that it was a feeling of indignation in reading about the reserve clause, for example. Someone said of me that I converted what had been an exclusively economic issue into an economic and moral issue. That came from my reading. And I wasn't reading just text, I was reading Bill Veeck. I was reading *The Hustler's Handbook* and *Veeck as in Wreck* and picking up the flavor. And as I say, my strongest memory about that time is a feeling of, why didn't I know all of this?

I had been with the Steelworkers at this point, end of 1965, I had been there more than fifteen years, going on sixteen. And I was attending a meeting in California. I was involved with the Kaiser Steel Tripartite Committee. The chairman of the committee was Dr. George Taylor, who had been the chairman of the National War Labor Board during World War II, who was an economics prof at the Wharton School, University of Pennsylvania. And out of the clear sky, in an elevator, he asked me, do you know Robin Roberts? And I said, no, but I know who he is. He's one of the great pitchers of our time. Why do you ask? He said, well, I'm not sure I know all the facts, but Mr. Roberts called me. I don't know him and he said something about they've got an organization of players in baseball that has never been able to do anything for them. It's been controlled and financed by the owners, and they want to change it. They've got a committee they call a search committee and they're looking for somebody experienced to be the first executive director and so on. Taylor wanted to know if I'd be interested. And I said, I don't know. But I said I'd be willing to talk to Roberts.

And from that came a meeting in December of '65 in Cleveland with Robin Roberts and Jim Bunning and Harvey Kuenn. And that began another phase of my education about baseball.

The meeting was a peculiar one in the sense that I was doing my best to find out what problems they had and how they viewed them and what they thought they could get out of a more solid organization. And the harder I tried, the less information I got. They seemed focused on the pension plan. What I came to understand is that the pension plan, which I found to be most inadequate, was nevertheless the one accomplishment they felt that they had achieved. And they felt it was threatened at that time. The pension plan had been financed by a share of the television money from the All-Star game and the World Series. And the value of those two attractions was getting more and more apparent, and television money was moving up and up.

The pension plan went into effect April 1, 1947. And they agreed with the owners' people that the only people to be covered were those who had been on a major league roster on the last day of 1946 or the first day of the 1947 season. Now, to give you some idea of how drastic that was, you could have a twenty-year major leaguer who was released late in the '46 season and he was not eligible. That cut them off completely. In addition, you needed five years of major league service after that point to be eligible for a pension.

There were some health-care benefits, too. There were some maternity benefits. There was some hospitalization. There were no dental benefits, no eye benefits. But having known something about baseball conditions and, more than that, having done a cram job just before this meeting with the search committee, I was amazed that until I brought it up, nobody talked about the reserve clause. Now, for people down the road, let me explain what that meant. Under the reserve clause, players came into the game mostly by being drafted by a major league organization, as if the major league organization were the government. In most cases, it was when you came out of high school, so you were of quite tender years. Some few players went to college in those days, but not many.

Having been scouted, your name would be placed in the draft and you had no say about who was going to pick you. And the major league organization would in the course of the draft select John Doe and they would then try to sign you into a contract. Agents were not allowed. It was considered to be perfectly fair to draft a kid out of high school and match him up with a general manager who might be typically middle-aged, who had negotiated hundreds, if not thousands of contracts, who had enough data, comparative salary data on hand to know everything about the salary structure. If he didn't have it at hand, he could get it with a phone call or two or three or four with the other general managers.

It was considered perfectly fair to sit down with an untutored eighteen- or nineteen-year-old and forbid them to have an agent. If the player accepted what was offered, and most of the time he had a theoretical option of saying no and going into the next year's draft and wasting a whole year or part of a year, but realistically, he was made to understand he had no choice, so you accepted whatever the club offered. Once you signed that contract, you became the property, literally, the property of that organization and remained the property of that organization for all the rest of your career unless they decided to sell you for cash or to trade you for another player or players to another organization.

You had no say when that happened. When it happened, you went where you were told. And you could not say no at that point. If you didn't sign a contract for the next year, under the contract you had previously signed, the club reserved the rights to your services indefinitely. That reserve language is why it's called the reserve clause.

Anybody who would think about this will know why salaries were fairly miserable. If you don't have any bargaining power, in most cases, you're gonna be discriminated against in terms of salaries and benefits. You have no place else to go.

In that first meeting with the search committee, Roberts, Bunning, and Kuenn, Roberts had said at some point in the meeting, what about strikes? What I said to him was, look, in any negotiations, a strike is the last, last, last, last, last resort. But sometimes it's necessary. Now, Robbie has written a book recently in which he suggests that I told him that there never would be a strike.

Well, what negotiator with experience in the trade union movement is gonna say in advance that there's never gonna be a strike?

That's like saying, I surrender and here's the white flag before we start. Of course I would never say anything like that. Yeah, the question came up at several of the meetings with players, and I responded in the same way, that that is positively the last resort. You try everything short of that and only when there are no alternatives.

I talked to them about a lot of antiunion propaganda, about how unions like strikes, et cetera—nothing further from the truth. That's the biggest strain that can be on a union and its membership and its treasury and its staff. All income stops. Anybody that tells you that people like strikes is crazy. But I said to him early on, I do want you to know that strikes happen but you never should look at it the way you view a strike in steel, autos, or in the corner grocer or laundry or whatever.

And I said, the reason is I have never before seen a group of employees who are so essential to the operation of their industry, that this is not like a group of employees going out and worrying that the employer is gonna hire scabs and they're gonna take my job, et cetera, et cetera. This is one of the essential things union members worry about. I said, I have never before seen a group like this. It may exist somewhere else, but I have never before seen it. So my point is, if it does come to that, you are not going to have the same fears as other people who are forced into a strike. I remember saying at each of the meetings, when this came up, I'm not gonna tell you that because of this kind of power you're gonna get the moon. But I am gonna tell you that whatever is within reason and fair, you can have with this kind of solidarity.

It was clear from the conversation back and forth that Roberts, whom I had never met before, was my most important backer. He was fairly impressed with me. That was clear. And he began to talk about what was ahead. And he said, you know, there are other candidates. I said, how many? And he said, well, five others. Okay.

And he said, we are gonna have to go back to the player reps of each club, the elected player representative, and they will make a decision on who their nominee will be. I said, nominee? He said, yes.

Robin Roberts

And then he'll be subject to an election by all of the players in the major leagues. And I said, okay. And he said, and all the coaches and all the managers and all the trainers, the management employees. I said, how did that come about? And he said, well, you know, they're covered by the pension plan. And so, you know, when you negotiate pensions, you'd be representing them. So, that was the first time I realized there's gonna be management people voting on this.

And then Roberts, who clearly had done the most thinking about this whole problem, he said—these are not his exact words but his meaning was—I'm quite impressed with you. I'd like to have you. But you have to remember that the players are basically conservative, and you come from a union. And they are not unionists. And he said, I don't have to tell you about antiunion propaganda. It's all over the place.

So he said, we had the idea—although he said "we," I think it was his idea—that we'll have a ticket, a voting ticket, and you will be the candidate for executive director and we need a conservative, a balanced ticket, in other words, who would be general counsel. At this point, I felt the other shoe was about to fall but I listened. And he said, as a matter of fact, we've already been to see someone who is interested. He would not be the general counsel himself but his firm would be. And he is a conservative and we think it would be a good ticket. I said, are you gonna tell me his name? That's when he said, Richard Nixon.

Well, at that point, I said it couldn't work. And Robbie's face just fell. Politically, he was sound, he was doing the right thing. And why wouldn't it work? he asked. So I said, well, consider, you've got a budget, we had already discussed that; you're gonna have just two professionals. You're gonna have a director and a general counsel, and there'd be one secretary and maybe one administrative person. That's it. I said, in that kind of a small organization, you can't have two people who are as incompatible as Richard Nixon and me.

I said, the Steelworkers Union had a staff of one thousand people, and you want diversity, and you can tolerate diversity among one thousand people. With two, you can't. And I said, besides, I don't think he's really the person for this job. You have stressed to me how important the pension plan is. I don't think he would know the difference between a pitcher's mound and the Empire State Building and a pension plan.

I got up and I shook hands all around and I started to leave. And I came back, I said, look, I'm going to do something I've never done before. I'm going to give you advice you haven't asked for. Whoever you get for director, let him pick his own counsel. It's only going to be the two of them there. They have to really be compatible. Sure, hold him responsible for whatever happens and the activities of his counsel, but let him pick him. And I walked out. I went back to Pittsburgh, and my wife and sons and daughter were anxiously waiting and I said I blew it. We're not going back to New York. But I was wrong. Various things happened that are not important. And they came back to me and said, okay, if you will be a candidate and if you are elected, you pick your own counsel. The arrangement was made before the players, coaches, trainers, and managers voted. I said, I want an opportunity to meet with them all. I want them to see who I am. I want to be able to talk to them. They said, okay. We arranged a spring-training trip. It was already late when they nominated me, March was already here, but they arranged for a trip. There were then twenty clubs in the majors. And it was decided that I would start in California, where the Angels were training, because I had a meeting with Kaiser Steel the next day, and then from there to Arizona, where three other teams train in the West, and then to Florida, where the final sixteen teams were.

If a Steelworkers Union official wanted to meet with the entire membership, he'd have to live to be older than Methuselah, just impossible, a million and a quarter people. But here, you're going to be on an active roster, there are going to be five hundred people. And the thought came to me that I could meet with them not just once a year, I could meet with them several times a year. I could meet with whole clubs. I can meet with part of a club. This was really going to be an opportunity to test some theories I have.

It had been agreed that the players would vote on my candidacy and the establishment of what they called an independent office of the Players' Association. But they would vote after I had talked with them. I thought that was a good idea. I could meet with them, I'll leave, and they're free to vote however they want. So the result was when I met with the four clubs that trained in California and Arizona, I did not know how they had voted.

The arrangement was that all of the player reps of the twenty teams would call the vote results to Frank Scott, who was kind of an administrative assistant there, and he would not release any of the vote results until he had all twenty teams'. The result was I did not know at that point in time how those four clubs had voted. If I had known, I'm not sure what would have happened, because, I don't remember the exact totals now, but the California Angels voted something like 32 -1 against me.

The Giants were unanimous with one abstention, against. Cleveland had, I don't know, one vote for me, I think. And the Cubs, training in Arizona, maybe four or five votes for me. I learned later that a campaign had been organized against me; I didn't know about that. And these four clubs, leaflets had been circulated, printed on the club's mimeograph machine. A whole campaign had started. The National League president had told the players that I was from the Teamsters and that the Teamsters was gangster-run. And this was going to mean endless strikes, et cetera, et cetera, et cetera.

I was being informed about the campaign that had been run against me before I got to the California and Arizona clubs, and I was being informed by players in the know that Warren Giles, the National League president, had been making the rounds of the teams in Florida, saying, he comes from a gangster union. I had players come up to me after the meeting and say, I've got to tell you something. Based on what we were told before we saw you, we thought we're gonna see somebody about six-four, wearing a black derby and smoking a great big cigar, and surrounded with an armed bodyguard and who talked English with a dese, dems, and dose, and we were convinced that that's what we're gonna see. And then you walked in. He said they overdid it. I learned that they had a habit of over-doing it.

But what I had said to the players on all twenty teams was that I understood that the organization had started many years ago and was basically without accomplishment. And that what I hoped was that we could create a new organization, one that would be solidly in line with what players wanted. I said that I hoped when I finished talking with them at each meeting that we could spend the last fif-teen, twenty, thirty minutes with them talking about whatever comments they wanted to make and whatever questions they had because I always believed in operating with a lot of input from the people I represented.

I said, I don't know what we're going to be able to accomplish but I want you to know that no matter what you think about your working conditions, they're terrible. I said, I recognize that a lot of you have stars in your eyes, you always wanted to be a professional ballplayer, you always wanted to make it to the big show, to the major leagues. And I understand that players had told me the general line that the owners had always given them was that you're lucky to be able to play baseball for a living. You play in a game.

And the line was that the owners don't make any money, they were all sportsmen. And if they don't like what happens, they'll pick up their bats and balls and go home. I said nothing can be further from the truth. This is an important industry. They make a lot of money. Your salaries—by this time I had done enough research to know—are a far tinier proportion of what they take in than people who work in a factory. This is what is known as a labor-intensive industry, where all the cost, almost all the cost, should be labor because that's what it is. And yet, you don't come anywhere near having the proportion of the revenue that an ordinary worker has, a steel worker has, et cetera.

Remember, we're talking now in the year 1966. Major League Baseball's first minimum salary was established nineteen years before that, 1947. It was $5,000 a year in the major leagues. Nineteen years later, when I'm coming through camp, it's $6,000 a year. In nineteen years, it went up by $1,000. This covered periods of some of the most horrendous inflation the United States had ever seen, and it wasn't just the minimum salary. It ran all the way up.

One hundred thousand dollars was the ceiling and it didn't matter whether you were Ted Williams, Joe DiMaggio, Mickey Mantle. In '66, you may recall, was the Koufax-Drysdale holdout, the first dual holdout in baseball history. Its purpose was to break the

$100,000 ceiling. Sandy Koufax did not make $100,000 at that point, and '66 was his last year, so figure, all his peak years and he still wasn't at $100,000.

Counting negative vote totals in the West, the overall vote total in favor of my candidacy was 489 to 136, which is kind of a remarkable total in the sense that included among the voters were 120 management employees. And with a total negative vote of only 136, it looks like the players supported me throughout after all.

In talking to the players in those first meetings, I remember talking about the reserve clause. The last thing I wanted to do was to set a target that was too high to reach fast, but I couldn't not talk about

Curt Flood

the reserve clause because I had run into so many players who really just had been brainwashed in terms of, you know, this is a sport and not a business.

Curt Flood was a star center fielder of the Cardinals, who a few years later wanted assistance from the players' union to file an antitrust lawsuit against Major League Baseball after he had been with the Cardinals for, I think, thirteen or fourteen years. They suddenly traded him to the Philadelphia Phillies. Philadelphia, at the time, according to the ballplayers who played there regularly, was one of the most anti-African-American cities that they played in in the North, and he decided not to go.

Flood did not talk to me about the reserve clause and the antitrust laws in '66, but I do recall, maybe the following year or the year after that, not raising it during the meeting, but he was one of those who would come up after the meeting and ask questions. And I do remember Curt talking about, has anybody ever taken this to court? And I said, yeah, unsuccessfully, and so on.

When I got to Fort Lauderdale, I met with the Yankees and I talked about the reserve clause, et cetera. When the meeting was over, one of the players came up, talked to me. And this wasn't just any player. This was one who was known as being quite liberal and quite rebellious, Jim Bouton. What Bouton said to me was, you talked about the reserve clause and changing it. But wouldn't that mean that one or two clubs will then get all the stars and win all the pennants and all the World Series? And he was sincere. And I looked at him; I smiled. After all, we're meeting in the Yankee clubhouse. I said, you mean like the Yankees? So even a forward-looking person like Jim Bouton was, on this score at least, most conservative. You can't touch the reserve clause because it would just mean terrible imbalance; one team gets all the stars, et cetera.

When we negotiated the first basic agreement, which became effective in '68, Spike Eckert was still the commissioner, Bowie Kuhn was associate counsel of the National League at that time. He was there in the negotiating committee, as was Joe Cronin as president of the American League, and Warren Giles, who was the president of the National League at the time, and the counsel for both leagues. And when the issue of recognition came up, to my amazement, there was hardly any discussion at all. There was no objection. The Players' Association was recognized as the sole collective-bargaining representative of the players.

The pension and insurance agreement was due to expire March 31, 1967, and I started in the summer of '66. My idea was to start the negotiations early, but I soon ran into one of the baseball truisms: You can't do anything while the season is on. It takes people's attention away from the ballfield, so it has to be in the off-season. So, I waited until the end of the '66 season.

At some point during the season, even though I knew we were not gonna start negotiations until the season was over, we drew up a questionnaire to all of the major league players, coaches, trainers, and managers. It was not just a blank questionnaire. It kind of set forth what we had with an evaluation of how adequate, how inadequate the plan was to be made by the players, and with a space on it for things that weren't in the plan that they thought ought to be there—questions like the level of benefits, the level of permanent disability benefits, what should a widow's benefits be, should it be 50 percent of the primary benefits, should it be 75 percent, should it be 100? We got into complete detail on everything.

When we asked players to sign membership and dues-checkoff cards, we included all the managers, all the coaches, and all the trainers, explaining that we still don't have a basic agreement, this is just on the pension plan. And since they are members, we will be negotiating their terms and conditions in the master plan.

With the pension plan, you had to be age sixty-five before you started it. You were eligible when you're aged fifty, but if you wanted the maximum, you had to be aged sixty-five. And in between, you got moderate increases for each year that you held off starting to draw the benefit. At age sixty-five, it was roughly about $200 a month.

When it came time to negotiate the basic agreement covering all terms and conditions of employment outside of pensions and insurance, we ran into a roadblock. The owners' committee said that these were management people, and of course, some of them were. The field managers were obviously management people. The question of whether coaches are management or not is a dicey question. Trainers probably would be considered management, too. The owners took a position that we're not gonna have a basic agreement covering the players unless we agree in writing that we don't represent the others.

And I refused. I said that I'm not gonna do that. I'm not gonna insist in this first agreement that, on all these other working conditions, that the coaches and trainers and managers be covered. We'll have to resolve this maybe by going to the National Labor Relations Board and have them tell us which are employees and which are management. But I'm not gonna sign it away without talking to the coaches and managers and trainers. And it was decided on that basis. The agreement said we represent the players. It did not say we represent the others.

In December 1966 we took a pension plan, which was then nineteen years old, and we more than doubled the benefits in one negotiation and added an awful lot of additional benefits, especially in the health-insurance area. We followed that up with the first basic agreement, which, among other things, was the first increase in the minimum salary since 1962, I guess; raised it from $6,000 to $10,000 with additional increases for future years. We took all of the spring-training and in-season allowances and made up for lost time by increasing them largely.

We added the cost-of-living provision so that each year it would go up automatically even when there were no negotiations. We raised the reserve clause issue and eventually settled on a two-year study labeled as a study to consider alternatives to the present reserve system. We tried negotiating a reduction in the number of games. They had increased the season total from 154 to 162 some years before that. And what I got from the players was that it was just enough of an increase to make the schedule far more onerous than it had been before. We were not successful in that, but we set up a study committee on that as well.

We did a whole overhaul. For example, this is just an example of what happens when an employer really dominates the scene. In Major League Baseball, the number of rule books can fill a library. You have the major league rules and you have the major and minor league agreement, and you have the contract of the commissioner, which is an agreement with rules of its own. You have the American League constitution and bylaws and the National League constitution and bylaws, and on and on like this. The old Uniform Player's Contract, which every player was required to sign—this is before the union—said that all these rules and books, and they specify them, will govern the player and he was acknowledging that that was so by signing the contract. Well, in practice, not only was he agreeing to that, but when they would change it in, say, midseason, they would say that since he had agreed to be bound by the major league rules or the major/minor, whatever, he was bound by the changes, too, even though his signature had occurred before the changes.

Worse than all of that, when I inquired, I found out that nobody had ever furnished the players with copies of these things, which they were asking them to sign, comply with. It was that bad. We changed all that.

It was more than they had let themselves believe was gonna happen. But my own feeling was that they had not set their standards high enough. And in part, I blame myself that perhaps I had been too conservative in indicating what was possible. So I had both feelings that, yeah, it was going well because the players were happy with what had been done, but inside me I was unhappy in that I didn't consider it a lot of progress yet.

By the time we got to 1969, Willie Mays was in his last few years as an active player, and it's pretty clear that Curt Flood at that point was the greatest center fielder in the game. That's just to set the stage for this. When he was notified by a newspaperman that he had been traded, which was kind of typical in those days, he telephoned me and told me what had happened and said that he had discussed this with his personal attorney in St. Louis and he wanted to file a lawsuit, an antitrust lawsuit, and could he discuss it with me.

I said, okay, sure, and made an appointment, and he came in with his St. Louis attorney. Richard Moss, who was the first general counsel of the Players' Association, and I met with the two of them. And we met all day long. And the best way I can summarize it is to say that Flood had made up his mind that he was gonna file this suit. He was not gonna report to the Philadelphia Phillies, and there was no arguing with that. He was gonna do it. And really, all he wanted from me was an indication that the union would back him. From my point of view, the most important thing was to make sure that Curt Flood knew what a million-to-one shot this was, winning this case. Because if he lost, then he'd never play again.

I said, I don't want to get into your personal life and I don't want you to tell me anything, but I just want you to think about it. If there's anything in your personal life that you don't want to see on the front page of the newspaper, be cautious here because you're gonna see it. He thought about it and he said to me, but if we win, it would benefit all the players in the future and all the players to come. I said, yes. He said, that's good enough for me. Then we go full steam ahead.

The Phillies sold his contract to what was then the Washington Senators. And Bob Short, who was one of the owners of the team, wanted to sign Flood. There was a problem because we were concerned that if he played, a court could throw the case out as being moot at that point. We discussed it with Arthur Goldberg [who represented Flood when the case went to the Supreme Court], and Goldberg met with Bowie Kuhn on that point and they agreed that they would not argue that the case was moot. They wanted Flood to play. This by no means ensured that a court wouldn't say it was moot, because the court has a right to make its own decision, but at least MLB was not going to argue with that. Curt came back, and a contract was negotiated with Bob Short. As predicted, we lost five to three votes [in the Supreme Court].

We know that the attorney general of the United States has the right to enforce the antitrust laws. That doesn't need Congress. There's nothing in the Sherman Antitrust Act that exempts baseball. There's nothing in the Clayton Antitrust Act that exempts baseball. So the chief law enforcement officer of the United States always was in a position to break up the baseball monopolies.

Andy Messersmith was a star pitcher, first for the California Angels, and then for the Los Angeles Dodgers, a twenty-game winner in both leagues. In the year 1975, in trying to negotiate a contract with the Dodgers for that year, he failed, and the Dodgers used the reserve clause and renewed his contract for the '75 season without his signature.

They were in disagreement on two things. One, on salary, and that was not the major disagreement. Andy Messersmith was kind of shocked when the California Angels traded him to the Dodgers. He loves California to this day. What he wanted was to be assured he wasn't going to be traded again somewhere else. So he asked the Dodgers for a no-trade provision. The irony of this, here's a player who eventually becomes a free agent and leaves, and the thing that would have kept him from being a free agent was his desire to stay, but the Dodgers would not give him a no-trade provision.

The owners, I learned partly then and partly later, were being given advice by John Gaherin [chief negotiator for Major League Baseball] that this was not a good case to go to arbitration, that this business of resting the whole reserve system on a provision which says—these are not the exact words—if the club and the player can't agree on next year's contract, then the club shall have the right after a certain date to renew it for one additional year. The first time I read that, I did a double-take, back in '66.

This is what they based the right to renew this year after year after year on, throughout a player's entire career and after that. Impossible, but there it was. And John Gaherin and his attorney saw the same things I did.

If we had tried to make a grievance of the trade of Flood against his will, it would have been heard by the commissioner of baseball, who was an employee of the owners. That was fruitless. In the first basic agreement after the Flood case was filed, we negotiated the first impartial arbitration of grievances involving the interpretation of the contract. It changed the whole relationship between owners and players. It really did. At any rate, that made the agreements on arbitration procedure available to Messersmith and not available to Flood because we didn't have it back then. John Gaherin was absolutely correct, in my opinion, in the advice he gave the owners that you're going to lose this case.

They, in effect, said, okay, it goes to arbitration. We're going to win the arbitration. They said, okay, we'll appeal the arbitrator's decision, for the federal court, circuit court, et cetera, as being not in conjunction with the contract.

We were in the process of the hearing and the arbitrator, Peter Seitz, a veteran arbitrator and very experienced, knowing the importance of the whole reserve clause issue and having that hot potato in front of them, proceeded to say to the parties, look, in any case, I'm always in favor of the parties' resolving important matters themselves rather than having an arbitrator. You have to live with the eventual outcome of this, and what better way than to negotiate a settlement. Furthermore, he said, it's fortuitous, but your basic agreement expires in a few weeks, and that's it. It's time for you to be negotiating this. I think Peter Seitz at that point when he did this, because most of the evidence was already—and I stress, this is only guesswork—I think when he was doing this, he was giving the owners signals. Negotiate. Don't wait for a decision here.

Those who later second-guessed this—saying, Peter Seitz had stars in his eyes, he was going to change the American national pastime, et cetera—he had no such desire. He was begging, take this case away from me. After the decision of the arbitrator, Messersmith and Dave McNally and other pitchers became free agents. And we still had to negotiate a whole new basic agreement and a whole new system. I knew that I was not going to take the position that Messersmith's being a free agent meant all you had to do was play one year under a renewed contract and then you're a free agent.

To me that meant far too many free agents at any given time to do much with the salary structure. I believe in the basic economics, a balance between demand and supply. But if the supply is limited and the demand is great, that's when you're going to see the salary structure move.

After the '76 agreement, we did work out a whole new agreement, a whole new pension agreement, a whole new reserve system. We finally agreed on a six-year major league requirement for free agency and all of the surrounding details about how do you become a free agent a second time and many things like that. And when that agreement was reached—and it was reached just in time for the All-Star break in '76—following that was a unique experience for me.

Usually when an agreement has been worked out, especially one where there's been no stoppage, usually there's an air of good feeling for a while. This was different. Almost before the ink was dry on that '76 agreement, the owners started a whole campaign to get rid of free agency. They wanted to do it in any one of several ways, including compensation for the loss of a free agent.

We narrowly escaped a whole crisis in 1980, mostly by agreeing on a whole new agreement, but also giving the owners the right to reopen the issue of compensation for the loss of free agents. That was the only issue opened in 1981. And it was a disaster because, frankly, the media just bought every argument being raised by the owners, that what they wanted was minor, that it wasn't worth having a struggle over something that would affect only two or three players. The media bought all the nonsense, none of it true. It would've finished free agency almost in its infancy if they had been able to force that down the players' throat. So it was an extremely serious issue.

Imagine the year before, having negotiated that entire collective-bargaining agreement, an entire pension and insurance agreement, without a strike during the season. And now, you've got only one issue open, nobody can raise any other issue, neither the employer nor the union, and you can't make a settlement because they were determined they're either going to break the union or get what they want on the free agency. So that began it. And then we get involved in the injunction and the court proceeding.

The cohesion was so strong in '81 because success breeds success. The tremendous progress that had been made in every phase of ball-players' working lives through the union was an important factor. But I think I'll take a little credit. I always had a feeling, even when I was with the Steelworkers and couldn't do it—and here, I could do it—I've mentioned this before, to have really close contact with the players. And I had encouraged the players through the years to remember that this is your union, not my union, not anybody else's. It's your union.

The union office has been placed in New York for a reason. Initially all clubs came through New York three times a season, later only two times a season. But it meant that all members had access to the union office. And whenever I saw the players or whenever I wrote memos to them, I kept saying, when you get to New York, if you have a problem, you come to the union. If you have a comment you wish to make about something that either annoys you or you think should be done, come to the union. If you have an idea that you think ought to be adopted, come to the union. And if, when you get to New York, none of these things applies, come in and we'll shoot the breeze, anyway.

Major league ballplayers are the most competitive people I've ever met, and the owners always made the mistake of trying to face them down. You don't do that with major league players. I think you can do all kinds of other things, but you don't challenge them and face them down. And I have to admit I, at every opportunity, when I saw the owners doing it, I would translate it and I would make sure the players understood what they were doing.

When you have a fifty-day strike, that's long enough in any industry, but if you do it in a seasonal industry, that's like a hundred days anywhere else. And when you do it in an industry where your whole career is limited, by the time you get to your late thirties, you begin to look the way somebody looks who's approaching retirement age in another industry thirty years later. The solidarity of those people in that dispute in 1981 is, it's just hard to imagine.

There was one point where the government intervened. The secretary of labor got us all to go to Washington and asked us, both sides, to make a pledge not to talk to newspapers or radio or TV about the dispute. I made a major error: I agreed. Previously, in crises, I had utilized the media to communicate with a far-flung membership. You know, this is not like having a strike in a plant where everybody lives around the plant. This is the whole of the United States and Canada. And I used the media to bring people up to date. The absence of that, because of the pledge I had made, pretty soon, there were one, two, three players at various times speaking out in frustration. I don't know what's going on, et cetera, et cetera.

In some of the earlier days, the usual propaganda against the union person is, he's an outsider. And that propaganda kept up. I was from outside baseball, he's an outsider. Until one day, I found out that out of all of the owners, I had more seniority in baseball than all but three of them. I was still the outsider.

I still would like to be remembered as somebody—and I'm hopeful that this will be so—as somebody who built a very solid union from the beginning, working with some bright people but ones without labor experience, without union experience, who became a really solid, united force to the point where today theirs is still considered one of the strongest and most democratic unions in the country. How will it be fifty years from now? I hope the same.

INDEX

Page numbers in *italics* refer to illustrations.